THE
COMPLETE
LOFT CONVERSION
BOOK

THE
COMPLETE
LOFT CONVERSION
BOOK

Planning, Managing and
Completing Your Conversion

Julian Owen

THE CROWOOD PRESS

First published in 2009 by
The Crowood Press Ltd
Ramsbury, Marlborough
Wiltshire SN8 2HR

www.crowood.com

This impression 2013

British Library Cataloguing-in-Publication Data
A catalogue record for this book is available from the British Library.

ISBN 978 1 84797 156 2

Disclaimer
The author and publisher do not accept responsibility, in any manner whatsoever, for any error, or omission, nor any loss, damage, injury, adverse outcome or liability of any kind incurred as a result of the use of any of the information contained in this book, or reliance upon it. Readers are advised to seek specific professional advice relating to their particular property, project and circumstances before embarking on any building or installation work.

Diagrams by Keith Field and Julian Owen.

Photographs by Julian Owen unless otherwise stated.

Front cover photographs by The Loft Company (top left), Julian Owen Associates Architects (bottom left) and Telebeam.

Back cover photographs by The Velux Company Ltd.

Frontispiece image courtesy The Velux Company Ltd.

Typeset by Jean Cussons Typesetting, Diss, Norfolk
Printed and bound in Singapore by Craft Print International Ltd

Contents

Dedication

For Paul, Zoe, Judy, Nick, James, Derek and Sue at Julian Owen Associates Architects

Acknowledgements

I would like to thank Richard Owen for his comments and advice and Sue Mercer for her invaluable help with administrative matters.

Thanks are also due to the following firms for providing photographs as illustrations for the book:
Absolute Lofts
Attic Designs Ltd
Room Maker Loft Conversions
Telebeam
The Loft Company
Julian Owen Associates Architects
The Velux Company Ltd

CHAPTER I

Introduction

Loft conversions are usually one of the first options considered when looking at ways of increasing the floor area of a house. The weather protection and floor are apparently already in place and it may be possible to stand up in the loft and look around at what seems to be a large potential bedroom. Up to 30 per cent of the floor area of the whole house may be gained, only needing a floor and staircase to make it complete. It is usually cheaper than adding an extension, as well as being relatively quick and less disruptive. But as you might expect having picked up this book, it is not quite so simple.

The loft space is believed to have first appeared in the fifteenth century and developed in parallel with the chimney. Until chimneys were invented, a large open roof was needed to disperse the smoke from internal fires. Once the smoke was being piped directly to the outside through a chimney, it was logical to reduce the space that needed to be heated by introducing a ceiling, creating a separate space above – and so the first attics were created. Soon these spaces were made use of and even small buildings were able to have two storeys. The ceilings were supported by the main trusses, which were also carrying the roof and consisted of planks of wood on thin wooden joists. Plaster ceilings followed later, supported on thin strips of wood ('laths'). As living standards improved, the two-storey house became the commonest form of dwelling, even for the less well-off, and the roof-space was mostly used for storage.

All these roofs were built up from timber on site and often improvised by the carpenter as he

Lofts are a modern invention and are generally used for storage. The Velux Company Ltd

A successful loft conversion is an asset to any house. The Velux Company Ltd

---

Good Reasons for Converting a Loft

- There is a large existing roofspace with plenty of space to stand up in.
- There is limited space around the house to add an extension.
- Other people in the area with similar house designs have already done it.
- You would like a slightly unusual space with lots of natural daylight.
- The cost of moving to get more space is more than the cost of a loft conversion.
- There is a lot of space on the ground floor compared to the first floor, or the building is a bungalow.
- Planning restrictions limit the addition of a normal extension or are difficult and complex to negotiate.
- The space is needed quickly.

When to Consider not Converting a Loft

- You can hardly stand up in the highest part of the loft.
- You have assumed that it is a quick, easy way to increase the value of the house before selling.
- You have assumed that it will be very cheap because it will need minimal building work to create a bedroom.
- It is easier to add a two-storey extension.
- You will end up with far too many bedrooms relative to the other rooms in the house.
- You need the loft for storage and there is nowhere else to put it.

---

built it, but just after the Second World War, when timber for building was scarce, the Timber Development Association produced a range of standard roof truss designs to use as little timber as possible as efficiently as possible (known as a TDA truss). By the mid 1960s the fink truss, or trussed rafter, began to be widely used. This is a development of the TDA truss, which uses the minimum amount of timber reasonably possible to span the house from one side to the other. A trussed rafter is prefabricated off-site in a factory. Most importantly, it uses small sections of wood that interrupt the roofspace and is designed to be just strong enough to support the ceiling of the room below and roof. These two characteristics make it more difficult to convert than a traditional roof and the problem is made worse by the introduction of shallow pitch roofs, made possible by the introduction of the concrete interlocking tile.

Many people start by using a loft for storage with access provided via a simple ladder. Improvements begin with the addition of a chipboard floor, followed by a better ladder, a roof light and a plasterboard ceiling fixed to the underside of the rafters. Eventually a new room is created. Although relatively cheap and easy to do, this approach will leave a room that is cold, that has condensation problems in winter and that may be a fire risk. When a house with such a room is offered for sale, potential purchasers are likely to raise questions and ask for proof that it has received Building Regulations approval. If it turns out not to have been approved, the house may be unsaleable.

A conversion that is well designed and constructed will increase the value of your home, provide an interesting, unconventional space to live in but also change the character of the house as you move around it. If it is not well designed and constructed, a property can be blighted and dogged with maintenance problems for the rest of its useful life. A badly converted loft can even endanger the health and safety of the occupants. The purpose of this and the following chapters is to assist anyone who is considering a loft conversion to make the decision and then, if the work is to go ahead, to explain the crucial issues that should be dealt with as the project proceeds.

There is no doubt that some lofts naturally lend themselves to being converted. The following issues are dealt with in detail in separate chapters later on, but often it is quite easy to identify whether a roofspace will be straightforward to turn into a room or whether it is probably best left well alone.

HOW TO DECIDE WHETHER TO CONVERT A LOFT

Is it Worth It?

The main reason for considering a conversion is usually that more space is needed for an expanding family. Another reason is that the existing house is not selling for the amount hoped for by the owners and it may be a way to make more money. Some people consider making use of the loft as a temporary stop gap to cover a time when a bigger house is needed but is too expensive at that point in their lives. Whatever the objective, the financial implications should be examined at a very early stage – certainly before starting to follow up the idea with enthusiasm. The danger at this point is that a simple loft conversion may be cheap to build, but some house plans will benefit more than others from the addition of an extra floor level.

You will get contradictory advice from estate agents on this subject. A favourite phrase is something like 'it will certainly add value to the property', along with 'it would help the property to sell more quickly'. Both these statements are unhelpful, because the crucial question is: 'How much will the conversion cost compared to the extra value that is added?' The answer will vary depending on the type of property, its location and the suitability of the loft for conversion, factors that are explored in more detail further on in this book. But it is possible to look at a typical situation and see how cost-effective a loft conversion is likely to be.

First of all, in terms of cost per square metre, a typical loft conversion is usually cheaper than adding the same floor area with an extension or a conservatory. However, it is not always as cost-effective, since it may not add as much to the value of the house as these alternatives. A loft conversion tends to add between 10 and 20 per cent to the value of the house. For example, converting the loft of a three-bedroom semi-detached house worth £180,000 would increase its value by between £18,000 and £36,000. If the cost of con-

An extra bedroom can add value to a home.
The Loft Company

verting the loft to add an extra bedroom is between £30,000 and £40,000 there is a clear possibility that the project will not make money. This is especially likely if the existing structure does not make the building work easy to carry out or a high standard of fittings and finishes is required. So anyone undertaking a loft conversion to generate a profit needs to investigate the costs and the ultimate sale price in some detail before committing to the project. Generally speaking, most roads have a 'ceiling' price, which represents the maximum possible price a house there will sell for, regardless of its size or quality. If you own a three-bedroom house in a street of mainly four-bedroom properties it will probably add significant value if you upgrade yours to a similar size. By comparison, if all the houses have three bedrooms and a loft conversion will increase yours to five bedrooms, it will generate less of an increase in value.

From the point of view of a family who needs the space but either cannot afford to move or does not wish to, the figures should be looked at in a different way. Moving house is not cheap and trading up from three to four bedrooms could easily cost £30,000–£40,000. Once expenses such as estate agent's fees, solicitor's fees, stamp duty and other general costs are added into the equation, the final cost of acquiring extra space by moving house could be between £40,000 and £50,000 – in other words well above the cost of a typical loft conversion. If the family are happy to live in the house for at least a few years after it is completed, it is an entirely sensible financial decision to convert, even though all the money spent will probably not be recovered.

What are the Other Options?

Even if a loft is a good candidate for a conversion, there may be other, better ways of increasing the number of rooms in the house, or improving the design. The alternatives and their relative benefits and disadvantages should be at least briefly considered. An extension to the ground and/or first floors is probably the best way to increase the floor area of a house. If the extra space is not for a bedroom, but for extra living space such as a children's room or a study, it is definitely a better option to build a ground floor extension, which is far more flexible in use than a loft space. However, many houses do not have sufficient space on their plot to allow an extension to be built at ground level, while planning restrictions often prevent them from being added on the first floor because they will overlook or overshadow a neighbour's house or garden. If you simply want an extra bedroom on the first floor, you would still incur the hefty expense of constructing an unwanted ground-floor room to support it. In terms of

The most common reason for a loft conversion is because more bedrooms are needed.
The Loft Company

adding value to the house, an extension will typically add around 10–15 per cent to the sale price of your home. This is significantly less than the cost of building such an extension, which is why in most cases extensions should not be added to generate a profit.

In an area where there is no space for an extension, such as near a city centre, another option is to excavate under the house, either from scratch or by enlarging an existing basement with low headroom. This is a very expensive undertaking and will only pay for itself where land values are very high and there is no other option, so a loft conversion, however difficult it may be, is likely to be a better option.

Too Many Bedrooms

The distribution of rooms around the house is another important consideration. If a house has a large number of bedrooms compared to limited ground-floor space, adding what is effectively a further bedroom in the form of a loft may be a bad idea. This situation typically occurs where there is an integral garage built into the body of the house, which restricts the amount of space available on the ground floor. Unless one of the first-floor rooms can be released to become something other than a bedroom, such as a family living room or study, adding a loft conversion will leave the house with a disproportionate number of bedrooms compared to general living space. This problem is made worse if the number of bedrooms is increased to more than five or if there are not enough bathrooms. A house that just about runs effectively with three bedrooms and one bathroom may become unworkable if the family expands into a fourth bedroom without adding at least an en suite. Living in such a house with all the bedrooms in use will feel cramped and the property will be less easy to sell when the family finally decide to move on.

You and Your Family

How the family adapt to and use the new space should be carefully considered. If the extra floor is being added to a two-storey house, the addition of a third level may bring benefits or disadvantages.

What will your family use a loft conversion for?
The Velux Company Ltd

Is the Loft Suitable?

Assessing the suitability of the loft is dealt with in the next chapter, but even a quick look can give you a strong hint as to how difficult the venture is likely to be. Some roofs naturally lend themselves to conversion and others make it an uphill battle. The less building work that is necessary the better. This doesn't mean that a difficult conversion should always be avoided, but it may sway the balance in favour of moving or extending instead. Some loft spaces almost seem to cry out to be converted and others promise little return for a lot of effort. Because it is sometimes quite difficult to judge how much space will be created from the drawings used to plan the work, one of the major mistakes people make is to spend a great deal of time and money to create a relatively small room

Any parents of young children know that they require a lot of looking after even when they are supposed to be asleep, not so easy to do if the adults are trying to sleep a flight of stairs away. Older people, or anyone who expects to grow old in the house over time, should realize that the effort needed to circulate between three levels instead of two is significantly more tiring for weaker muscles. Sometimes the staircases up to the loft are so limited in size that they are not suitable for a stair lift to be fitted.

In an ordinary house, the space in the loft is a vital storage area. Lack of storage space is a common complaint heard from owners of modern houses. Rather than disposing of their unwanted possessions, many families are used to sticking them in the loft to be dealt with later, or kept in case they become useful again. If the loft is to become a bedroom, the contents will have to be removed or stored somewhere else in the house.

Some lofts are more suitable for conversion than others. The Loft Company

It takes a good imagination to visualize a dark, dirty storage area as a new living space.
The Velux Company Ltd

that hardly has space to walk around a single bed without knocking your head on the ceiling.

If a house is particularly suitable for a loft conversion, it will reduce the disruption to the family living in it during construction and the building work itself will be relatively quick. This contrasts with the construction of an extension, which can interfere far more with the running of the household and usually is a longer and more complex process, particularly if a planning application is necessary.

As well as the space available within the roof structure, the condition and standard of the construction are important. As long as it is all basically sound, it will not be a problem, but if there are existing problems, such as rot in the timbers, defective roof slates or undersized rafters, these will have to be put right to make the project worthwhile. Of course if the condition is so bad that major remedial work is required anyway, it may be well worth spending a bit more money converting the loft at the same time.

Planning and Building Regulations

In the UK planning approval from the local authority is sometimes necessary to alter the external appearance of a roof. Whether or not permission is necessary depends on a number of factors. In rare cases alterations to the interior of a loft may also need consent from the planning authority. If a building is deemed to have historic value it will be listed to protect it from unacceptable alterations and this may prevent any kind of building alteration. Another example is if there are bats roosting in the roof void. Bats are a protected species and disturbing them without permission is a criminal offence.

The Building Regulations have some very specific requirements that cover aspects of the design and construction such as fire escape, fire spread, headroom, heat loss and structure. There is very limited scope to deviate from the standards set so if there is something about the construction of the existing loft space that makes it impossible or, more likely, very difficult to satisfy the regulations, the project may have to be abandoned. The classic 'killer' problem is the inability to achieve sufficient headroom, particularly over the staircase. Even if it is possible for most people to stand up without bumping their head, if the requirement for 2m at the head of the stairs is not met, the plans are unlikely to get the approval of the building control officer.

For full details of the likely effects of planning and Building Regulations requirements, *see* Chapter 5 on local authorities.

How Will it Look?

Assuming that all the practical aspects have been dealt with successfully and it appears to be a viable project, a final aspect to consider is how a new room-in-the-roof will look and how it will relate to the existing building and its neighbours. Even if you are not concerned at all with the appearance yourself, a poor-looking conversion can wipe thousands of pounds off the value of a house, despite satisfying all of the functional requirements such as the Building Regulations and providing adequate space. In its simplest form, a loft can be made usable with the only change visible outside being some windows that follow the line of the roof. Once extra features such as dormer windows are added, the character of the house will be affected. Sometimes the only way to get the desired space involves ruining the appearance of the building.

If in doubt the best thing to do is to consult an architect to get the opinion of a trained designer as to whether the end result will be acceptable. It may be that a professional can suggest a way of rearranging the design to make it more pleasing to look at. Ultimately, whether or not to proceed with alterations that damage the appearance of a home is up to its owners, but they may lose out in the long run if they get it wrong.

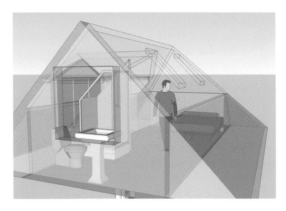

It may be worth investing in an architect to produce a considered three-dimensional design if the final appearance is important.
Julian Owen Associates Architects

STEP BY STEP

Any significant home alteration project can seem daunting to a family when it is first contemplated. However, like any project, the best way to approach it is to break it down into a series of steps or stages that have to be completed. The serious commitment doesn't have to be entered into until an instruction is given to a building company to carry out the work. Up until this point, although there may be some expenses, these are relatively minor compared to the actual construction cost. If the project does not live up to early expectations, or proves to be generating a lot more aggravation that planned, it can be halted and the whole thing put down to experience. What is more likely is that as you progress through the process, you will gain confidence and enthusiasm for the transformation that is about to occur in your standard of living. Unless there is an urgent reason for the project to be completed quickly, it is very important to take the time to go through each stage properly. Too much impatience may lead to problems later on if there is not enough advance planning.

Step 1: Make your Own Appraisal

Most people can at least make a basic check on the feasibility of a conversion. Using a book such as this, it is possible to make a fairly considered appraisal and avoid paying out for professional advice for a project that could never be viable.

Step 2: Talk to the Experts

There are many building companies that will carry out loft conversions. Some are only interested in straightforward, easy work that they can carry out quickly before moving on to the next, others relish a challenge. They will usually come and look at your house for free and make some comments on the viability of a conversion. It is not reasonable to expect them to provide a detailed design without being paid, but they should be able to explain how it would be done in principle and describe the problems that will have to be solved. If your house has particular architectural quality, or you are unhappy with commissioning a builder right at the start you can consult an architect, who may charge for the time but will offer impartial advice and may be able to offer some more creative solutions.

With smaller houses, there is a limited combination of room layouts that are possible and a professional with experience should be able to tell straight away whether or not it is a good idea to proceed. At the end of this stage you should have a clear idea of what is possible and a shortlist of firms that you are considering using.

Step 3: Commission a Design

This is the point where you will have to commit to paying out some money. There are two ways of employing a designer. You can engage the builder right at the beginning, who will in turn pay the designer as part of his total costs, or you can pay your own designer and use the resulting drawings to get competitive prices for the work. The design process and the relative benefits of the two approaches are discussed in Chapter 4.

Step 4: Get Planning Approval (if Required)

If a project requires planning approval or a related permission such as listed building consent, work must not start until it is in place. Even apparently straightforward applications have been known to hit unexpected snags in the approval process so it is not sufficient just to assume everything will be fine until you have the signed permission in your hand. From the date that the application is submitted to receiving that approval can take eight weeks or longer, so it can delay the start of a project. Fortunately, most loft conversion projects do not need formal permission from the council.

Step 5: Get Building Regulations Approval

All loft conversions need approval under the Building Regulations. It is possible to get the work approved by the building control officer as it is actually being built but the more sensible option is to have detailed construction drawings prepared and submit them for approval before the building work starts. The building contractor may deal with this process, but it is your responsibility to ensure that the regulations are complied with, and you are entitled to see all the paperwork. The regulations are mostly for your benefit, to ensure safety both during construction and once the new spaces are occupied.

Step 6: Agree a Price

If you have used a builder from the very beginning, before the design was prepared, you will probably have a good idea of the cost. However, most contracts allow for some adjustment to the price once the detailed construction has been finalized and even during construction. If you have used an architect to prepare plans and used them to invite competitive tenders, you will have fixed a price before agreeing to the work proceeding. Either way, you should have a proper written contract that does not allow the contractor to add to his charges without very good reason. If the only price stated is an estimate, or the likely cost is not absolutely clear, do not instruct building work. Just as important is a proper programme of work with a fixed completion date.

Step 7: Start Building

A typical conversion can take between five and eight weeks. There will be some disruption, particularly when the staircase is built, but at least it will be less fuss and quicker than an extension.

Step 8: Completion

A completion date should be agreed between the builder and the client before the work starts. It usually triggers the final large payment to the builder so it is important to walk round and check that everything has been done, to an acceptable standard. Most builders are anxious to get on with the next project and occasionally the final few tasks are rushed or forgotten. Once payment has been received, it is much harder to get any outstanding issues dealt with.

When the going gets tough it helps to focus on the end result – a useful and attractive addition to your home. The Velux Company Ltd

Common Pitfalls when Converting a Loft

- **Going over budget** This is the biggest risk of any building project. Advance planning and a proper contract with the builder are the best ways to reduce the chances of it happening to your project.
- **Starting before planning permission is in place** This occasionally happens, either through the ignorance of the building team or a desire to cut corners. It is almost always spotted by neighbours. Any competent builder knows the rules and will build in the time and cost needed if they quote for a design and build service. If work is well underway and the expected planning permission is not granted and the local authority either refuse to allow the work as proposed or at all, you will be left with a major problem.
- **Poor design and construction** Doing the conversion too cheaply will probably cost more in the long run when it has to be upgraded later. The local authority building control approvals process protects you from poor building work to some extent, but this is a safety net imposing only minimum standards. It is essential to use a professional team.
- **Failure to appreciate the impact on the house** A classic example of this problem is when on completion you find that the staircase has filled most of the new loft space created and drastically reduced the space on the floor below. Avoid this by ensuring that the designer is experienced in this type of work and can visualize three-dimensional space.

Two-dimensional plans can be deceptive and sometimes three-dimensional drawings such as perspectives or card models can give a better idea of how the rooms will look.
- **Realizing too late that the loft does not comply with Building Regulations** Some roof-spaces cannot accommodate a conversion to a habitable room without major rebuilding work. Very occasionally the plan of the existing house makes adequate fire escape impractical. Basic checks early on in the process can usually establish this.
- **Staircase too steep and too tight to get furniture up** The tightest possible staircase allowed by the regulations will easily allow a person to use it and a lot of modern furniture is designed to be carried through a house and up typical staircases, possibly in parts that are assembled in the room. The same is not true of older furniture, especially if it was made for up-market homes.
- **Creating an 'unlivable' loft** This is one of the commonest mistakes, often seen by surveyors who are valuing a property for sale. It is where the loft has been gradually converted over a period of time, with floorboards, plasterboard linings, a window and then a better ladder all being eventually fitted. This sort of room is not considered 'habitable' by a purchaser's solicitor or an estate agent and will not get Building Regulations approval for use as a bedroom. The only solution is to rip out most of the work and do it all again properly.

CHAPTER 2

Assessing a Loft for Suitability for Conversion

Before getting too far into the process of converting a loft or incurring the cost of hiring professionals the suitability of your roof should be assessed. For many, the best way of doing this may be to contact a builder or architect and ask them to take a look at it. However, it does no harm to do your own research first. Some aspects of the roof design and construction, such as the headroom available, may prevent a loft conversion from being carried out at all unless the roof is rebuilt. Other limitations, such as the structure of the roof, may not prevent a conversion, just make it more expensive. Provided that they can get into the loft safely, most people are able to check the key elements themselves. The detailed design work that will be needed is covered in later chapters, but at this

This loft has sufficient headroom, but will need some structural alterations to carry out a conversion. Attic Designs Ltd

early stage it is possible to visualize how a finished conversion might look and identify the area of the existing construction that will have to be altered.

The key questions to ask when considering a loft conversion:

- Is there enough headroom?
- Where will the staircase go?
- Where will windows go?
- Is the roof structure in the way?
- Are there any services to be altered, for example electrical wiring, water tank?
- How easily can it be insulated?
- What will happen to all the junk currently stored in the loft?

HEADROOM

The first, basic test for the feasibility of a loft conversion is to go up into the roof and try to stand up without bumping your head. If you can't, conversion is unlikely to be cost-effective because you will have to put on a new roof or lower the ceiling of the floor below to get enough space. This may seem an obvious point to check, but some lofts can be inaccessible because there is no loft hatch. Also the infirm or disabled are not able to climb up a ladder easily, or if the house is being inspected by a potential buyer access may not be immediately available. Roofs look higher than they actually are if only seen through a loft hatch whilst standing on the landing.

Assuming that it is possible to stand up comfortably, the next question is, 'How much space is

What to look for in a loft.

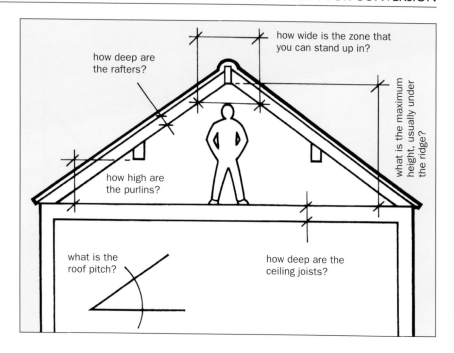

how deep are the rafters?

how wide is the zone that you can stand up in?

what is the maximum height, usually under the ridge?

how high are the purlins?

what is the roof pitch?

how deep are the ceiling joists?

there above your head?' If your head is tucked into the space under the ridge of the roof, with little space around it, a conversion is going to be difficult. Even if you have reasonable clearance, the finished conversion will need a stronger floor, raising the floor level, and the roof must be insulated, which usually means that the insulation will be deeper than the existing rafters. The result is that the space that you stand in before the conversion will shrink once the work is complete. There are ways to add more space, such as adding dormer windows, but if the roof is too low in the first place, they will not necessarily help unless they involve extensive alterations to the roof.

The minimum height that you need from the top of the existing ceiling joists to the underside of the ridge (the highest point of the roof) is about 2.3m. In most cases this will allow just enough width to move around in the narrow corridor of full height space under the ridge and should allow some dormer designs to extend the volume of the room. If the height is less than this, some roofs may still be convertible, but it will depend on the design and construction of the alteration work. Because the Building Regulations require that there is at least 2m clear headroom over most of the top of the

new staircase, if the clear height under the ridge would be less than this once the work is complete, the roof is not suitable for conversion into a habitable room and a new roof structure would be the only way to create sufficient space.

How to Estimate a Roof Pitch

If you want to work out the approximate pitch of your roof, there is a simple method using the '3:4:5' relationship between the sides of a 90-degree triangle that you may have learned at school: that is, if one of the angles of a triangle is 90 degrees, then the ratio of the length of the sides is 3:4:5. If this is too complicated, the following chart will help make a more approximate estimate. If you measure 1m from the point where the rafter meets the ceiling joist and then measure the height of the underside of the rafter at this point, the table indicates the approximate roof pitch. If you want a more precise measurement, you can use an angle finder. There is an electronic version of this tool, which is quite expensive, but the more old-fashioned manual version cost only a few pounds, is quick to use and may be worth investing in if you are going to construct a roof or need to measure the angle of a lot of rafters.

Chart for Estimating Effect of Roof Pitch and Span on Headroom

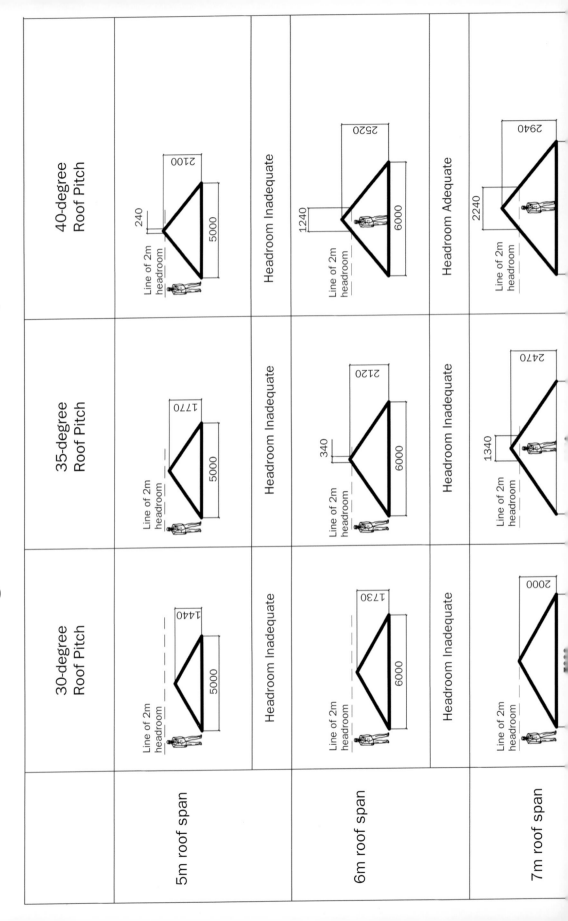

	30-degree Roof Pitch	35-degree Roof Pitch	40-degree Roof Pitch
5m roof span	Line of 2m headroom — 1440 / 5000 — Headroom Inadequate	Line of 2m headroom — 1770 / 5000 — Headroom Inadequate	Line of 2m headroom — 240 / 2100 / 5000 — Headroom Inadequate
6m roof span	Line of 2m headroom — 1730 / 6000 — Headroom Inadequate	Line of 2m headroom — 340 / 2120 / 6000 — Headroom Inadequate	Line of 2m headroom — 1240 / 2520 / 6000 — Headroom Adequate
7m roof span	Line of 2m headroom — 2000	Line of 2m headroom — 1340 / 2470	Line of 2m headroom — 2240 / 2940

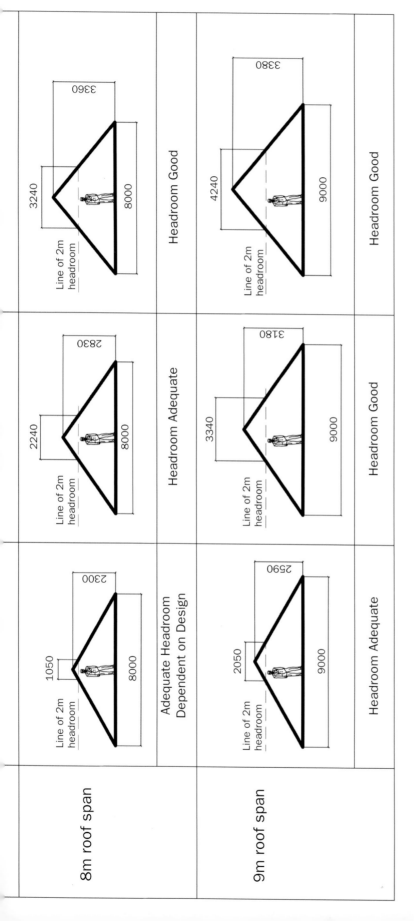

8m roof span

Line of 2m headroom — 1050	Line of 2m headroom — 2240	Line of 2m headroom — 3240
2300	2830	3360
8000	8000	8000
Adequate Headroom Dependent on Design	Headroom Adequate	Headroom Good

9m roof span

Line of 2m headroom — 2050	Line of 2m headroom — 3340	Line of 2m headroom — 4240
2590	3180	3380
9000	9000	9000
Headroom Adequate	Headroom Good	Headroom Good

Chart for estimating effect of roof pitch and span on headroom. These dimensions are very approximate. Some roofs are built with slightly different pitches to each side. The diagrams show the internal line of the existing roof, so the headroom shown here will be reduced by the new floor and linings under the rafters. Dimensions are in millimetres except where otherwise stated.

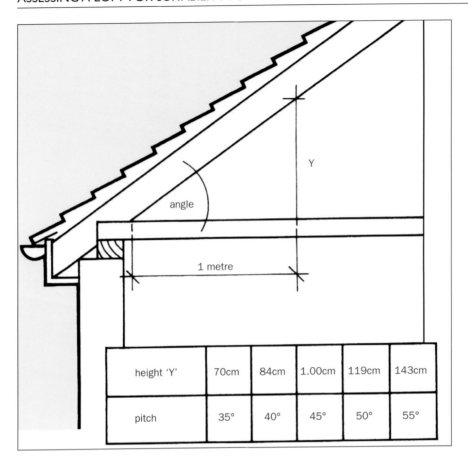

How to estimate a roof pitch.

height 'Y'	70cm	84cm	1.00cm	119cm	143cm
pitch	35°	40°	45°	50°	55°

The chart on pages 18–19 shows the relationship between the pitch of the roof, the span and how much loft space is available. It shows that to be sure of getting a workable loft conversion with a 30-degree roof pitch the span must be around 8m or 9m. With a 40-degree pitch, it is just possible to create a room when the span is around 6m. It can be seen from this table that where the roof is on the borderline of being convertible, it is essential that accurate measurements are taken when making an assessment of its potential. Sometimes the difference between success and failure is decided by a matter of a few centimetres. An added complication with older houses is that the pitches on different sides of the roof can vary by several degrees – something that is not immediately noticeable, even to the experts, unless an angle finder is used to check each pitch. Very old

houses are also often not built square in plan as well. These inaccuracies in the construction are usually irrelevant unless the loft conversion is very short on headroom, in which case they should be checked to make sure that the headroom at one end of the building is the same as at the other. This is why some smaller loft conversions can take more time to survey and design than larger roofs with plenty of headroom.

If the headroom is not sufficient, it may still be possible to create a loft conversion, although relatively elaborate solutions are required. One is to replace the roof completely and either make the roof pitch steeper or build up the main walls of the house. Apart from the significant extra cost, planning approval will be needed to do this, which may not be granted if your house is one of a row of identical properties. The alternative is to lower the

Plenty of headroom is essential for a successful loft conversion. Room Maker Loft Conversions

ceiling of the rooms below. To do this there must be sufficient headroom in these spaces and structural work will probably be required to prevent the rafters of the roof from pushing out the tops of the walls. It may be possible to form a mezzanine level to avoid the roof height becoming oppressively low.

STAIRCASE ACCESS

Assuming that there is adequate headroom, the next issue is the location of the staircase. For a house with two storeys or more, this should ideally be directly over the existing staircase. Unfortunately, in many houses, the staircase is sited at the edge of the house under the eaves, where the roof is at its lowest and so a dormer window is usually needed to allow the extra headroom. If it is not possible to position the new stair over the existing one, space will probably be lost from one or two of the existing bedrooms. In the worst cases a whole bedroom can be lost in which case clearly the new loft space has to be significantly bigger to make the project worthwhile. When trying to work out the staircase locations that are possible, it can be helpful to start by identifying whereabouts the top step can go in the loft. Because there should be 2m headroom at this point, the number of possible locations is fairly limited in all but the largest roofspaces.

There must be sufficient headroom at the top of the stairs. Attic Designs Ltd

If the house already has two floors, the Building Regulations require that there should be a safe escape route in the event of a fire. This can be achieved by creating a route from the loft room to the front or back door that is completely fire protected for 30 minutes, or a similar route to the

Sometimes it is necessary to cut through the existing structure to create a window at the right height. Attic Designs Ltd

first-floor landing with windows that can be climbed through.

WINDOWS, VIEWS AND DAYLIGHT

The new rooms to be created must have daylight, ventilation and ideally a view out. Roof windows that follow the line of the roof are the simplest and cheapest solution. Dormer roofs are also a well-used method, with the added benefit that they also add extra space with headroom. Sometimes where a main wall of the house extends up to form a side of the loft space, usually in the form of a gable, it offers an easy way of creating a conventional window. When making an initial assessment of the loft, likely locations for the windows should be considered. If possible they should allow a view but not significantly overlook a neighbour's garden. If they have to go on the front-facing roof of the house, they may need planning approval. Sometimes, to position a roof at the right height and location, it is necessary to cut through a significant element of the structure, such as a purlin (one of the horizontal beams that supports the rafters). It is usually possible to do this, but you will require some extra structural supports, such as steel beams, to compensate for the missing sections.

SERVICES

Many lofts have water tanks of some kind in them, especially in houses that have older heating systems. If there is no space for them once the conversion has been completed it will be necessary to fit a new system. Some boilers work on mains pressure, without using a water tank, which means that there is a good chance of getting hot water up to a bathroom or WC in the roofspace. Systems that rely on a large water tank providing a 'head' of water cannot provide enough pressure to supply water to fittings that are at the same level or above. In the former case, it may just be possible to get taps to a washbasin to work, but a shower will never have sufficient pressure unless you introduce a pump system, such as a power shower.

Water tanks often have to be moved as part of a loft conversion. Julian Owen Associates Architects

How well insulated is your loft? The pigeons know, because a badly insulated loft provides the perfect warm roost in winter. Much of the heat energy paid for by the house owner escapes to the outside. Julian Owen Associates Architects

INSULATION

Modern standards insist that any habitable room in a house is insulated to reduce heat loss – but with rising energy costs it is an important part of the building work regardless of the rules and regulations. Consequently, a new layer of insulation is needed immediately below the roof covering. The line of the new ceiling will be lower than the underside of the existing rafters because they are unlikely to be deep enough to accommodate the thickness of insulation that is needed. This means that the overall headroom of the space may reduce by anything from 50mm to 100mm.

If a loft has been used only for storage, it may not have any insulation in the roofspace at all, especially if it is an older property. It is more likely that it will have some insulation laid directly above the ceiling below, between the ceiling joists. The latest Building Regulations require that an extra layer of insulation is laid over the top of the ceiling joists as well. Apart from insulating against heat loss, the insulation can also reduce noise transmission between floors, so it does some good to leave it where it is rather than lower the height of the new floor. It is unlikely to be thin enough to be reused to insulate between the rafters.

STORAGE

Most unconverted lofts are a handy place for storage. There is little enough space in modern houses and it is easier to put items up there than get rid of it. However, there are also things, such as suitcases, books and memorabilia, that are not needed in everyday life but the family do not want to lose. In some cases, the amount of such clutter can be considerable. Even after a major de-cluttering process, which is time-consuming and is best started as soon as the decision to convert is made, there is likely to be a need for a sizeable amount of extra storage space. This can be dealt with by incorporating new cupboards in the house as part of the project, or building a new shed in the garden or by hiring long-term storage space elsewhere.

Most lofts are full of junk that needs to be thrown out or stored elsewhere.
Julian Owen Associates Architects

Some Definitions

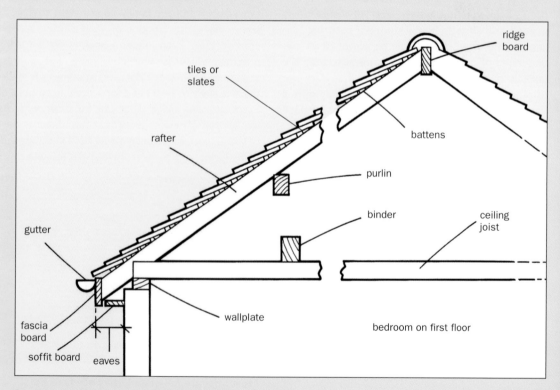

Typical terms for parts of a roof.

Section showing some typical components of a roof.

Barge board This board follows line of tiles at the gable end of roof to conceal the joint between roof and wall.

Ceiling joists These span between wallplates on top of the walls at either side of roof. They carry the weight of ceiling and insulation only, and if there is extra load such as a water tank, extra support is provided. They also tie the feet of the rafters together to stop them from moving outwards and pushing over the tops of the walls. They are often too slender for the distance that they span, so a binder spanning between cross walls provides intermediate support.

Common rafters The main structural element of the roof, spanning between ridge and wallplate, supporting battens for the roof. They are birds-mouthed over wallplate.

Dormer A way of increasing headroom in a roof and also forms a vertical window.

Eaves The section of roof that overhangs the top of the external wall.

Fascia board Board that is fixed to the end of the rafters, supporting the gutter and the last row of tiles.

Gable end The triangular end of a double-pitched roof.

Hip roof An extra slope to the roof in place of a gable end.

Purlin This provides intermediate structural support to the rafters when they are too thin to span distance on their own. They are supported off walls. If a purlin is cut before it is properly supported a roof could collapse.

Ridge The top of the roof, where rafters meet.

Soffit board Closes off the gap between the fascia and the top of the external wall.

Valley Where two roof pitches meet and form a drainage channel, usually made with glass fibre or lead flashing.

Wallplate Typically 100 × 50mm in size, this softwood section supports the rafters and ceiling joists. It is bedded on mortar on top of the external wall. Modern wallplates are fixed to the wall with steel straps, with the rafters and ceiling joists nailed to them.

Two of the most basic structural components of the roof are the rafters, which follow the slope of the roof, and the purlin, a horizontal beam that the rafters rest upon. Julian Owen Associates Architects

TYPES OF ROOF

Although the pitch and construction are also important, some roof shapes are easier to convert than others. Assuming that there is at least one part of the roof that is high enough for someone to stand up in, the arrangement and shape of the roof will partly determine how easy it can be converted.

Gable Roof

This is one of the simplest forms to construct and, in terms of shape, is one of the easiest to convert. The triangular walls at the end allow the pos-

sibility of ordinary windows and there is a long section of continuous usable space. Dormer roofs can be added easily, although there are often purlins in the way that will need to be cut to allow this.

Hipped Roof

Along with gable roofs, hipped roofs are the most common type of shape in the UK, particularly in the suburbs. They are slightly more difficult to convert than a gable, because the extra sloping roofs reduce the space available and also reduce the option for locating a staircase. For a standard three- or four-bedroom detached house, it is likely

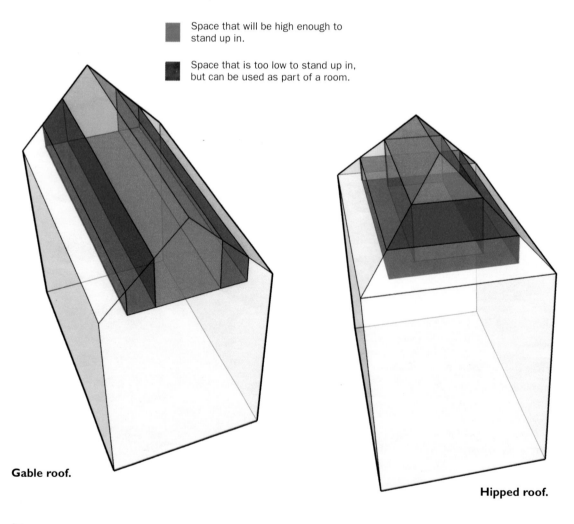

Space that will be high enough to stand up in.

Space that is too low to stand up in, but can be used as part of a room.

Gable roof.

Hipped roof.

Monopitch roof.

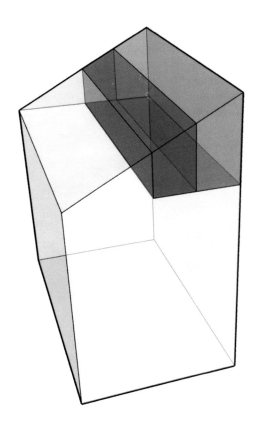

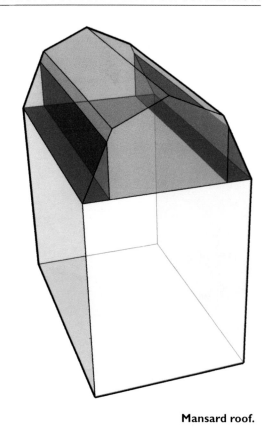

Mansard roof.

that this type of roof will require a dormer or other roof alteration to allow the staircase sufficient headroom. Because the roof structure all leans into the centre of the building, any purlins have to be supported off internal walls with props, which makes the roof structure slightly harder to alter.

Monopitch Roof

Monopitch roofs are often found over single-storey ancillary rooms and spaces such as utility rooms at the side or back of the main building on traditional houses. If a monopitch roof spans across a whole house, the end at the top of the roof can be disproportionately high relative to the other side, which is at eaves level. To avoid this problem, some modern roof designs tend to

reduce the pitch and span of a monopitch, but this leaves little or no space for a conversion. If the monopitch does have a steep enough pitch and is over a ground floor only, it may be possible to get to it from the first floor. Staircase access is tricky to this type of roofspace unless the void is unusually large.

Mansard Roof

Mansard roofs are usually created at construction specifically to allow the roofspace to be used. If it has not been made use of, it is a prime candidate for conversion. If an existing roof is too low to be converted and a new roof has to be built, a mansard is a good way to increase the height and volume of the roofspace whilst keeping the ridge relatively low.

Butterfly and Four-Pitch Roofs with Parapets

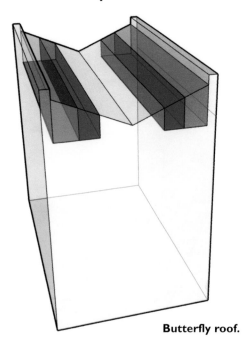

Butterfly roof.

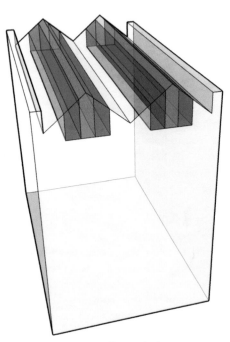

Four-pitch parapet roof.

These are more common in the grander traditional terrace houses, such as those in the Georgian style. If there is any space at all with adequate headroom, it is not usually in the ideal location for conversion. It may be possible to 'fill in' the space between the valleys, by constructing a new roof, but this may make the ridge height of the roof unacceptably high from the point of view of the planners, particularly if it is visible from the street and contrasts with its neighbours'.

STRUCTURE AND CONSTRUCTION

Provided that the geometry of a roof is appropriate, most of the structural alterations that may be needed to convert a loft are usually possible. The question is whether these alterations are so elaborate that the cost and disruption do not jus-

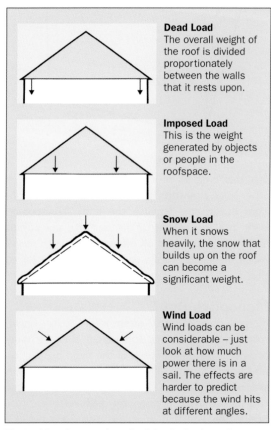

Dead Load
The overall weight of the roof is divided proportionately between the walls that it rests upon.

Imposed Load
This is the weight generated by objects or people in the roofspace.

Snow Load
When it snows heavily, the snow that builds up on the roof can become a significant weight.

Wind Load
Wind loads can be considerable – just look at how much power there is in a sail. The effects are harder to predict because the wind hits at different angles.

Typical loads associated with pitched roofs.

tify the end result. An important step in the assessment of an existing roof is to understand the structure and construction, so that the effect of possible alterations can be identified and the best solutions chosen.

Roof Triangulation, Loads and Forces

The same structural principles apply to any type of double-pitched roof. The weight of the roof covering and construction, such as the roof tiles, battens, insulation and 'self weight' of the rafters rest on the structure. As well as the weight of the structure, the roof also has to support occasional extra loads, such as snow or people walking up it to make repairs. All these loads have a tendency to push the bottom ends, or feet, of the rafters outwards. Except when the span of the roof is very short, the force of this pushing out of the feet is significant enough to push out the tops of the walls they are sitting on and even collapse the whole roof.

The simple solution to this problem is to securely tie the ends of the ceiling joists to the ends of the rafters. Then, in order for the roof to

spread, it would have to pull apart and snap the joists. Fortunately timber is very resistant to being stretched, so even relatively thin sections of softwood will easily resist this tension. This means that apart from supporting the ceiling, these joists also play a crucial role keeping the roof above stable. This simple structural system is a fundamental building technique that has been used since humans first began building and is known as 'triangulation'. The most basic arrangement of this type of roof is called the 'couple roof', which will not usually span far enough on its own to raise the ridge to a height that will allow space for a conversion.

If the ceiling joists are cut without proper regard to the consequences, or the fixings that secure them to the rafter feet are weakened, a perfectly strong, well-built roof structure may fail. Usually it is possible to cut some of the ceiling joists in a limited area, for example to create a loft hatch or even a stairwell, because the structure of most roofs is far stronger than the loads and forces that they usually have to bear. However, some roofs, particularly on older houses that have been cheaply built, are more easily damaged.

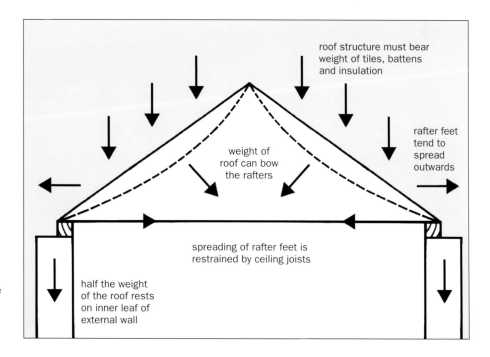

roof structure must bear weight of tiles, battens and insulation

weight of roof can bow the rafters

rafter feet tend to spread outwards

spreading of rafter feet is restrained by ceiling joists

half the weight of the roof rests on inner leaf of external wall

Forces that are acting on a typical roof structure.

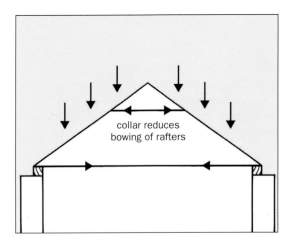

Effect on roof structure of introducing a collar.

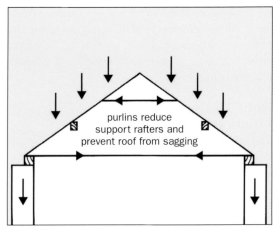

Effect on roof structure of introducing purlins.

There are a number of ways of increasing the span of the roof by introducing extra timber members to the design. The introduction of a collar to the roof will prevent the rafters from sagging, allowing them to span further. As with the ceiling joists, if too many collars are cut or removed from a roof, there will be damage to the roof structure and movement will occur. However, collars are not always needed all along the roof and it is not unusual to find that the original builder used one only on every fourth rafter.

The structural system of a roof can be further improved by adding purlins. These beams are larger in cross-section than the rafters, ceiling joists or collars and span at 90 degrees to them. Purlins have to be supported off walls that are at right angles to the walls supporting the other structural timbers. In a small house this support may be provided by external walls, but more often internal walls, or 'cross walls', are used or steel beams. In a traditional two-storey house, the cross walls have to have foundations and therefore will run from ceiling level through the first and ground floors. The removal or disturbance of these walls must only be carried out with the advice of a building professional to avoid harm to the structure of the rest of the house.

A modern development of the structural principle of triangulation is the trussed rafter, where many smaller timber elements support the roof, using the minimum amount of timber to maximum effect. They are cheaper, because less materials and labour are needed to create the roof, but they make conversion far more difficult to carry out because the roof void is filled with a criss-crossed network of timber.

The most important concept to understand when contemplating alterations to a roof structure is that all of the timbers that make it up are performing some sort of important function and many are doing two or three jobs at once. Before any of them are removed the likely effects must be understood and allowance made for them. Sometimes this may only be strengthening the remaining structural elements to make up for the loss, but quite often extra structures, such as new steel beams, are needed to prevent problems.

Construction Types

There are two main methods of roof construction used for modern houses in the UK: the traditional, or 'cut', roof and the trussed rafter roof. A hybrid of the two is the TDA roof truss, in which a smaller number of larger, stronger roof trusses were used to support thin purlins between them, which in turn support rafters. The latter is not as common as the main types.

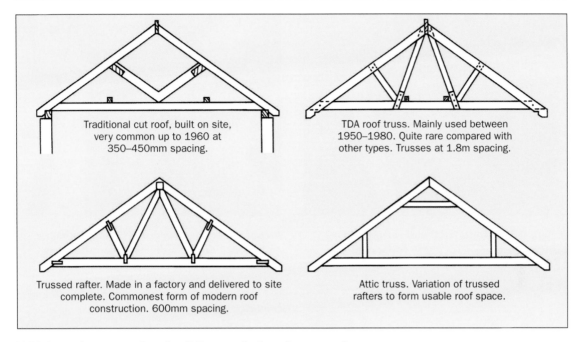

Traditional cut roof, built on site, very common up to 1960 at 350–450mm spacing.

TDA roof truss. Mainly used between 1950–1980. Quite rare compared with other types. Trusses at 1.8m spacing.

Trussed rafter. Made in a factory and delivered to site complete. Commonest form of modern roof construction. 600mm spacing.

Attic truss. Variation of trussed rafters to form usable roof space.

Which one is your roof made of? Four typical roof constructions.

The type of construction used for your roof will determine how easy it is to convert and each type requires quite different approaches to alter their structure successfully.

Traditional Cut Roofs
Traditional roof structures are constructed from rafters, ceiling ties, purlins, collars and struts by sawing up timber and building it all on site. The

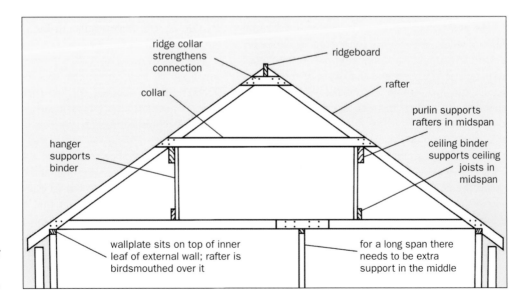

ridge collar strengthens connection

ridgeboard

collar

rafter

purlin supports rafters in midspan

hanger supports binder

ceiling binder supports ceiling joists in midspan

wallplate sits on top of inner leaf of external wall; rafter is birdsmouthed over it

for a long span there needs to be extra support in the middle

Typical cut roof cross-section.

31

A typical traditional roof, with rafters and purlins. The purlins are partly supported by props. Julian Owen Associates Architects

A roof under construction showing the rafter ends sitting on the wallplate. The rafters are not notched onto the wallplate because the detail for the eaves is corbelled brickwork and the rafters do not overhang the outside face of the brick wall. Julian Owen Associates Architects

typical cross-section shows how these might be assembled. There are many combinations of these basic elements that are used, depending on the span of the roof and knowledge and skill of the carpenter building it. Most houses built before 1960 have this type of roof, other than those which could be called 'historic', where larger sections of timber were either affordable or more readily available.

The main roof covering is supported by the rafters, which are in turn supported by the walls below. Sometimes the only support for the roof structure is the two external walls that it spans across, but more often an internal wall is used to support the ceiling joists to prevent them from sagging. If the ceiling joists are not long enough to span the whole distance between the feet of the rafters so that two lengths are needed, they should be securely joined together to ensure that they retain the ability to resist roof spread. The rafters are invariably too shallow to take the depth of insulation required for a conversion even if the gaps between them are completely filled. The ceiling ties will normally be of inadequate strength to take the extra weight that will be imposed by using the loft space to contain furniture and people. If

there are normal collars, fixed to the rafters at regular intervals, they will probably be too low and will need to be removed. Assuming that they are preventing the rafters from bowing, extra support such as steel purlins will be needed to take their place. Sometimes collars are higher up the roof, where they perform a slightly different structural role – strengthening the connection between the tops of the rafters. In this case they often do not intrude on the main usable space and should be left in place.

The feet of the rafters sit onto the inner side of the external wall, and if the roof overhangs the eaves, they are notched to help them to make a good connection and increase the area of timber that is in connection with the top of the wall. To help get a good fixing, the top of the wall is usually formed from a timber strip called a wallplate. This is bolted securely onto the wall and makes it relatively easy for the carpenter to nail the rafter in place, as well as ensuring that the load is spread evenly.

Purlins are major structural supports and although it may be possible to shuffle them further up or down the roof, they are most effective when they are positioned in the middle third of the

Typical traditional roof construction of a terraced house.

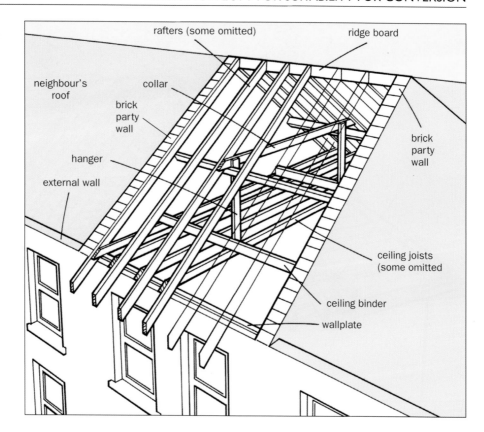

rafters (some omitted)

ridge board

neighbour's roof

collar

brick party wall

brick party wall

hanger

external wall

ceiling joists (some omitted

ceiling binder

wallplate

BELOW:
Traditional cut roof – typical construction inside a hip.

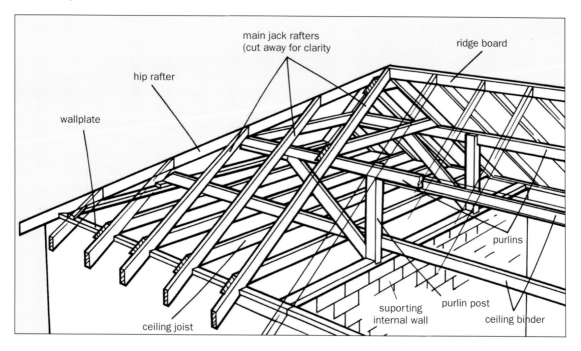

main jack rafters (cut away for clarity

ridge board

hip rafter

wallplate

purlins

purlin post

suporting internal wall

ceiling binder

ceiling joist

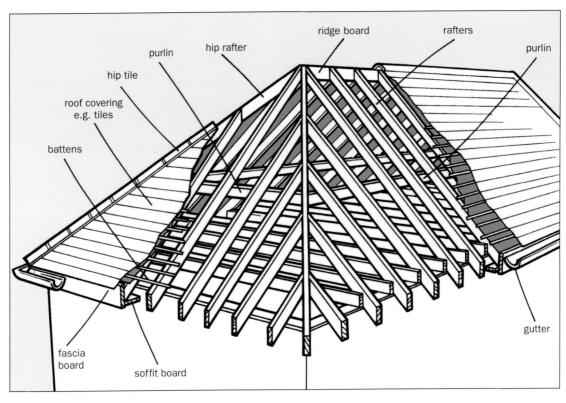

Traditional hip-roof construction from the outside.

The corner of a hip roof. Unlike a gable roof, there is no wall to sit the ends of the purlin into, so the purlins on each side are fixed to each other at the corners.

Julian Owen Associates Architects

rafter. This is often exactly where the new windows are to go and so they have to be cut, requiring significant extra structural support to replace the missing sections.

An alternative to using internal walls to support ceiling ties that would otherwise be too thin for their span is to add larger timber beams, called ceiling binders, spanning at 90 degrees to the rafters and joists, supported by lengths of timber hanging from the purlins.

The form of traditional roof that is easiest to build is the gable roof. This is basically two roof pitches resting on each other, with triangular sections of wall to enclose the ends. It is used a lot for terraced houses because it is cheap and quick to build in comparison with other roof shapes, but is also used for detached houses and occasionally semi-detached.

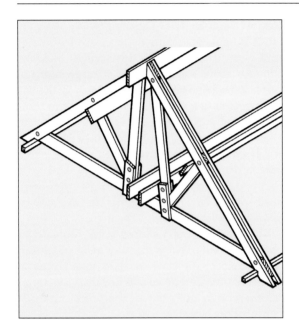

A TDA bolted truss.

The disadvantage of a gable roof as far as modern planning controls are concerned is that where the walls of houses are close to a boundary, the ridge is more prominent compared to the main alternative, the hipped roof. The benefit of the latter is that the ridge is kept away from the edge of the house and therefore appears less dominant to its close neighbours. This is one reason why houses built in the UK during the expansion of the suburbs in the middle years of the twentieth century tend to have hipped roofs. From the point of view of the builder, the disadvantage of hipped roofs is that they are more complex structurally and more expensive to construct. From the point of view of someone contemplating a loft conversion, the disadvantage is that the volume of existing roof available is greatly reduced. A further, less obvious problem is that the roof structure lacks the walls at each end that are available for support in a gable shape and so the purlins rely entirely on props resting on the internal walls for their support. This makes structural alterations slightly more complex.

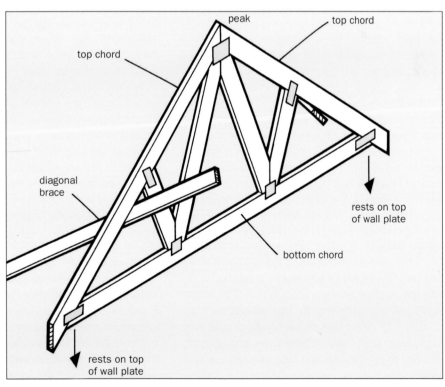

A trussed rafter.

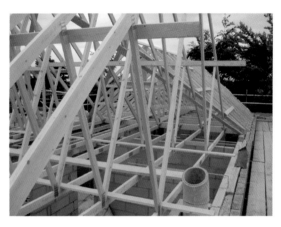

A trussed rafter roof under construction.

TDA trusses

These are named after the Timber Development Association that devised them, were used after the Second World War in an effort to make use of the scarce supplies of timber more efficiently. Sometimes the timbers were bolted together, using double-sided 'tooth plate' connectors, and sometimes plates of plywood were nailed on to join them together. They were standardized so that they could be used without needing an engineer to carry out a detailed design.

Trussed Rafters

The modern way to form a roof is an elegant solution from the point of view of structural design – the trussed rafter, or fink truss. This is designed to use the minimum amount of timber possible, in the form of relatively small cross-section, standard timbers. Computers are used to calculate the optimum arrangement of these timbers, which are held together by galvanized steel-toothed connecting plates. Because the sizes are so precisely calculated, the timbers must not be cut or drilled in any way once the truss is complete or they may be significantly weakened. Each truss is manufactured in a factory and delivered to site, where they are hoisted into place, held together and braced with extra lengths of timber. These roofs are generally cheaper than a traditionally built one and can span significantly further without needing any other

support – up to 12m. They are widely used for modern housing and are the standard method of roof construction for speculative builders, although some experienced roof carpenters still prefer the traditional version. Obviously all the ties and struts fill the roofspace, which therefore cannot be used as an attic room without major alterations. However, it is possible to use 'attic trusses', which are like standard trussed rafter roofs with a hole in the middle large enough to be used for a room. Attic trusses are fine as long as you don't need to join two roofs together, for example to make an 'L' shape in plan.

The conversion of a trussed rafter roof into an open roofspace requires specialist assistance. It can be achieved by inserting standard steel beams to replace the timber struts and ties that have to be removed or by using one of the proprietary systems that are available.

Historic Roof Construction

In the construction of many older properties, particularly one-off constructions built before the nineteenth century and rural buildings such as barns, large, widely spaced trusses were used to support thinner rafters than those used for the traditional cut roof described above. Very old buildings tend to be made from very large sections of timber. This is because up until the seventeenth century oak trees were in plentiful supply, growing across huge areas of the country. Softwood, which tends to come in more slender sections, gradually began to be imported and the demands of the industrial revolution led to a shortage of heavy timbers available for housing. This in turn led to the adoption of the cut roof, which makes good use of the thinner sections of softwood. If the roof of a house has traditional oak trusses such as those shown in the illustrations, it may be possible to incorporate them into the design of the new loft space without removing them, turning them into a feature wall by infilling between the timbers. However, it is likely that the trusses will be in the way and will need to be cut or removed to achieve a successful conversion. If this is the only option, the date and type of truss should be established before carrying out the work. With a venerable old

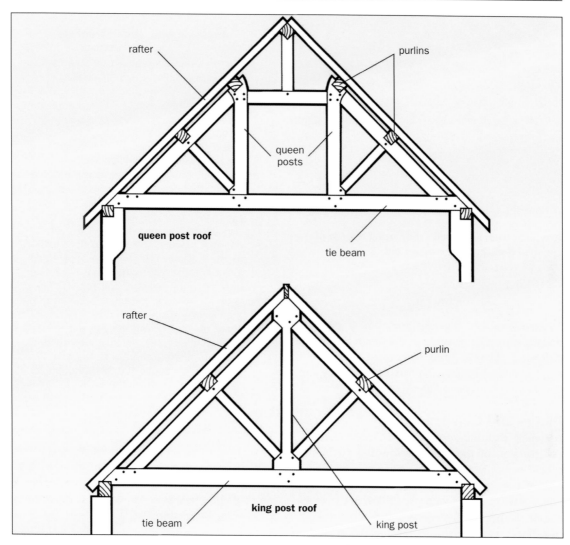

ABOVE: **Eighteenth-century roof trusses.**

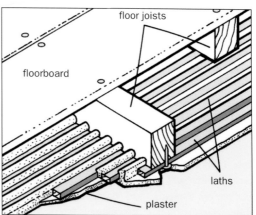

RIGHT: **A lath and plaster ceiling.**

A typical truss and purlin roof, using a form of construction that is centuries old.

Julian Owen Associates Architects

Assessing the Roof Structure

- Identify which structural type your roof is and work out how it is triangulated.
- Look for the way that the timbers are joined together – whether they are nailed, bolted or held by plates of steel or plywood.
- If the roof has purlins, what height are they and will they interrupt windows?
- Work out how the loads from the roof are transmitted down to the walls.
- Check to see if you can identify the structural walls that may be useful to provide support to the new design. This can be done by tapping walls on the floor below to check if they are stud or masonry and looking in the loft to see what is resting directly on the walls.
- Look for hangers and binders supporting the ceiling joists.
- Look at the ceiling joists and check whether they span the full width of the house or whether there are internal walls that they are supported on (as opposed to simply passing over them).

---

construction, held together with timber pegs or dowels, it may be possible to dismantle and reuse it. If the building is listed, however, it would be a criminal offence to alter the trusses in any way, and could result in a severe fine.

Floors and Ceilings

Assuming that the roof is not boarded out, the construction of the ceiling below the roofspace should be easily visible. The ceiling is likely to be one of two types of construction. In a modern house it will be lined with plasterboard, a layer of plaster sandwiched between cardboard to make a rigid board that is fixed to the underside of the ceiling joists. The plasterboard is then either given a thin coat of plaster to finish it, or the joints are taped and filled and the surface is covered with wallpaper.

Older buildings, pre-1960s, will probably have a 'lath and plaster' ceiling, which consists of strips of softwood nailed at 90 degrees to the joists and coated in plaster to form a smooth surface, either for painting or wallpaper.

A lath and plaster ceiling, especially an older one, is more prone to damage during the building work, which will involve a lot of disturbance to the ceiling by banging and hammering and putting unusual loads on it. If the ceiling is particularly poor

it may have to be removed and replaced. This may be necessary regardless of its durability in order to achieve fire protection between the new room in the roof and the spaces below that is required by the Building Regulations.

Surveying the Condition of the Construction

Having made an assessment of the capability of the existing roofspace to allow a successful conversion, the condition of the construction should be checked. Apart from needing to know how well the structure will stand up to the indignities of the building work, if some areas of the roof are in poor condition, this may influence the decisions that are made as well as the total cost of the project. For example, if a roof has extensive rot and the tiles are deteriorating, it may be a better option to replace the entire roof rather than spend a lot of money trying to repair and strengthen it.

Assuming that as with most projects there is a limited budget, once a defect is identified, someone has to decide how to deal with it. Often this is the builder or architect, but it is perfectly possible for the homeowner to identify the biggest items at an early stage and then be ready for the discussions that may ensue when the schedule of works is being prepared.

Health and Safety

At this point, it is worth mentioning that care needs to be taken when inspecting a loft, especially if it involves moving about in areas that have not been visited for some time. Strictly speaking, to follow current health and safety recommendations, anyone entering a loft should wear an approved safety helmet, industrial quality gloves, protective goggles and a face mask with a filter. The reality is that most people, even professional contractors, do not do this, regardless of what is suggested by prudence or stated by the health and safety laws. Most risks are easily avoided by using your common sense, but it is sensible to be aware of some of the less obvious risks that are unlikely but dangerous if encountered.

The most likely risk when the ceiling joists are unboarded is that of stepping directly on the ceiling instead of the joists. This can result in a foot and leg breaking through into the room below. Although this type of accident is much beloved by the writers of TV sitcoms, it can actually cause some nasty injuries. The risk is increased where the insulation layer covers the top of the joists, making them difficult to locate in a gloomy loft space.

Never venture into a loft without a good source of light, either by electric light or a good torch, with a smaller pocket torch as a backup. If you are taking on a DIY project and expect to spend a lot of time up there, it may be worth investing in a proprietary head-mounted torch that looks a little strange, but has the benefit of leaving both your hands free. Look out for service runs and electric wires that are often laid over the ceiling joists and can trip the unwary.

Mineral wool, one of the commonest materials to be used in insulating lofts, is an irritant. This

A thorough survey of the existing roof is essential. Julian Owen Associates Architects

means that although it has no harmful chemical effects and has no known effect on the long-term health of anyone who comes into contact with it, it can irritate the hands, eyes and throat. If someone is particularly sensitive to it, a temporary rash may result from contact. So if mineral wool is to be moved about, lifted or handled in any significant way, gloves, goggles and a face mask should be used if you want to avoid the risk of any discomfort.

If a loft has been infested with pigeons for any period of time, their droppings present a serious risk to health, particularly once they dry out and are then disturbed, sending dust into the air. There are many very nasty illnesses and parasites that build up in droppings, some of them fatal. If there has been significant infestation, the roofspace should not be entered unless an appropriate facemask is worn. This is another instance where expert help is required, in the form of a pest control company. If bats have taken up residence in your roof, they must not be disturbed without permission from your local council even if you think they are a health hazard, because they are a protected species. It is a criminal offence to upset them in any way.

Asbestos is occasionally present in the roofspaces of houses in the form of lagging to pipework. If there is any doubt an asbestos survey is essential, particularly if the material is to be disturbed by the work in any way. Asbestos is also sometimes present in older, cheaper cement-based roof tiles. Provided that they are not crumbling and are not sawn or broken in any way, they do not present an immediate health risk, but as with any type of asbestos, the law requires that they are placed in special sealed bags and disposed of separately from other building waste.

If the roof is to be inspected from the outside by climbing a ladder, especially for houses more than one storey high, precautions must be taken. A ladder should be at an angle of no more than 11 degrees to the vertical, weighted at the bottom by a person or other method to prevent it moving and ideally secured at the top as well. Do not consider venturing out onto the roof itself without experience and appropriate equipment to reduce the risks of a fall. This is a dangerous manoeuvre even for professionals – more building workers are seriously injured or die from falls from roofs than in any other type of accident on construction sites.

Rot and Where to Find it

In the UK, because of the climate the main threat to timber used in a roofspace comes from fungal decay. In hotter, drier places, insects are more of a threat, particularly termites. Wood rots if fungi are

A common place to find rot is at the ends of the rafter feet where they rest on the top of an external wall, because this area is often the first to be exposed to damp if the roof covering begins to fail or a gutter leaks. Another common location for rot is where the ends of a purlin are built into the external wall.

Julian Owen Associates Architects

Dealing with a Building Defect

Which of the following is the best treatment for any defects identified? The further you go down the list, the more it is likely to cost.

1. Leave it alone as it won't get any worse. For example, timber may have rotted slightly on the surface, but this stopped long ago and the wood is generally sound.
2. Carry out remedial work. It is not beyond repair and repairing will restore it. If the problem relates to a feature that is hard to replace, such as period detail like an original timber truss, it may be cheaper to cut out rot and replace it with new timber and/or wood filler, and it will look just as good once painted.

3. Remove the damaged area all together and replace with a modern alternative. You may do this if something is beyond repair, and it will not be detrimental to the appearance or function of the building. For example, you might remove an extensively rotted timber truss in the roofspace and replace it with steel purlins.
4. Remove the damaged area and replace it with an exact copy. You may be compelled to do this if the building is listed, or decide to do this if you think that it is an important part of the appearance of the house. For example, if some old facing bricks have crumbled, using modern, metric-sized bricks to replace them will never look attractive.

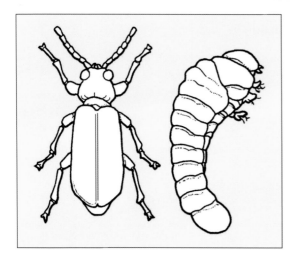

The furniture beetle.

present and break down the wood as they extract sugar-rich elements such as carbohydrates. Wet rot is the commonest form of fungal attack, although the other form, dry rot, is the one that provokes the most fear and excitement.

Wet rot can be identified by the dark brown staining it causes to the wood, with olive-green or dark brown fruiting bodies. It only survives in the immediate area of the damp that has caused it, and dies as soon as the source of moisture is removed. A classic case of damp in a roof occurs at the feet of the rafters, where a gutter has overflowed or the final few tiles are dislodged or defective, allowing rain to soak the top of the wall plate. A roof that has extensive rot can remain structurally stable for some time, especially if the damage is confined to one area. Failure of the timbers that are rotting takes quite a long time and the weakening of some of the timbers may be compensated for by the surrounding ones taking on extra load.

Dry rot has a characteristic mushroom smell and produces extensive strands of white root-like threads across the timber that eventually develop into off-white sheets. The final stage of development is a fruiting body that looks a bit like a pancake in shape, mostly dark rusty brown in colour with white fronds at the edges. The dry rot can

spread its tendrils behind walls, through plaster and even across apparently solid barriers such as brick and concrete. It also releases spores into the air that will flourish if they land on any other areas of damp timber. Dry rot is very destructive and will reduce apparently strong structural timbers to crumbling dust. It is much harder to eradicate than wet rot and specialist advice should be sought immediately if it is discovered in a roof.

To an inexpert eye and when in their early stages, it is not always easy to tell the difference between wet rot and dry rot so if there is any doubt a professional should be called. If you are standing in a roof structure and you identify that any significant rot of either type is present, retreat immediately and do not place any extra weight on the structure until you are sure that it can support it. If it is dry rot that you have discovered, assume that all the other structural timbers in the building are at risk unless you can prove that they have not been affected.

For either dry or wet rot to survive there must be a high moisture content to the timber – usually at least 20 per cent – while in a modern heated house the moisture content will usually settle down at about 10–13 per cent. Denied its principal requirements of warmth and dampness, rot will not establish itself.

Infestation of the timber by insects is unlikely in a roof construction built to modern standards because the timber preservative treatments effectively prevent it. Many of the potentially damaging species only affect hardwood or newly felled timber. Even for the older untreated roofs, provided the moisture content of the timber is below 20 per cent, the other insect types are unlikely to become established. The ubiquitous woodworm or furniture beetle can infest drier timber, but is deterred by well-ventilated, warm dry timber found in most UK homes, which tend to have central heating. Woodworm infestation is revealed by boreholes on the surface of the timber between 1mm and 2mm in diameter, and has to be fairly extensive to cause any structural weakness. The house longhorn beetle is established in a very limited area of the UK, south and west of London, where the threat is serious enough for there to be

A Condition Survey

You can tell a lot about a roof by a simple inspection if you know what to look for. The following table is a condensed version of the sort of checklist that a surveyor or architect would use. It is by no means exhaustive, but covers the major points that will affect a conversion.

Element of the Building	Comment
Roof	
What is the roof geometry?	For example, gable, hipped, or several sections of roofs that join into each other.
Has the roof been built using separate rafters and purlins on site or were trussed rafters used?	Trussed rafters are made from thinner sizes of wood and usually zigzag across the roofspace.
Height within the existing roofspace.	2.2m is the minimum requirement, but you must allow for thicker roof insulation and deeper floor structure.
Sizes of roof timbers and ceiling joists etc.	Look for unusual timbers that may play a structural role such as bracing.
Are any of the roof timbers bent or bowed?	Do the ceiling joists deflect or bounce when walked on? Which walls are they resting on?
What is the pitch of the roof?	It may vary slightly on different sides of the roof.
Is the ridge line straight and level?	If not, the rafters may be sagging, due to overloading or failed joints. Generally, if any of the lines of the roof are not straight they should be investigated.
Roof covering type	For example, clay plain tile, pantile, slate or concrete interlocking.
Are there many cracked or damaged slates or tiles?	Slates do not last as long as tiles. Concrete tiles fade but last longer. If the nails are corroded the disturbance that results from work to the roof may dislodge so many of them it is better to replace the whole roof covering than attempt repairs. Tiles or slates that 'chatter' loudly in the wind indicate a potential problem.
Is there 'torching' between the slates or tiles and is it intact?	Houses built before underlay was introduced in the 1940s had lime mortar fillets between the tiles to reduce the amount of rain getting under them. Over time this tends to drop out, and lie on the floor of the loft. If still in place torching attracts and stores damp and can rot the battens of the roof.
Are there any signs of damp or rot?	Typically indicated by clues such as soft woodwork or a musty smell. Look particularly at the ends of the timbers where they are resting on walls and around junctions of the roof covering. If there is rot present, get it assessed by a surveyor.
Is there a roof underlay?	The sheet directly under the roof tiles on top of the rafters, usually black in colour.

Element of the Building	Comment
Is the roof insulated?	Current standards expect 250–300mm depth of mineral wool quilt between and over the ceiling joists.
Is there good ventilation?	Older roofs without underlay are well ventilated by the gaps between the tiles. If replaced with a new underlay, new ventilation paths may have to be created at the ridge and eaves.
Is the external timber in good condition?	Timber eaves and bargeboards are particularly vulnerable. They are harder to reach when the house is decorated and so tend to get missed out.
Are any flashings secure and in good condition?	Flashings are the lead strips that seal the junctions of a roof, for example where there is a chimney. If flashings become loose they will let in rain, causing rot.
What service runs and pipes are there in the roof and will they need to be diverted?	Look for water, electricity, soil pipes venting the drains and water tanks.
Gutters and downpipes.	Apart from dripping water in when it rains, a sign of blocked gutters (visible from below) is grass and weeds growing in them.

Walls

Which walls are supporting the floor, first-floor walls and roof structure?	These are structural walls and will need steel beams in their place if they are to be removed.
What is the condition of the mortar and pointing of any walls forming the loft?	If the mortar is partly missing it may let in driving rain. If the mortar is soft, it is probably made from a lime mix and should be replaced with a similar mix, not a modern hard cement mortar.
Is there a party wall and if so, how thick is it and how well sealed around the edges?	The party wall is the wall between your loft and your neighbour's. Sometimes there are beams running from one side to the other. Beams that are on the neighbour's side may rest on the whole wall and be exposed on your side.
Are there any cracks in the internal or external walls?	If they run through to the internal walls, or are getting bigger every year they could be a serious problem. In older houses in clay areas, cracks sometimes open up in summer and close again in winter.
Are the walls all straight, particularly at the top where the walls and edge of the roof meet (known as the eaves)?	You can dangle a string with a weight on the end out of the window or from a ladder to find out. If a wall is more than a third of its width off being plumb, it is technically unstable and in danger of collapse.
Are the walls bowing out along their length?	Stand at a corner and look along the surface of the wall to see if they are.
What is the condition of any external surface treatment, such as render?	Once render is cracked and gets water behind it, it will deteriorate and will need to be completely replaced.

continued overleaf

continued from page 43

Element of the Building	**Comment**
Are the lintels over windows and internal and external doors all level without cracking above?	Older houses may have timber lintels, or even rely on the window frames to support the wall above. They must be strong enough to bear the extra loads that result from a loft conversion.
Is there any insulation in the walls?	Modern Building Regulations require about 100mm of mineral wool, but more efficient insulation materials can be thinner.
If there is no insulation, is there a cavity that can be filled to provide it?	If there isn't, insulation would have to be fitted to the inside of the walls and covered with plasterboard, or on the outside and covered with render.
Are any chimneys that are to be kept functioning sound?	Older chimneys may leak gases into the roofspace and should be swept regularly if they serve solid fuel fires to prevent soot build-up. Above the line of the roof older chimneys may need repointing to keep them sound or even rebuilding if they are becoming unstable.

Staircase

Is there space above the existing staircase for the new one?	This is usually the best place for a new stair because there is no loss of the existing floor area.
Does the existing staircase comply with current regulations?	If it does not, it may be possible to correct it whilst the rest of the work is being carried out.

Ground Floor

Does the stair exit directly into the hall or do you have to go through a downstairs room to get outside?	A quick and easy route to the outside is essential for anyone in the loft in case of fire.

First Floor

Which walls on the first floor are structural?	These should be checked to make sure that they have not been weakened or altered since the house was built.
What is the first-floor ceiling made of?	Traditionally either lath on plaster or plasterboard in a modern house.

Other General Considerations

Space around the house	How near are neighbouring buildings? Is there space to get a scaffold up the side of the building and carry materials around the back of the house if necessary? Can a ladder be set up for someone to escape from a loft window if there is a fire?
Is the rest of the building generally structurally sound?	The new work is likely to increase the loads on some parts of the existing structure, so if there are already problems, such as foundation settlement, they should be put right beforehand or they may be made worse.

special provisions in the Building Regulations for these areas. If boreholes are found in a roof timber, it may be a relic from an infestation from long ago. For evidence of a current problem, look for new timber powder (or 'frass') around the holes.

Rot is usually treated with chemical insecticides, but the only cure for severe cases is to remove the damaged sections and replace them with new, pre-servative-treated timbers. Sometimes the whole structural element may have to be replaced. If the roof is part of a structure with any historic value, as much of the existing timber should be retained as possible, with new pieces spliced into the old. If the building is listed, any remedial work that involves the removal of any part of the construc-tion will need approval from the council. Once the timber has been treated or replaced, the causes of the damp, usually a leak or lack of ventilation or both, should be dealt with. It is usually fairly straightforward to locate the source of a leak by careful inspection and the timbers of the new roof that results from the conversion will have to be well ventilated to comply with modern regulations.

Although it is recommended that expert advice is sought if a rot problem is suspected, there are unfortunately a number of unscrupulous compa-nies that advertise their services in this field and offer a free diagnosis. Although many firms that offer this are perfectly reputable, after the survey some will greatly exaggerate the extent of work required to remedy the problem and imply that your roof may collapse onto your heads if they are not commissioned to carry it our immediately – at great cost, naturally. Do not be intimidated and get several quotes from firms that you know are rep-utable, or employ an independent consultant such as a surveyor to advise you.

> **Possible Sources of Damp in a Roof**
>
> - Overflowing gutters.
> - Disintegration of the back of rainwater pipes (only detectable by close inspec-tion).
> - Missing, damaged or dislocated tiles.
> - Failure of lead flashing where services pass through the roof, for example chim-neys.
> - Failure of the lead flashing around junc-tions between the roof and wall.
> - Leaking water pipes.
> - Condensation, caused by lack of ventila-tion in the roofspace.
> - Seeping through a brick gable wall where the mortar pointing has been worn away.

Sometimes it is only possible to confirm that the timbers of a roof are sound by exposing them for visual inspection.
Julian Owen Associates Architects

CHAPTER 3

Setting Up a Project

Having made an assessment of your loft and decided that it will be probably be suitable, you are ready to get your project underway. Unless you are an experienced DIY expert, with plenty of knowledge of the regulations and building techniques required, not a lot more will happen until you involve the professionals, but before you actually commission a firm to help you, a careful look at the budget is advisable.

BUDGETING AND COSTINGS

How to calculate the maximum you should spend on a conversion before it ceases to pay for itself has already been discussed in Chapter 1. Having gone through that exercise and decided that you

Even a small loft conversion will cost more than most people expect. Attic Designs Ltd

wish to carry on, you will need to estimate the extent of the work and try to identify the range of cost within which the work is likely to fall.

Managing the cost is the hardest part of any building project and going over budget is the single biggest risk that you face. At the early stages the calculations will all be 'best guesses', but you should review the budget calculation at every key point in the process. As you progress, the figures will become more accurate as you add to your knowledge and start to get a clearer idea of actual costs. The current budget calculations should be at the forefront of your mind whenever you have a key decision to make. There is no doubt that many building projects run into difficulties, when the actual costs are finally revealed.

Unfortunately, there is no magic formula that can guarantee you will not go over budget, though you can do a lot to reduce the risk of it happening. A popular but generally true mantra in the building industry is that a project can be any two out of cheap, fast and good quality, and the relationship between these three elements decides how much it eventually costs. Assuming that the project is not needed urgently, the real balance that has to be struck by most people is between cost and quality. No early cost estimate can be relied upon unless you have a clear idea of the quality of the finished rooms that it allows for. There are several ways of getting early cost estimates and the ideal is to use two or three of them and compare the results – which will almost certainly be contradictory. The consensus seems to be that even a small loft conversion will start at around £18,000–£20,000

Budget Planner for the Start of a Project	
Item	*Cost (£)*
Local authority fees	
Planning application	
Building Regulations application	
Plans approval fee	
Inspection fee	
Legal costs, for example Party Wall Act	
Initial cost estimate (based on cost/sq m) for:	
General building work	
Plumbing and heating	
Electrics	
Decorations	
New furniture	
Carpets	
Maintenance, for example the existing roof	
Work to the rest of the house, for example upgrading fire escape	
Architect	
Structural engineer	
Finance cost	
General expenses, for example cost of copying plans	
Contingency (10–15 per cent at this stage)	

plus VAT if it is to a reasonable standard of construction (2009 prices).

If the figures seem very low, be suspicious, because there are no easy bargains in the construction business, and you really do get what you pay for. There are a few costs that you cannot influence, like VAT and local authority fees, so you just have to accept them. But many are in your control, to a greater or lesser extent. The biggest single influence on the price of your home is you – how you run the project and the choices that you make as you do it. To set a budget, you need to pick a realistic target figure, and then aim for it. Then check it regularly as you work through the process and adjust your next actions accordingly.

Talk to Builders

Sadly, at the very beginning of a project, no one, not even the smartest, most experienced local builder you can find can tell you accurately what the cost will be at the same time as guaranteeing quality. Such a person will be able to predict a range of cost with reasonable accuracy. However, if you were to engage them on the spot without a clear idea of a scheme and without agreeing a standard of materials and finishes beforehand, they would rely on adjusting the quality once the project is on site to ensure that the job will make a profit for them. This is why many prices given by builders at this stage are fairly heavily qualified. As a result of the uncertainty, it is not unusual to get wildly differing prices at this early stage, which can add to the confusion rather than be helpful. The better organized firms may be able to provide a schedule of the standard fittings and finishes that they use for their projects. Advice on how to find reliable builders and get prices that can be properly compared is offered later in this book.

Ask an Architect

Like builders, architects who do this type of work will also have some knowledge regarding the likely cost of a conversion, but will have a similar problem trying to make an accurate prediction. If you employ an architect directly they will obtain fixed prices from builders using very detailed information about the project, but this will not be until later in the process. Architects tend to work with a wide range of builders and may be able to advise which of them will suit your likely budget.

Pricing Books and Quantities

It is the job of quantity surveyors in the building industry to estimate cost. They are not magicians, producing figures from the ether, but methodical professionals who break down any building project into a list of work and then use their knowledge of current prices to calculate the overall costs. Information on building costs is collated nationally by organizations such as the Royal Institute of Chartered Surveyors and can be obtained to a very high level of detail, with breakdowns given for every possible operation that may be needed on a building site. In the early stages of a project, quantity surveyors use average statistics, again compiled from real, recently completed projects across the country, to estimate typical costs per square metre. This information is available at great expense online, but also in book form.

Most of the publications are too complex for loft conversions or refer to larger building sites, where costs are quite different from what the average, locally based builder working on private houses is likely to incur. However, there are a number of publications aimed specifically at the latter sort of work (see Recommended Reading at the end of the book). So if you want to estimate the costs for yourself and can buy or borrow one of these books there are two approaches that you can use. The first is to look up the approximate costs per square metre for the closest project description to yours.

For example, the following is a typical cost estimate from a pricing book (based on cost information published in 2008):

- Clear out existing loft, including services, water tank, etc.
- Insulate between rafters and to walls
- Plasterboard finish
- Softwood floor

- New staircase
- New electrics and heating
- New dormer windows 4m × 5m in size = £1,000–£1,300 per square metre
  To add two dormer windows allow £11,000.

This is a useful ball-park figure to start off with, but be aware that there are shortcomings to this kind of estimate.

The second way of using the pricing books is to break the work down into as much detail as is possible at this stage, measure the extent of the work required and compile a detailed schedule listing every operation that will be needed and the area, volume or numbers involved for each of them. This is how builders work out their prices, is fairly laborious and relies on some guesswork at the early stages, but can produce some useful information. If the project is to be a DIY exercise, these calculations will have to be carried out by the homeowner at some point anyway. It is only recommended for someone who is experienced in home alterations and used to lots of work with a pocket calculator or spreadsheet.

Many popular magazines feature articles and tables suggesting building costs. These are generally unreliable and should never be used as the only basis for setting a budget for a real project.

Prices in Books and Magazines

Home-improvement literature can be a great source of inspiration but you should treat any hard figures quoted with caution. Ask yourself the following questions:

- How current is the information? A book could take six to twelve months between writing and appearing on the shelf, so even if the publication date is recent, it could be out of date.
- Do the prices relate to your area of the country? Prices vary significantly depending on where the project is – for example, Wales may be generally 15–20 per cent cheaper than Greater London.
- What is included in the price stated? Costs per square meter include everything necessary to

do the job, but are designed for typical situations and do not stand up to close scrutiny. For example the difference between a conversion with six large roof windows and one with four smaller ones cannot be accounted for by this method. Prices for individual operations should include materials and labour time, but what about disposal of debris and equipment? The builder's overheads and profit often have to be added on to the calculations before the total figure is reached.

- What is the source of the information? The most authoritative cost information is compiled by surveyors' organizations such as the BCIS, which is a cost information service run by the Royal Institute of Chartered Surveyors. They compile data sent in regularly by surveyors from across the country, as do some other organizations and publishers. But not many of the suppliers of this cost data work for the very small builders who carry out loft conversions. Also, bear in mind if you are going to use a small builder that they rarely use pricing books when preparing quotations, preferring to rely on their own experience, knowledge and judgement.

Other People's Projects

Aside from being a good source of potential builders for your project, friends, relatives and acquaintances may be ready to show you around their new room-in-the-roof and reveal the costs of the venture to you. Assuming it is accurate, this is probably the best way to gauge the likely bill that you will face for you own project. However, be aware that, particularly if there was an over-spend, it is human nature to talk up the project and omit some aspects of the cost rather than admit to having lost control of the budget.

Factors Affecting the Cost of Your Conversion

Project Size Versus Quality of Specification
The bigger the area of the loft conversion, the more it is likely to cost. The better the quality of materials and fitting, the more it is likely to cost. Both of these are in your control, and should be

---

Don't Forget VAT

It is a convention in the building industry not to include VAT in any prices quoted. It also helps salesmen not to mention it, particularly when discussing cost, although if it is to be charged it should be stated clearly on any written quotation. Some smaller firms, especially those that leave a lot of the fitting-out to their customers, may not be registered for VAT and will therefore not charge it at all. Also if you own a listed building and get approval to convert the loft, any aspects of the work that are considered alterations (as opposed to maintenance) are zero rated for VAT.

---

the subject of careful thought and examination. If you aim at the minimum quality to achieve the maximum size, you are likely to be disappointed because most people would not be happy with the very lowest standards of construction and finish. It is likely that you will want to increase the standards as the project progresses and go over budget.

Cost-Effective Versus Cheap
Be aware of the difference between these two concepts. For example what seems to be a cheap material may lose you money in maintenance costs and in the long run is actually a very expensive choice. Buying the cheapest available will be a false economy if you end up with an unsatisfactory end result, or could get a much better product for a small extra outlay, or you have to rip something out and replace it because it is so unattractive.

Finance Costs
How you arrange your finance, how good a deal you get, and how interest rates fluctuate will all affect your budget. Most people finance a home alteration project by extending an existing mortgage. It may be a good time to shop around and move the mortgage for the whole house to a new lender with a better deal than the current one.

A large loft conversion will be more expensive if you also want a high standard of specification.
The Velux Company Ltd

Management

How well you manage your project will be crucial to keeping on budget. Careful planning and taking care to research and consider decisions before acting are all likely to improve your chances of keeping the costs down. The single simplest way to get good value is to ensure that when you get prices from competing contractors or suppliers they are quoting on exactly the same work and materials, so that they can be accurately compared.

Building for Profit or for a Better Life?

Some people start with idea that their conversion will be a money-making venture, but end up creating their dream home, without much in the way of profit materializing. This is fine, as long as the decision is taken deliberately along the way. It is difficult for the average homeowner to totally detach themselves from the process and make the hard-nosed, money-making decisions that developers do in the course of a project. If you are carrying out the building work speculatively, you only spend money where it will help get a better sale price and you have to avoid personalizing the design too much. If, like most, you are trying to steer a middle course between following your own tastes and getting a good return on your investment, be aware of the dilemma and ensure that you understand the implications before making decisions that affect the cost.

How to Keep on Budget

With any one-off building project, there can be no certainty of price. The people who do best financially are usually the ones who identify and manage the risks most effectively.

Be Realistic

The biggest problem you face in trying to control the budget is your natural optimism – few pessimists ever get to the point of actually embarking on this sort of project. Sales people, pundits and professionals that suggest it will all be simple and profitable sound attractive and convincing. You may desperately want to believe that everything will be easy and you will end up with a wonderful addition to your home that will cost very little. In short, a part of you wants to be lied to. Get lots of advice, read up as much as possible and then try to be brutally honest with yourself. Don't work to the most favourable figures you can find, but pick realistic ones. With a bit of luck, you may do very well financially, but count this as a bonus and keep your expectations realistic.

Monitor and Discuss

Constantly revisit your budget, and keep doing this until the work is finished. Discuss it regularly with your family, professional advisors and builder. Update it and replace your assumptions with real figures as you go along.

Control Small Decisions

It is quite rare for a single, big decision to unexpectedly drive up costs. If you decide that the bath taps must be gold plated, or that you need an extra dormer window, you will probably guess that it will cost more money. The reason that costs go up is

A loft conversion may be a lifestyle choice rather than to increase the value of your home. The Velux Company Ltd

because a whole lot of small decisions are made, each of which, on their own, have a negligible effect on the total cost. But collectively they result in tender prices coming in over budget, and then have to be taken out of the contract. Be aware of the likelihood of this pushing you over budget and try to prevent it from happening.

Have a Contingency

It cannot be stressed enough how important it is to have some financial reserves for unexpected costs. At the very start of a typical project this amount should be 10 per cent of the total budget. As building work is about to start and costs are more certain, it should be at least 5 per cent. It will be spent at some point even if it is on a nicer bed or some fitted wardrobes right at the end.

Professional Team

Pick your team with care. If you are sufficiently self-aware, identify your own weaknesses and make sure that you get help to cover them. A good builder or architect will easily pay for themselves in money saved, quality achieved and stress relieved. A builder who is honest, reliable and efficient but more expensive will usually be cheaper by the end of the project than another who quotes a very low price initially and has none of these qualities. The delight in getting building work for an extra low price will fade after a month or two, but the distress and irritation caused by cheap and shoddy workmanship may have to be lived with for many years.

Good Design
Design is not just about how things look. A well-planned design will get the best end result for your money. Good design will also ensure that problems are anticipated and designed out where possible, allowing you to save money, or spend it on other aspects of the building. An ingenious designer will work out how to use the limited space available to its best effect and without excessive cost.

Preparation, Preparation, Preparation
You cannot be too well-prepared for building work to start. The more that has been worked out, agreed and specified in advance, the fewer extras there will be once the builder starts work and the better chance a project has of keeping to its budget.

Manage the Invitation of Tenders Correctly
The rules for obtaining prices are covered later in this book. If this crucial stage is not managed properly, the budget can go awry as building work progresses. If you choose not to get accurate tendered prices for the build, you will probably have to pay more for this luxury. If there is only one builder or supplier that you want, at least give them the impression that you are getting other prices keep their price competitive.

Changes of Mind
If you change something after you have agreed a price, it will be a bit more expensive than if you asked for it to be included in the tender. If you change your mind after something has been built, it will be a lot more expensive. If you are unsure, you can ask for two or more different options to be priced as part of a quotation. If the doubtful item is a fitting or component, you can exclude it from the contract and give yourself the option of getting it

from somewhere else. If you are completely undecided, identify it in the tender information as an item that may be changed, and get the builder to check with you before it is ordered or built.

Accommodation Costs
If the work on the loft is part of a major refurbishment of the house, you may have to move out. If this is necessary don't forget to include the cost of renting in your calculations, and allow for the project overrunning when agreeing a lease. A short increase in the rental period negotiated at the last minute can be expensive.

Get the Loft Surveyed Thoroughly
An earlier chapter has covered the potential defects in the house that should be checked at an early stage in the preparation of the schedule of work. If a thorough survey is not carried out in the hope that if there are problems they can be dealt with as the work proceeds, this may lead to increases in cost at a late stage in the project.

Get the existing loft thoroughly surveyed before work starts. Julian Owen Associates Architects

Never Pay in Advance

It may not be possible for this rule to be strictly applied in reality, because there may be some specialist components that are manufactured particularly for your project that will require a deposit of some kind. Otherwise, pay promptly, pay in stages if appropriate, but pay after the service or product has been provided. If you pay a builder large sums up front, they may lose the incentive to make the completion of your project a priority or, in the very worst case, disappear without completing the work to your satisfaction.

Keep Good Records

If there are arguments about money, such as whether some aspect of the work is an extra or whether it was instructed by you rather than improvised by the workman on site, a combination of clear tender documents and some well-kept contemporaneous notes of meetings and discussions will help you to win the argument and avoid extra payments.

PROGRAMME

An essential part of managing a successful building project is to understand how long things should reasonably take, draw up a programme and then attempt to keep to it. Right at the beginning, as with predicting cost, this is quite difficult to do because there are so many unknowns. Typical predictions of how long each stage will take are all very fine, but every project is different. The only

reliable prediction is that it will be longer than you expected when you first thought of the idea. But even though the first attempt at drawing up a programme is likely to be inaccurate, it is still worth having a go, not least because you will have to use your imagination to think through everything that needs to be done – a useful exercise in itself. Some stages are harder to guess than others, but there are a few that can be predicted with some reliability. For example, the planning process generally takes about eight weeks from submission to approval, assuming it goes smoothly. Building Regulation applications also tend to take a consistent period of time to be processed. Once you have a programme drawn up, you can monitor where you are and amend the dates as you go along, particularly once you get the professionals involved as they can usually tell you fairly accurately how long their aspect of the work will take.

The broad range of times indicated in the typical programme in the panel below are an attempt to cover a range of project sizes. Some of the stages can be greatly reduced or may not be needed at all, such as planning approval, but the import thing to note is that early comments from builders that your loft conversion will take 'about six weeks' are not necessarily telling the whole story. Unless there are some pressing concerns it is unwise to rush things unnecessarily. Getting things done properly takes time and a few weeks here or there are of little consequence when compared to the total time that the new space will be used, possibly for decades to come.

A Typical Programme for a Loft Conversion Project

Feasibility study	2–4 weeks
Interview architects and/or builders	3–4 weeks
Design work	3–6 weeks
Planning approval process	8–12 weeks
Preparation of working drawings	4–6 weeks
Tender process/Building Regulations approval	4–6 weeks
Waiting for contractor to become available	4–6 weeks
Construction period	6–12 weeks
Completion and moving in	1–2 weeks
Total time from inception to completion	35–58 weeks

Feasibility Study

How long this stage takes will depend on the family involved and how much time they have available. Sometimes it is obvious that the only solution to the problem of lack of space in a house is to convert the loft. In other cases it may be necessary to look at alternative ideas before settling on the way forward. A basic check on how much money can be afforded will probably be carried out and the suitability of the loft assessed as much as possible without expert help.

Interviewing Architects and Builders

If you are lucky enough to know the right company already, this time will not have to be allowed in the programme. But most people want to talk to more than one professional to get a feel for the best person to carry out the work, and to decide whether to go for an all-inclusive service from a builder or get an architect to prepare a tender package first. If one or more of the decision-makers in the family work full time, this exercise can take a while due to busy diaries on all sides.

Design Work

You may be employing your own designer, or using the builders' consultant, but either way the processes of measuring up the existing roofspace and other affected areas of the house, discussing your requirements with the designer and drawing

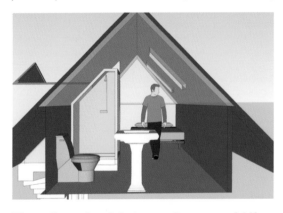

Three-dimensional design studies are useful if you are not able to visualize the end result before it is built. Julian Owen Associates Architects

up plans will all still have to be gone through. It is particularly important that you take the time to consider the design proposals carefully, to ensure that you understand what is being proposed and that it fits in with your wishes and budget. If necessary, you should have simple three-dimensional design studies prepared so that you can appreciate how the finished conversion will work.

Planning Approval

There are some stages of the process that require the same time regardless of the scale of the project. A good example of this is the planning approval process. Planners aim to process an application from submission to decision in eight weeks. Surprisingly, this period is nominally the same for an office block as for a modest domestic project. There are quite a lot of changes that a private homeowner can make to a house without needing planning approval. The provisions in the legislation that govern when approval is not needed are called 'permitted development rights' and are explained in Chapter 5. The time saving that is possible if planning approval is not needed is significant. Sometimes fairly minor changes in the design will move a project from being permitted development to needing an application, so it is important that your designer knows if you want to avoid the wait for a decision.

If a relatively minor alteration to the outside of the roof is going to be very visible in a conservation area, it may take longer than the eight weeks' target to get a decision, since amenity bodies like local conservation societies may be involved and more neighbours may object than usual.

Preparation of Working Drawings

For a very simple project an experienced builder may not need the detailed construction working out in advance. If you wish to get proper competitive tenders by using your own designer, or the work is more complex, construction drawings will be necessary and often essential to work out how the alterations will be built and ensure that all the necessary regulations are complied with. At this stage calculations are needed to work out the sizes of structural steel beams and similar elements and a structural engineer will normally be employed for this.

Tender Process/Building Regulations Approval

If you are using a builder to arrange the design as well as the construction, the process of inviting tenders, or quotations, for the work will occur near the start of the pre-construction stage. If you are asking for accurate quotes based on drawings that you have commissioned yourself it is normal to allow the builders three or four weeks to get their price back. Once the detailed drawings have been prepared they can be submitted to building control for full plans approval, a process that takes a few weeks, but typically not as long as it takes to get prices back from contractors and get them started on site. If a builder is skilled and the work straightforward it is possible to avoid submitting drawings to building control and get them to check that the design is correct when they are inspecting the work as it progresses on site. This may not particularly save you any time, however, and has some inherent risks, relying as it does on the construction being entirely straightforward.

Waiting for Contractor to Become Available

Most good builders tend to be busy and are not able to start work straight away unless another project has unexpectedly fallen through, so you usually have a wait between instructing them and work starting. How long you have to wait will vary enormously, depending on the economic climate and how good the builder is at organizing his workforce.

Construction Period

How long your loft conversion takes to build will depend on the size and complexity of the project and the resources available to the builder. A larger firm, or a well-managed specialist loft conversion company can complete a project much faster than a small builder, although there may be an extra cost in exchange for the time saved. Smaller building companies are notorious for overrunning on the

The construction time is difficult to predict in the early stages of a project. Attic Designs Ltd

agreed completion date but this is not always their fault. Sometimes an over-critical or indecisive client can delay progress on site significantly. Whatever the cause, there are usually a few good reasons why work does not proceed as quickly as everyone hopes, so it is sensible to allow an extra week or two onto the date promised by the builder when work starts. You can reduce the risk or scale of overruns by asking for a detailed construction programme before you finally agree the contract and checking regularly on progress during construction.

Completion and Moving in

Once the builder is finished there are inevitably some extra tasks to be completed before the space can be fully occupied. For example, carpets may have to be laid and furniture moved up into the rooms. Some people prefer to decorate the rooms themselves, often an easier job in a loft compared to an ordinary room because the area of the walls is less and the ceiling is within easy reach. This can take a week, or a lot longer if you are slow off the mark.

So the times indicated on the table can be reduced, but it is better to work out a realistic timescale at the start and aim to reduce it as the project develops, than to be over-optimistic at the start and end up disappointed or inconvenienced.

ARRANGING FINANCE

Most people have to fund their project either from savings or a mortgage lender, or both. It may be possible to cover some of the costs of the earlier stages such as local authority and architects' fees from day-to-day living expenses, but unless you spread the work out over a long period or do it yourself there will clearly be significant payments to be made to the builders once construction work starts. One of the jobs to be done as you plan the budget at the start is to find out exactly how much money you can make available. Many people have equity stored up in their existing house, that is their mortgage is a lot less than the sale price of the building. Lenders are usually quite happy to finance alterations in these cases, provided that the end value of the property is not less than the total money eventually owed to them. At some point they may send in their own valuation surveyor to check this and approve the release of the money. This is not a bad thing because you will get an independent opinion as to how worthwhile it is to proceed. It is not a good idea to take on a greatly increased mortgage that you will struggle to pay in order to carry out improvements that add little value to your home. You may end up living beyond your means and become very vulnerable to interest rate rises, or even worse end up with negative equity, where your house is worth less than the mortgage you are paying off.

Never take up loan offers from specialist home improvement companies or builders without looking at all the other options and getting alternative advice first. However attractive they look at first glance, most of these loans are on far less favourable terms than the high street lenders and should be avoided.

If you are in the fortunate position of funding the whole project from savings then you are in more danger than most of going over budget, since you won't have the discipline imposed on you that results from having to make a case for what you want to do to persuade a bank or building society to lend you the money. Try to get some professional advice on your budget from someone who understands building projects and is prepared to

---

Ways to Pay for the Work

- **Savings** Keep some of your own money available in case of an emergency.
- **Credit card** Not recommended unless it can be paid back quickly.
- **Mortgage increase** The easiest and safest method (could change building society to get a better rate).
- **Bank loan** Terms may not be as good as a mortgage and larger amounts will have to be secured, that is the lender can take away your house if you don't pay it back.
- **Builder's scheme** Usually much higher interest rate and less favourable terms than high-street lenders. Treat with great caution.
- **Grants:**
  Disabled You may be eligible if the alterations make life easier for a disabled person (planning and Building Regulations fees may be waived by the local authority)
  Renovation Local authority schemes that subsidize things such as extra insulation
  Conservation/historic buildings Listed buildings of note may be funded by English Heritage, or by the local authority for buildings of local interest (usually very small amounts). Will want to control specification and design of elements of the work covered by funding.

---

give unbiased advice rather than just talk you into using their services.

PREPARING A BRIEF

A 'brief' is the information that you give to a designer or architect that explains your needs, along with an idea of the budget and timescale. Sometimes the brief can be given verbally, but even if this is the case, the designer should write down everything that you say and identify those parts of it that are the most important. If you prepare your own list before you meet the designer it will be a useful starting point and will save time. Apart from being of enormous assistance to them, it will help you and your family think through what you would like to do in more detail, and will bring to light any areas of disagreement.

An enjoyable exercise, which is also very useful, is to compile a scrapbook of pictures from magazines or your own photos of styles or designs that you particularly like, or that you think are relevant to your project. Just as important is a similar collection showing things that you positively hate – it is quite demoralizing for an architect to spend several hours on an ingenious way of using a dormer window to increase a roofspace only to find on presenting it that you dislike dormer windows. Obviously it is best if you make your passionate hatred of dormer windows clear before the design drawings are started. This principle holds good for all your important requirements, right down to the detailed construction if it is of particular interest to you. It is important to prioritize your needs and decide what your absolute minimum requirements are, without which it is not worth your while to proceed. This is in contrast to those things that you would like but would be prepared to sacrifice if practicality or lack of money make them unattainable.

There are quite a few decisions that should be made before design work begins in earnest. You may not want to have to think about some of them, and prefer to launch straight into briefing a designer to see what they come up with. For anything aside from a very simple project, this can waste time, because it is rather unfair to expect your ideal scheme to be produced without a thorough briefing process – any success by the designer in guessing what will suit you would be down to chance rather than skill.

One of the basic rules of preparing a brief is that you share your ideas with the rest of the family who are involved. This can provoke some unexpected discussion or disagreements, but it is better to have these arguments early on rather than in front of the architect who has just spent several days preparing an unwittingly controversial design.

What to Include in a Design Brief

The short answer is to include anything that you think is important. If the only thing that really mat-

---

Typical Design Brief

- Budget: £30,000–£40,000 plus VAT

Essential Extra Space Needed
- Bedroom, compact, for a double bed (visitors only), also to act as a study with good daylight levels.
- En suite bathroom.
- New rooms that would be desirable: separate study.

Furniture to be Accommodated
- King-size double bed.
- Dressing table.
- Shower, wash basin, toilet and bidet in en suite.

Appearance
- To blend in with existing house in scale and materials.
- Traditional design outside, modern interior.
- Lots of light, to give an 'airy' feel to the spaces.
- Photos of buildings and features/details/ materials that you like.
- Photos of buildings and features/details/ materials that you do not like.
- We dislike: dormer windows, concrete tiles, stripped pine and the colour green.

Other Important Considerations
- House will be occupied during the building work, so bathroom facilities will need to be available the whole time.
- We do not get on with the neighbour on the other side of our semi.
- We are in a conservation area (which means special planning controls).
- Energy efficiency is important but not to an extreme level.

Possible Work to Existing House
- Smallest bedroom on first floor can go to make room for the staircase.
- New boiler so that water tank in loft can be removed.
- Redecorate hall, landing and affected first-floor rooms.

ters to you is that there are at least two bedrooms, or that there is space for your train set, that is all you have to put into it. Most people have more to say than this, of course, because the brief goes to the heart of the matter – getting specific things is the whole reason for embarking on the project in the first place. Some briefs have been known to run to several A4 ring binders, but this is counter-productive. The whole point is to identify the important things that are essential and record them in a way that is intelligible to someone else.

Appearance

The style and appearance of your home are the most subjective things in the brief. The subject of style is highly emotive and may lead to the biggest disagreements among the family, but try to keep an open mind. One person's design feature is another's carbuncle. There is a huge range of choice of styles available, and some people find this intimidating. But everyone knows what they don't like, so this is one possible starting point, and it is just as important to communicate this to whoever designs your house as letting them know what you do like.

The best way to record your inclinations is to find some illustrations – a picture really does say a thousand words. Cut out and keep photos from magazines. Keep a camera handy and take your own pictures of houses that interest you. If you have time, go around the show houses on the local new estates (with your camera). Talk to architects and designers, visit exhibitions and read as many magazines as you can get hold of.

If you examine the information that you have collected, there are likely to be some consistent themes, for example particular styles and features that crop up more than others. Using these clues, you should be able to take a stab at completing the form listing your preferences.

Whose Room is it?

Who is to use a room is usually obvious, but not necessarily – asking this question may spark a discussion. Who uses the room most will perhaps be allowed to decide how it is designed, equipped and finished off, in the event of a disagreement. Many people prefer the bedroom to look over the back of the house, to enjoy the view of the garden and have some privacy, or keep an eye on young children playing.

Furniture

At the beginning, you may not be all that sure what the fitted or loose furniture may be that you want in the rooms, but it is worth making some edu-

A good way of choosing colours and materials is to get actual samples and compare them.
Julian Owen Associates Architects

If possible, it is a good idea to work out the furniture that you will be putting in the space at an early stage, to ensure that it will all fit.
Julian Owen Associates Architects

cated guesses. Your designer needs to be aware of the likely contents of the room and warn you if it will not fit. You will have to be able to get the furniture up the stairs and then find space for it in rooms with limited headroom. A classic mistake is to allow space on the plan for a large double bed, only to find once it is in place in the finished room that there is not enough headroom to walk around it and climb into it from both sides.

Electrics and Lighting

A regular complaint about many newly created rooms is that they do not have enough electric sockets in the right locations. A little thought at an early stage will help ensure that your conversion has enough power and phone sockets. Another area neglected in many homes is the ability of the lighting design to contribute to the quality of rooms and spaces in the house. This is especially important in a loft, where normal fittings will not work either because they can't be fitted to a sloping ceiling or because they end up so low people hit their heads on them.

Sustainability and Energy Efficiency

An issue that is important to many is how green or eco-friendly the construction and design should be. If this is a high priority for you, it is vital to identify the fact as early as possible. Current Building Regulations already acknowledge the need to make modern homes respectful of the environment and natural resources. However, there are many ways you can improve on the minimum requirements – it is a question of how far you want to go and how much you can afford. Sadly, many of the more radical options are expensive, and do not work out as economic for the average home-builder, but by careful design it is possible to incorporate some of them at no extra cost. For example, putting a high proportion of the windows on the side of the house that faces south will get the maximum benefit from the sun's heat and reduce the amount of energy needed to heat the house in winter.

You may need to do some investigation before you decide how far you want to go down the green route, and you may face some interesting dilemmas, usually as a result of the cost. If you have to choose between a luxury bathroom or a solar-powered heating system, which would you go for?

If you are going to look at this in hard financial terms, you should calculate the 'payback' time. This is how long it takes for an element of the construction – such as a solar panel – to pay for itself in efficiency savings. For example, if extra insulation saves you a certain amount on your heating bill, you can calculate how much you save a year and thus how long you have to wait until you have got back the money spent. At the moment, people buying houses do not seem to value energy-efficiency measures, in that they will not pay extra for them. So although energy-efficient design is something to be encouraged, if you decide that you want an unusually high level then you should be aware that there is a cost and have allowed for it in your budget.

The simplest and probably most cost-effective measure is to increase the thickness of the insulation between the rafters to well beyond the minimum required by the Building Regulations, but this may lead to a loss of headroom.

MANAGING THE DESIGN AND CONSTRUCTION OF THE CONVERSION

A crucial part of your brief for your project is the way that you will get it built – who takes responsibility for the various stages of the work. This is known to construction professionals as your 'procurement route'. The choice you make will affect the budget, how much risk you will accept, how much of your time is devoted to the project and most importantly, your peace of mind. Whatever you decide, it is a false economy to try to make savings by cutting out professional help that you really cannot do without due to your own inexperience.

There are several basic routes and which one is right for you will depend on several factors. All kinds of people from all kinds of backgrounds have successfully completed projects with all of these methods, but occasionally some over-confident

	Main Contractor Design and Build	Main Contractor Build Only	Managed Subcontractors	DIY
How Your Choice of Building Method Affects Your Project				
Price	Usually fixed at an early stage	Fixed at tender stage	Updated as building proceeds	Updated as building proceeds
Quality	Completely under contractor's control	Strictly controlled by you, often through an architect	Controlled by project manager or you day to day	Controlled by you day to day
Amount of drawings and specification required	Drawings by builder, outline specifications only, no detailed drawings	Full working drawings and specifications, all worked out before tenders invited	Either Building Regulations drawings only, or tender package	Usually Building Regulations drawings only, produced by an architect
Site management	Contractor	Contractor	You, or your project manager	You
Choice of materials	Mostly selected from a range chosen by contractor	Mostly chosen by you, sometimes with an architect advising	You, helped by each subcontractor	You
Insurances	Contractor	Contractor	You	You
Health and safety responsibility	Contractor	Contractor	You or your project manager	You
Payment	At agreed stages	At agreed stages	At stages or end of each week	As needed or with an account at a builder's merchant
Payment certification – if required	Provided by builder	None or by an architect employed by you	Usually none	Usually none
Detailed programme	Controlled by contractor	Controlled by contractor, sometimes monitored by an architect	Controlled by you or your project manager	Controlled by you and your family

converters have got into difficulties by wrongly assuming that they will have the resources and abilities to do everything.

DIY Self-Build

Taking on most of the building work yourself is an option that should only be pursued by the most determined home improvement enthusiasts. It is perfectly possible, but rare for anyone to actually complete every task personally – not least because certain tasks are definitely for people with training or qualifications, such as electrical wiring or roof work. The chief attraction of working this way, apart from the challenge, is the reduced cost from cutting out the profit taken by the main contractor and the expense of hiring labour. The benefits have increased in recent times due to the lack of skilled building workers and the consequent increase in their wages. However, these savings can be offset by the builder's merchants and suppliers charging higher prices. They are reluctant to offer the DIY enthusiast the same level of discount available to long-term customers.

Apart from the reduced costs, the other common feature of the DIY route is the extra time required to complete the project. It can take two or three times longer than using an experienced contractor. The pressure to complete means that most leisure time is taken up working in the loft. Progress is slowed as new skills have to be learnt and old ones brushed up. Apart from the building work, all the management side has to be dealt with as well. Safety, insurance, ordering of materials and dealing with building control officers all need to be taken into account. Sometimes, to avoid these kind of difficulties, a hybrid of the full DIY route is used, where the structural work is built by a professional contractor, leaving a watertight shell for the self-builders, who then arrange the electrical installation, plumbing, plastering and decorating themselves.

Although you should have a carefully monitored cost plan and you must comply with planning and Building Regulations, you are free to make design decisions and change the specification as work progresses. Any design decisions taken from an early stage must allow for ease of construction, and products or construction methods that require a high level of building skill not possessed by the DIY enthusiast are best avoided. For example, structural alterations should be kept simple, and new roof shapes should be kept straightforward (possibly avoiding hips in favour of gables).

Self-Manage

Rather than carry out all the work, you can hire individual trades, either on a fixed price or daily rate, to do most of it for you. You then will take on the role that is usually played by the main con-

Taking on a DIY loft conversion can be more complex than it seems at first. It may be better to leave a job that requires extensive structural alterations to the experts.
Room Maker Loft Conversions

tractor – that is buying some of the materials, finding and employing individuals and subcontractors, performing the site management role, and possibly doing some of the less critical work (such as decorating). Money is saved because you do not have to pay as much for overheads as a contractor, and you keep all of the profit they would otherwise take out of the project. The total of both these typically amounts to 10–20 per cent on the building cost. However, the loss of builder's merchants' discounts, which cannot be achieved by domestic customers, may reduce savings in the same way as for someone carrying out a DIY project.

It is a mistake to think that builders earn their profit easily. It is usually hard-won by crafty bargaining, shrewd business acumen and the skilful management of people. A self-manager will have to go some way to matching these skills in order to make the exercise worthwhile. As well as management skills, you also need time to apply them – not just a certain number of hours in the week, but sometimes at specific times of the day as well. If a problem develops it may have to be sorted out straight away, and deliveries of supplies may require you to be there to check and sign for them. For this reason, many self-managers tend to be people whose job allows them flexible working hours, such as the self-employed or senior management. A common problem for self-managers is that sub-contractors and trades fail to turn up on the appointed day, or leave a job part way through. This is because they can afford to offend (and lose) a one-off client, and will do so rather than let down a contractor who employs them regularly.

Apart from assuming the role of the contractor, you also assume the risk taken. A builder who quotes a fixed price for a thoroughly described job gambles on their ability to accurately price and properly manage the project. If they do well, they make a profit. If they do badly, they will lose money – the price to the client is the same. If you are managing the project and you get it wrong, you will lose money, or in the worst case, run out of finance and have to stop the whole project. Conversely the rewards are high if you are successful at it.

If you are going to take this route, it is sensible to have the design and specification worked out well before each stage or trade is started, so that payment can be agreed and the work programmed in. However, you may be able to incorporate products and materials that you come across as the project proceeds on site, since you can make design changes later in the programme than if you are using a single contractor. You can also trim or expand the amount you spend on fittings and finishes more easily towards the end of the building work.

Main Contractor

Most people will choose to employ a builder to do all the work. There is an extra cost to doing this, but assuming that you have chosen the right firm, work will proceed quickly, in the hands of experienced builders who can anticipate and solve the inevitable problems that develop in the course of a project. Speed is important because the disruption caused to the everyday lives of a family as building work progresses is considerable, even for a loft conversion where a lot of the work goes on above the living areas. To get the full benefit you must agree a fixed price before you agree to employ the builder. This way the risk of extras and unexpected problems lies mainly with them, and although extra costs are almost inevitable in any building project, they should not be excessive.

Working with an Architect

The very simplest loft conversions may not need detailed drawings for a contractor to price and the local authority may not require them for planning or Building Regulations approval purposes. But most projects will need to be worked out in advance by someone to be successful and avoid problems such as the budget being exceeded or last-minute alterations on site.

There are two basic options for working with a designer. Either you can find your own architect to prepare a design that you then use to get competitive prices from a selection of builders, or you can choose a building firm right at the start who then employs their own designer.

There are benefits and disadvantages to both of these options.

Employing your Own Designer
You can employ someone directly to prepare all the necessary drawings and manage the project for you up to the point that the builder is employed. Apart from contributing design ideas and expertise, the architect can obtain planning and Building Regulations approvals and create a tender package for builders to price competitively. The contractor submits a fixed-price quotation (as opposed to the more approximate 'estimate') and then carries out the work exactly as described for the quoted price, finishing on an agreed date. The contractor can only ask for more payment if there are design changes, and may have to pay damages to you if the project overruns. Sometimes the architect is employed to manage the contract on the client's behalf, although this is not cost-effective

for many loft conversions (*see* section on architect's services).

Whoever is responsible for actually hiring the architect, the homeowner still pays for the preparation of the drawings and the administration needed to submit local authority applications. Any extra fees charged by the architect to prepare a tender package should be recovered when you get competitive prices from builders. Because the quality standard and specification has been described in detail and exact, fixed prices are submitted, all the prices can be compared directly. This encourages contractors to submit keen prices and also ties them into all providing an identical standard of materials, fixtures and finishes, giving the homeowner a much greater level of control over the detailed building work.

If the architect does a good job, it also reduces the risk of extra charges being incurred once the work starts on site, since all the problems that can reasonably be predicted will have already been picked up by the design and drawing process. The architect will also suggest local building companies who have completed good work in the past and help you to avoid the cowboys.

Another little-known advantage is connected with the copyright of the design. If permission to use a design is withdrawn by the copyright owner, it cannot be built. If an architect creates a design he retains the copyright, but grants a licence to the client to use it for their project. If the builder employs the designer, the builder controls the copyright. So the homeowner who employs the designer directly has stronger rights to use the

Employing an Architect Directly

Benefits	*Disadvantages*
Complete control over specification and standard of work.	Most of the architect's fee has to be paid in advance, rather than being partly absorbed in the building cost.
Homeowner retains right under copyright law to use any builder to build the design.	Homeowner takes the risk on the budget being exceeded until design work is complete and tenders are returned.
Homeowner can choose the best designer to suit their taste and requirements.	Homeowner has to find the right architect for the project.
Creative ideas.	Many contractors specialize in loft conversions whereas architects tend to do all kinds of house alterations and few specialize specifically in loft conversions.
Everything is worked out before builders' prices come in so there is less chance of extras or corners being cut.	The project preparation time may be a few weeks longer where planning and Building Regulations are not needed. In that situation a builder might start immediately, without any drawings.
Competitive prices can be obtained from builders that can be directly compared.	Practical details may be solved earlier if an experienced builder is involved from the start.
Standard, unbiased contract can be used rather than contractors' own terms and conditions.	If there is a mistake, the homeowner has to decide whether the architect or builder is responsible.
Homeowner has more control on site.	
Independent, unbiased advice at all stages.	

design in the event of a falling-out of the building team. If the builder employs the architect the homeowner has to use that building company to carry out the work and cannot employ another, even if all the design work has already been paid for.

In order to minimize the risk of budget overrun once work starts on site, it is vital to ensure that a full set of working drawings is prepared, along with a detailed specification, before any prices are quoted. There is little benefit in employing a designer to prepare perfunctory drawings that simply obtain local authority approvals without going into the detailed construction. Projects run over budget and time when this advice is ignored. Getting detailed design work means that there is an unavoidable up-front cost that must be paid, but this will save far more money by avoiding extras or changes on site later.

If the project requires design ideas and some creative input and you want something other than a standard conversion, or it is part of a larger programme of possible works to the house, it is worth considering employing an architect, especially if you are looking for a 'wow' factor. An architect is essential if the building is unusual or complex in design or is listed.

Design and Build
Employing the contractor to manage the design process as well as the construction has the benefit of convenience. It should also offer the certainty that the early budget will not be exceeded, although this depends on the terms of the agreement that is signed. It also lifts the responsibility of employing a designer and places more of the risk with the contractor if the project hits problems. In exchange for these benefits, agreeing a price before the design and specifications have been worked out in detail, it may be more expensive. As mentioned earlier, once the plans have been agreed, the builder can prevent you from taking the drawing he has had prepared to other contractors and getting alternative prices.

There are plenty of contractors who do loft conversions and some that do nothing else. Consequently they build up a lot of expertise in assessing the likely problems and costs when they visit homes to quote prices. If the house has a fairly common, standard layout, a good design-build contractor should be able to quote a fairly accurate price at the beginning and keep to it. They usually have a designer who prepares drawings for them, or will have 'in-house' designers who specialize in loft conversion projects, unlike independent architects who tend to do a lot of other types of work. Usually the designer is not a qualified architect but a draughtsman or technologist. The cost of the design work may be buried within the overall bill from the builder and some of the project management costs will be incurred as part of the builder's service rather than the designer's.

The vast majority of loft conversions are completed successfully using the design and build route, without an independent designer being employed by the homeowner. This is partly because these builders are often easier to find than the designers but also because of the convenience and speed that they offer.

FINDING A DESIGNER

Even modest, small-scale projects can benefit from a designer's input. If you pay by the hour, you can use their design skills at the early stages to generate ideas and suggestions without commissioning them for a full service that is more appropriate for slightly bigger projects.

Choosing the right person or company to help you with the design is an important step and it is worth spending a little time to make the right choice. The architect must be able to understand your requirements, respect your budget, and put forward ideas and suggestions in a clear way. As with any creative project, good communication between client and designer is vital. In turn, you, as the client, should make your requirements clear as well as listen to your advisor's professional advice.

Types of Designer
There are several types of designer who may be able to help you. The custom for people outside the construction industry is to refer to all of them

How to be a Model Client

- Be sure that you really want the level of skills and assistance with your project that the architect you are considering is offering.
- Do your homework before you meet, and agree with the family what you are looking for from the design.
- Don't dismiss a new idea without at least giving it some thought. Part of a designer's job is to suggest things that may not have occurred to you.
- Don't go for the cheapest fee possible if you want an acceptable level of service. You will probably require someone with experience, expertise and skill – which come at a cost.
- Make yourself available during reasonable office hours for meetings with your architect and other consultants if possible. To you it is a hobby, for them it is work.

Membership of the Royal Institute of British Architects is only available to fully qualified professionals. RIBA

by the generic term 'architect'. As shown below, there are in fact a number of different types of people who design house alterations, all with different types and levels of skill. In the interests of brevity, generalizations are made here in describing them. However, there are many others factors apart from paper qualifications that will decide who is right for your project.

Architects
The title 'architect' is protected by law and only designers who have completed a tough seven-year course are allowed to use it. People who style themselves as 'architectural consultants' or 'architectural designers' are not architects and do not necessarily have any formal qualifications or training. An architect's training is rigorous, the longest of any construction professional and includes all aspects of the design and construction process, from small- to larger-scale buildings. Unlike unqualified draughtsmen, they also are obliged to carry professional indemnity insurance in case there are any errors in their design work.

All architects must be registered with the Architects Registration Board (ARB), a government organization that is responsible for dealing with complaints as well as keeping the register. Most architects are also members of the Royal Institute of British Architects (RIBA), although this is not obligatory. Members of RIBA are allowed to call themselves 'chartered' architects, because this organization has a Royal Charter. Architects are known for their ability to design, but also are trained in practical construction methods, project management and contract law. The majority of their time is actually spent designing construction details, sending out tender packages, running projects on site, and dealing with contractors on their client's behalf.

Architectural Technologists
Although their title is not protected by law in the same way as for architects, these professionals are usually members of the Chartered Institute of Architectural Technologists (CIAT), which requires its members to be trained and qualified. Academic training is much shorter and less broad than it is for architects, but has a more practical edge to it. Aesthetic design skills are not considered essential to qualify, although some technologists develop these through experience.

Surveyors

Surveyors come in many different guises. Their background may be in selling houses, estimating quantities for building, construction or property management. Some can and do design work, with their ability coming from experience rather than training. Again, the use of the title 'surveyor' is not protected, but most surveyors tend to be members of the Royal Institute of Chartered Surveyors (RICS) – for this, they must have adequate training and qualifications.

Consulting Structural Engineers

If you embark on any significant structural work, you are likely to need the advice of a suitably qualified engineer. Some designers can do their own structural calculations, but more often than not it is cheaper and more efficient to use a specialist for this work. They can also help to avoid over-sizing and get the most efficient design for the structure. Most engineers can do scaled drawings and some non-structural design work, although they are usually not the best people to approach if the appearance of the house is affected. The title 'engineer' is not protected and the professionals who use it may specialize in design for all kinds of areas, including buildings, roads or machinery. Look for membership of either the Institution of Civil Engineers (ICE) or the Association for Consultancy and Engineering (ACE).

Unqualified Designers

If you need to check that someone using the title 'architect' is genuine, you can contact the Architects Registration Board, but also look at the letterhead. Someone who is misrepresenting will not use the title of architect in writing since this would be a criminal offence. But anyone who claims that they have the necessary skills and training to design and oversee the construction of a house should be carefully questioned and investigated, regardless of their formal qualifications.

Where to Look for a Designer

Realizing how important the choice of the right designer is for the success of your project, how do you find one? To start with, aim to come up with a shortlist of several candidates, using some or all of the methods outlined below.

Personal Recommendation

This is a good way to find anyone who you need to provide a service, but most people do not necessarily come across architects in their personal or business life. If encountered at a place of work, they may not be appropriate for a relatively small-scale project (but they may know someone who is).

The Royal Institute of British Architects

RIBA have a Client Services section that will locate local architects for you, or practices with special skills, such as sustainable design, or straw bale construction. However, they list most small practices as being suitable for domestic work, so further investigation may be necessary to establish whether they will treat you as a key client, rather than a 'filler' between their regular work. RIBA Client Services can be contacted by phone (020 7307 3700) or through their website (www.ribafind.org), which has an online search facility.

ASBA Architects

ASBA was founded in 1993, to assist people to find architects with an interest and track record in house extensions, conversions, self build and other domestic work. It has a network of members across the UK, all of whom must be ARB registered and RIBA members (tel: 0800 38731; www.asba-architects.org).

ASBA is a network of chartered architects who specialize in domestic projects for home owners. ASBA

Specialist exhibitions offer an opportunity to meet architects and inspect their work informally. Julian Owen Associates Architects

A typical modern architects' office is now more likely to be populated by computers rather than drawing boards. Julian Owen Associates Architects

Yellow Pages and Yell.com

These directories are a useful starting point for many people but the problem is the sheer number of consultants listed with minimal information about them. Some of the professional organiza-tions have a separate display advertisement that lists their members in the locality. Yell.com allows a search by postcode (www.yell.com).

Other Projects in Progress

There will probably be other building work going on near to your site. Consider contacting the householders and asking about the builders and the designer.

Local Authorities

The codes of practice that planners and building control officers work within prohibit them from recommending designers and builders. Some may give an 'off the record' recommendation, but most will be uncomfortable doing so. However, the plan-ning register, kept on the reception desk of every local authority planning department, is open for inspection. This will list the names and addresses of the agents who have submitted applications recently, and your right of public access means that you can take a look at the drawings that they have submitted – an excellent way of judging the stan-

dard of work you are likely to get from the designer.

Magazines and Shows

The magazines dedicated to home alterations are filled with illustrations and case studies of proj-ects, which usually give the name and contact details of the designers. Likewise the national and local exhibitions and shows feature architects and designers. If a practice has gone to the time and trouble to attend a show and make themselves available to prospective clients, this at least indi-cates enthusiasm.

Others

There are many other incidental ways of finding your ideal designer. There are several websites that claim to be able help you, but it is important to check what architects have to do to get listed. If the answer is that all they do is pay a fee, there is little value to the recommendation.

Choosing the Right Architect

Once you have a shortlist, your next task is to nar-row it down to one. Naturally, you will want to do a bit of investigation, but the truth is it's the gut feeling that counts the most. Unless your project is high budget or unusually large, whittle the shortlist down to a maximum of two or three designers. If you do decide to do the rounds with more than this, the chances of any one of them actually getting a job are greatly reduced and they may feel it is a waste of time responding to your enquiry. Busy professionals will not rush to respond to standard letters or emails that have clearly been sent to a large number of companies.

Interviews

Firstly, be sure to spend a little time in the company of the professional under consideration. However, it is unreasonable to expect them to offer lengthy consultations or site visits without charge, particularly if your project is relatively modest.

Formal Qualifications

Ask some direct questions about their professional training and qualifications. If you do not understand what the initials after someone's name means, it is perfectly reasonable to ask for them to be explained.

Experience

Be prepared to ask some searching questions about the experience that the practice has had working with private clients on their homes. Do they work regularly with people like yourselves, on your scale of project, or you going to be a 'fill in' job whilst they wait for a larger commercial project to turn up? Do they have technical knowledge and competence as well as design flair? Some architects are talented designers and artists and have never bothered much with the practicalities, while the reverse is true of others.

Qualifications

Some letters after a name indicate that exams have been passed, for example 'BArch' (a degree that must be obtained to qualify as an architect). Others may simply indicate the payment of the membership fees of an organization, with no requirement for any qualifications.

Attitude

Sometimes designers, particularly architects, are accused of arrogance. In fact most architects are approachable, reasonable people, and would not be in business for very long if they were not. One skill that is not part of an architect's formal training, however, is the ability to listen – which is an essential characteristic for you to be able to work with them.

The Size of the Practice

Generally speaking, loft conversions are best dealt with by 'sole practitioners' (that is one person only) or small practices. A large practice will not put a priority on a comparatively minor project.

Completed Work

Aside from asking to see illustrations of previous jobs and talk to past clients, why not ask to see a set of drawings for a typical project? You may be surprised at the range of quality and quantity of work produced by different practices.

Indemnity Insurance

All registered architects are required to maintain professional indemnity insurance (PII) to cover the work that they do in order to use the title. There is not the same compulsion on unregistered designers. If architects make a serious error that costs you money, they are insured and the benefit of that insurance is passed on to you.

Appointing an Architect

Paying an Architect

The question of fees and charges should be raised early by the architect. You should insist on receiving a proper explanation of the fee structure, and be made fully aware of the services to be provided along with the payment terms, expenses charged and so on. Before you agree the fee arrangement, be sure that the level of services being offered is appropriate and has been agreed and tied into the fee.

Architects may calculate fees by the hour or by a percentage of the build cost or as a fixed fee. Which method is used will depend on how much

Questions to Ask your Designer

- Is the designer an architect or lesser-qualified professional?
- Do members of the practice have professional qualifications?
- How many loft conversions does the practice carry out each year?
- How many technical/professional staff has the practice got?
- Who will be working on the project, and what is their seniority/experience?
- Can you see examples of completed work and talk to previous clients?
- How soon after receiving an instruction can they start?
- How long should the project take from now to completion on site?
- How are fees calculated, and how much are they?
- Does the practice carry professional indemnity insurance?
- Is there to be a written contract?
- What would happen if you asked for a design change that the architect did not agree with?

What the Contract Should Cover

- The exact level of service being commissioned.
- Who gives the architect instructions.
- Who will be engaging consultants, such as the engineer.
- How fees are calculated and whether VAT is due.
- Expenses and how much they are (printing costs alone can be several hundred pounds for a larger project).
- When you will be invoiced and how long you will have to pay.
- What happens if you are unhappy with something and don't wish to pay the amount invoiced.
- How you can terminate the agreement, and what reasons you can have to do this.
- Who owns the copyright to the design.
- If a dispute arises between you, how it would be settled.
- Who you can complain to if you feel that the required standards of professional conduct have not been met.

information is available about your project at the time, what level of involvement the architect will have, and the management process to be used. Contrary to the popular myth, architect's fees rarely add up to 10 per cent of the build cost. If there is a partial service required, the project is a large one or the work is very straightforward, it may be quite a lot less than this. If the project is very small, or complicated (for example alterations to a listed building) or services over and above the standard range are required, it may be more.

There is a good case for not using an architect to manage the project on site if it is a typical loft conversion (say, up to £40,000 build cost at 2009 prices). Provided that you are using a reputable builder the extra tier of management is usually not necessary. However, regardless of the size of the project, if you have a heavy workload or currently live outside the locality and do not have time to spend on the project, then an architect can help by managing the builder for you.

Appointment Contract

If your designer is an architect, they will be obliged by their registration body to confirm the details in writing. Some use standard appointment documents supplied by the RIBA, but others will want to use their own version. Do not accept a simple letter stating the fee. This should be in a separate document, which you should have a copy of and which you should acknowledge your acceptance of in writing. You may get away with less than this, but if anything should go wrong, you will find that the absence of agreed terms and conditions could prove an expensive mistake.

FINDING BUILDING CONTRACTORS

Probably the most important decision in the whole project is deciding who will carry out the building work. You may intend to do a little or a lot of the work yourself, but for anything other than the

Sometimes a good builder can be found by spotting a sign and asking the homeowners for their opinion of the builder. Attic Designs Ltd

simplest project it is inevitable that you will need some professional help.

Whether you are looking for a company to do the whole job or someone just to do the plumbing, there are some basic rules to follow in selecting a builder that apply across the board. Obviously the less significant the role, the less intensive the selection procedure, and it is up to you to decide how many of the suggestions listed here to take up.

You should aim to get at least three realistic prices, more for a larger project. To achieve this you may consider and actually approach more builders than this. This is because whether or not a building contractor from a smaller company will submit a price is influenced by their workload, which can change overnight when they win a contract. It is not unusual for a contractor to agree to tender one day, and have a change of mind the next. They may let you know they have changed their mind, but are more likely to simply not bother submitting a price. Alternatively, they may inflate their tender to an unrealistically high figure so that if by some accident they do get the job, it will have a very big profit margin to compensate for the need to employ extra staff. A reasonable number of contractors to approach with a preliminary enquiry is four or possibly five, allowing for one or two to drop out or over-price. The minimum to aim for is three tendered prices.

If you ask for an unreasonable number of tenders, however, do not be surprised if many drop out – there is a lot of work involved in preparing a tender, and a builder wants a reasonable chance of winning. They can find out who else is tendering from shared suppliers or subcontractors.

It is also possible to choose a contractor before inviting tenders from others just to check that the price is reasonable, but this again is an unreasonable thing to do. A tender takes several hours to produce if the estimator is diligent and a builder who has no chance of winning the contract is left to bear the cost of the wasted time.

How to Find Builders

Unlike most of the professions, builders are not licensed, which means that anyone with a mobile phone and a truck can advertise themselves as a builder. Unemployed DIY enthusiasts, firemen, funeral directors and software designers have all done just this, with mixed results. Much like choosing your professional advisors, the strategy is to make up a list of likely firms and whittle it down by a checking procedure. Part of the problem is that contractors who are good at what they do don't always advertise – they get much of their work through personal recommendation.

Initial Checks

If you are going to hand your whole project over to one building contractor, it is absolutely crucial that you engage the right company, so you must apply some tough selection criteria. With the exception of those recommended personally by someone you know and trust, none of the methods on the list of sources to obtain names are particularly reliable in themselves, but they should get you a reasonable shortlist to work with. The next stage is to carry out some basic checks, followed by more detailed scrutiny of those who seem the best prospects.

First Checks

The following suggestions as to how to find names to shortlist apply only to general builders. They do not all apply to individuals who carry out very small building projects or hire themselves out as

> **Places to Look for Building Contractors**
>
> - Your architect
> - Yellow Pages
> - Local papers
> - Friends
> - Neighbours
> - Builder's merchants and product suppliers
> - Site boards by building sites
> - Internet sites that list contractors and have feedback from previous customers
> - Proactive contractors who contacted you after your planning application was submitted
> - Local authority planners and building control officers (strictly unofficially)
> - Local authority lists of approved contractors, which are sometimes available to the public

sole traders. These people usually run their businesses with minimum management but may still be highly skilled.

Address and Contact Details

If there is only a mobile phone number, and further details are not immediately proffered, cross the firm off straight away. If they do give an address, is it their home number or do they have a yard or an office, or just an accommodation address? If they are a small operation, this may help them to keep their prices down, but the lack of facilities would be a disadvantage for a complex or sizable project.

Membership of Organizations

There is a plethora of unregulated organizations for builders to join, some of which require members to fulfil superficial conditions, and others that just have a membership fee. Some conduct high-profile marketing and promotion campaigns, but they are not independent organizations – their main aim is to represent and procure work for their members. Mediation schemes often turn out to be more about protecting the interests of their members than resolving disputes or satisfying unhappy customers. The truly professional organizations that builders may belong to are the RICS (Royal Institute of Chartered Surveyors) and the CIOB (Chartered Institute of Building). Both these organizations require academic qualifications of their members and enforce codes of conduct. All the other builders' organizations, whatever grand claims they make about regulating their members, are effectively clubs or lobby groups. Once they have your details, a few will even try to sell you insurance or finance. Membership of this type of organization is not a guarantee of a good-quality service.

Track Record

How long has the company been in existence? This is different from how long they have been in business. Some organizations have a habit of winding up their business and starting a new company with a very similar name the next day, and employing the same staff at the same premises. This way they avoid all the debts and legal liabilities incurred by their previous incarnation. Occasionally, small building firms are made insolvent through no fault of their own, for example by the poor payment practices of larger companies.

Staff

How many permanent staff do they employ, as opposed to part-time workers and subcontractors? If their management team is just one person, what happens when that person goes on holiday or is sick?

Availability

Most good building contractors are booked up several months ahead. Some are booked up for twelve months by springtime. So if they are available next week, ask them why. Sometimes there is a genuine reason, typically that an expected contract has fallen through, leaving a sudden gap in their workload.

Behaviour and Communication

If the person who first picks up the phone doesn't listen properly, uses unnecessary jargon, or is evasive when asked straight questions, put a big question mark next to their company, and ask to talk to someone else if they are not in a senior position.

Readiness to Quote

Make it clear that you will require a fixed price, and will be using an industry standard contract. If they will not consider the latter, ask them why not and ask to see a copy of the terms and conditions that they intend to insist that you use. Builder's own contracts or those prepared by some of the organizations that represent them are usually biased in their favour compared to one of the independently published contracts, so make sure that you understand the implications before you put them on your tender list. Get independent advice if you are unsure. If they suggest that you don't need a written contract, bear in mind that all reputable contractors will insist that one be signed. Watch out for the writing in small lettering or grey ink on the back of a quote. Sometimes these contain contractual provisions that are blatantly in favour of the builder and unfair to the customer.

Brochures and Marketing Information

Invite the builders to send you some information on their company by post, but do not be too disappointed if you receive little or nothing. Many building contractors who are excellent builders are hopeless at marketing, and take the view that as long as they have happy clients, there will always be plenty of work to be done. Administration is often the weak point of a small business, where the boss is primarily concerned with ensuring the quality of work and is on site in person for most of the working day. Conversely, well-produced marketing brochures and websites have occasionally been found to conceal a business that cannot get work through any other means.

Research and Visiting

Once you have selected your preferred candidates you can move to the next stage and look more closely at them.

No contractor should make it on to your tender list unless you are quite sure that, based on what you know so far, you would choose them if their tender is the most favourable. To save time you may leave some of the second-stage checks until after you have got prices back, but proper checks are essential before you commit yourself by signing a contract.

Place of Work?
Try to visit their offices if at all possible. If they won't invite you, find an excuse to go, however briefly. In all likelihood it will not be a palace, but you will get a good picture of who you are dealing with. If their office is based at home, the size of their house and make of car will tell you a bit about the profit margins of the company.

References and Portfolio
When you visit them, ask to see photos of examples of buildings that they have worked on, find out where they are located, and then ask for references. Visit the properties and talk to the clients. A short telephone conversation will tell you more than any written recommendation.

Insurance
All building contractors must have public liability insurance and the other insurance necessary to run a construction site. It is acceptable to ask the contractor to confirm that they are current, and check the extent of the cover. It is perfectly reasonable to ask for documentary proof before you sign the contract.

Integrity
There are many ways to evade taxes and save money by ignoring legislation and it is tempting to collude with the builder when you could reduce the cost by several thousand of pounds. However, if a builder is prepared to evade the payment of taxes on such a large scale, they are likely to try to evade their duty to do a good, safely carried out job for you as well. The main reason so many people are killed and injured every year on construction sites is because companies of this kind fail to comply with the health and safety laws and other rules and regulations. You or one of your family could become one of those statistics if you allow your builder to cut corners.

How to Spot a Cowboy

- No address on flyers or letterhead.
- No proper telephone number.
- Use on letterhead of logos to which they are not entitled.
- History of regularly winding up companies.
- Immediate availability with no explanation.
- Poor standard of behaviour by staff.
- Insistence that you use an unreasonably worded contract.
- Reluctance to work with your professional team.
- Very few or no previous clients who you can speak to directly.
- Will not produce insurance certificates.
- Unrealistically low quotation.
- Demands for large amounts of money in advance.
- Offers 'cash in hand' deals to avoid substantial VAT payments.

Fortunately, contrary to the popular image of the small building contractor promoted by some elements of the media, there are many excellent ones who take great personal pride in their work and deal honestly with their customers. They leave nothing but well-constructed projects and a lot of goodwill in their wake. If you use one of these firms, you will find the experience of working with them an educational and enjoyable experience. We should all treat them well and pay them fairly, or they will become an endangered species.

Self-Managing Tradesmen or Subcontractors
If you are not going to use a single main contractor, but wish to organize you own project and perhaps do some of the building work yourself as well, you need to use a different method to deal with the tradesmen you will employ. Some of the approaches that have been suggested for the general contractors will work, but there are some important differences. These tradesmen are often

just individuals and as such are more difficult to find. They may give priority to their regular employers – the contractors who use them as part of a building team. They may not agree to a written contract, and any written record of your agreement will probably have to be made by you. They will expect to be paid weekly, not in stages as with a main contractor, and they will probably want cash in hand.

The best way to find them is through recommendation, but failing this the only way to find out if they are satisfactory is to actually take them on and sack them if you are unhappy. It is a daunting task to find good, reliable workers who will work for you directly, because even established contractors have trouble finding them, and fewer and fewer younger people are moving into the construction industry to replace the skilled older generation.

Getting a Price for the Work

Once you have your list of contractors you will want to invite prices from them. If you are doing this from design-build contractors without a tender package, as a very minimum you should ask them to include a detailed specification with their price and also ask them to make it clear whether the figure is an estimate that can be altered later on, after you have signed a contract with them, or a fixed quotation that will not change as the detail of the project is developed. As mentioned earlier, if a fixed price is quoted a sensible builder will either want the flexibility to vary the specifications or the price in the event of unexpected work becoming apparent later in the project as the detail is worked out. This will be less of a problem where the likely plan and design is fairly apparent right at the beginning or the house is a standard type for the area.

Checklist for Quotes Before the Design has been Prepared

The following is a list of aspects of the work that affect the price. If one builder has included something that another has not, the prices should be adjusted accordingly before comparing them.

- Accommodation – how many bedrooms, bathrooms and so on and approximate size.
- Staircase location.
- Number, type, material and approximate size of windows, for example two dormers with 1200 × 1200mm double-glazed UPVC windows, four 600mm wide × 950mm deep roof windows.
- Dormer cladding type, for example leadwork to gable, tiled sides, double-pitched roof.
- Materials to be used and how well they will match the existing house.
- Are there any necessary works to complete the job not included, such as tiling, finishes, sanitary ware?
- What works are included for the existing house, for example upgrade to the boiler, rewiring, new fire doors to bedrooms?

- Detailed specifications of doors, stairs, ironmongery, sanitary fittings, light switches, paint finishes.
- Level of insulation – will it be the minimum level possible under the regulations or more generous?
- Who obtains and pays for planning and Building Regulations approval?
- Are the designer's and engineer's fees included?
- Who is responsible for expenses and what are they likely to be?
- Will the builder provide welfare facilities for the workforce, such as a portaloo, and space for preparing drinks, or will they be trooping into the house?
- What security measures will be taken when the house is unoccupied?
- Type and level of insurance.
- What are the payments terms? Will money be asked for up front, at the end or in stages?
- How long they will take to complete the work, and when they can start work.

If you have your own design and construction drawings prepared, you or your architect will send out tenders to the selected builders requesting a fixed price. It is usual to allow a period of three or four weeks for this, as many contractors tend to deal with pricing in between all their site-related jobs for the day, and they will also want in their turn to put some of the work out to tender from their regular subcontractors.

When inviting builders to prepare a price, it is essential that they all base their calculations on exactly the same information, and that any extra details or changes of mind are confirmed to all of them. This is the only way that the prices received can be accurately compared. It is also important that they are not told which other builders are on the list. The reason for this is that if they know their competitors' pricing policies it is possible for them to adjust their tender price accordingly, or in very rare cases fix the price.

After Tenders

Hopefully, you will have filtered out any problem contractors before they are invited to price and have on your list only the best available companies. But when you receive prices back, you should consider the following.

Checking the Figures

The lowest building contractor should then be asked to provide a detailed price breakdown and you should check the arithmetic. This is to make sure that they have not made a mistake in their calculations, which does happen occasionally. It is better to find this out before you employ them.

Thoroughness

As the contractors carry out their costing exercise during the tender period, they will inevitably pick up small errors or ambiguities in the tender documents, or want clarification on particular points. If a contractor has been in touch with questions before submitting their price, this is a very good sign. If they have not, it is a sign either that they worked out their price very late in the day, or that they have not worked out a price in sufficient detail, or that they have guessed the answers to the questions that arose.

CHAPTER 4

Designing a Loft Conversion

THE DESIGN PROCESS

The approach to creating a good loft extension must be firmly rooted in the four basic cornerstones of a good design – respect for the budget, adherence to your requirements, practical thinking and an eye for what will look attractive. This may sound like common sense, but if any of these four aspects goes significantly wrong, the result is a bad design. There are several different ways for a designer to approach the design process, but generally they follow the same pattern.

1. Identify the budget.
2. Discuss and agree the client's requirements.
3. Measure and draw the existing building.
4. Sketch out ideas.
5. Discuss with the client.
6. Rework design in the light of client's comments.
7. Prepare planning drawings.
8. Prepare construction drawing and specifications.
9. Monitor the construction on site.

LEFT: **Although most people in the UK associate lofts with bedrooms, they are flexible spaces that have many other uses.** The Velux Company Ltd

BELOW: **Good design does not happen by accident.** Room Maker Loft Conversions

After getting a clear idea of your budget and brief the next step is for the relevant parts of the existing building to be measured and for these to be translated into drawings. The drawings must be as accurate and comprehensive as possible. Accuracy is important because they will be used to work out the design and detailed construction. If the design work is based on wrong dimensions, it may not be possible to build it, or may lead to some unpleasant surprises later on. One possible consequence of a poorly measured survey is that there is insufficient headroom to fit the staircase, which may not be realized until the builders begin work. Sometimes a few centimetres can make the difference between a design that passes Building Regulations and one that fails.

Once a reliable record of the existing building and any surrounding relevant features has been made, the design process can begin in earnest. Usually the first step is developing some preliminary drawings. For a simple scheme, there may a limited number of options, or even only one sensible way to proceed, in which case final drawings may be produced almost immediately. Where there are several options, with different benefits and disadvantages, more sketchy drawings may be used at first to examine the feasibility of each. Sometimes the only way to find out which route is the best one for you will mean abortive work, with a scheme being abandoned after it has been developed a fair way into the design process. This may seem like needless expense, but in fact it is considerably cheaper than finding out an idea doesn't work very well once building work is underway.

At this stage, as before, good communication between you and whoever is carrying out the design is essential. An architect may explain ideas using freehand three-dimensional sketches, computer drawings or, for a complex scheme that is difficult to visualize, models. But in addition to these there should be meetings where the designer can explain the thinking behind what has been presented. This is the stage when misunderstandings are most likely to develop between designer and client and the best way to deal with them is by talking it through.

Once a design approach has been settled on, it may have to be developed in more detail. Even if a planning application is not necessary, larger-scale design drawings will be needed before the construction details and specifications are drawn up. Who will carry out the detailed design work is up to you. It may be an architect, who can produce information in the form of drawings and specifications for the builder to follow. It may be the foreman of the building company, or even a bricklayer as he wields a trowel on site. But whoever it is, and whether they may realize it or not, they will be making design decisions and this should really be in consultation with you and your family if you wish to ensure that the finished work reflects your own aspirations and tastes.

'Envisioning' – How a Design is Described

As part of the essential communication with your designer, the developing ideas have to be described in ways that you can understand. And not just you, as it is necessary to illustrate the proposals to others, such as planning officers and councillors on the local authority planning committee. Two-dimensional (2D) drawings, prepared using ink and set square or by computer-aided design, are a central plank in this process. Drawn to scale, they can

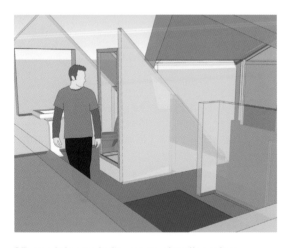

3D models can help you to visualize what it will be like to be in the new rooms.
Julian Owen Associates Architects

The style of a room is as much dependent on the contents and furnishings as the space created. Julian Owen Associates Architects

impression of what the completed space will look and feel like.

However, if you commission fully rendered drawings or accurate card models from your architect, be aware that they are quite time-consuming to create and thus expensive compared to 2D plans and elevations.

Cheaper, low-end computer packages that can be mastered by anyone with knowledge of computers are available, and can help to give an impression of a design. Although some programs are surprisingly sophisticated, they tend to have a restricted choice of materials, components and shapes. Scale models can also be created out of white card.

THE MAIN ELEMENTS OF A DESIGN

At the beginning of the design process, you are likely to have plenty of your own ideas about the style and approach that you would like to take, but try to keep as open a mind as possible. You need to decide how radical you are prepared to be with the alterations and consider which aspects of the design are most important to you. There are many details that need to be considered as a design is being developed.

be related directly to the building as it will be built and used as an accurate, measurable description of the finished building. However, they can sometimes be difficult to read, or even deceptive, to the untrained eye.

These drawings may be adequate, and cost-effective for simple conversions, but sometimes a design has been created in the mind of the architect as a three-dimensional (3D) form and this may not be apparent from elevations, sections and plans alone. Many people find it very difficult to judge how much room they will actually get from these sort of illustrations, particularly where the ceiling is sloping. Worse, this kind of depiction may actually make the design look unattractive. Simple three-dimensional computer models or card models may help to give a more accurate

What Features Make Up a Style?

- Design features, such as sash windows, moulded architraves.
- Scale and proportion, for example ceiling height, roof pitch, window proportions, sill heights, door openings.
- Materials, for example bricks of nineteenth-century sizes, terracotta details, size of glass panes.
- Building methods, for example timber frame, thatch.
- Structural constraints, for example short span of roof and ceilings on older properties.
- Age, for example the way that the building has weathered or sagged.

Style

This is probably the most immediately obvious feature of the interior and exterior of a house.

You need to make an appraisal of the style of house that you already have, and decide whether you wish to keep and enhance it, alter it completely so that it is unrecognizable, or create something as a sharp contrast to what you already have. The latter option requires some skill from your architect. If your taste is for a contemporary flavour, but the rest of your house has an attractive traditional appearance that you want to preserve, a style confined to the striking modern interior can be the solution.

Contemporary Style

The designs for older, traditional houses were evolved by craftsmen, using traditional local materials and building techniques. Creating a modern-looking design may well be more expensive than staying with the tried and tested route. The materials and products used may be unfamiliar to the builders that usually only deal with domestic alterations, and to get the best effect, a higher standard of workmanship than usual will be needed. Because there may be no architraves to hide the joints and junctions between materials, and there is a need for walls and other surfaces to have smooth unblemished surfaces, greater skill will be demanded from whoever builds it.

One simple technique used by designers is to paint all the walls white, in conjunction with a neutral colour scheme for the furniture and fixtures. Carefully controlled natural and artificial light can also be used to good effect. Plenty of background daylight can be concentrated into brighter areas to contrast with patches of shadow. Transparent and translucent walls, for example, using glass blocks, along with slatted screens and blinds will filter the light and add depth to the spaces.

Traditional details, which normally conceal the inaccuracies of the average building site, are dispensed with. So skirting boards and architraves, which could hide gaps and timber shrinkage, are often omitted. Services, such as pipework and electrical wiring, have to be concealed.

Older buildings, which already have a consider-

Designed properly, loft spaces lend themselves to interesting spaces. The Velux Company Ltd

able charm without any alterations, need very careful handling, even more so if they are protected in any way. For example, with a listed building everything within the site boundary is protected, including the interiors. Even if the inside has no features from the original construction, you may still need listed building consent to alter it significantly, and professional advice is essential before any structural alterations are made. If an older, unlisted building has interesting features, it may not be necessary to remove them to achieve a contemporary feel.

Ten Features of a Contemporary Home Interior

- Large, open-plan spaces.
- Lots of natural light.
- Smooth surfaces with minimal details at junctions.
- Clean, straight lines.
- Monochromatic colour scheme.
- Concealed storage.
- Natural finishes.
- Industrial materials, fixtures and fittings.
- Well-designed artificial light.
- Neat, orderly lifestyle of occupants.

Natural light can be maximized in a loft conversion. The Velux Company Ltd

Sunlight is a welcome feature in any room, as long as it can be shut out when it is too hot or there is too much glare.

The Velux Company Ltd

Space Planning

The volumes of the rooms that you are going to add or change are an important part of the design. It is hard to visualize how the new spaces will feel from looking at a 2D plan so you may ask for a 3D sketch or model, or try to relate them back to existing rooms that you are familiar with. If the proportions of a space are wrong, it will feel uncomfortable to people, perhaps without it being obvious why. We tend to relate the 'feel' of a space back to our own human dimensions, so a room that is high and narrow, or wide with a low ceiling as we stand in it will make us feel uneasy.

Structure and Construction

Traditionally built or 'vernacular' buildings were often not consciously designed. Their features and appearance were dictated by the limitations of the materials and building techniques available at the time. For example, at one time the roofs of barns and ordinary houses were limited to a span of 6m or so, because that is as far as the timber they were using would span. If you apply these rules to your design it will help to keep it looking and feeling traditional. However, for a loft conversion, this approach can reduce the structural options and in many cases modern structural components have to be used to create the best possible space.

If you decide that you want large, open-plan spaces or wide openings, you will need to use either steel beams or a modern laminated timber beams supported on masonry or a similar 'heavyweight' structure, because timber would have to have a very large cross-section to span the required distances. You then have a choice of cladding them to look like timber beams spanning impossible distances for their size, boxing them in or leaving them exposed. Each of these options will have strong impact on the design of the house.

Daylight and Sunlight

These are free natural resources that are on offer to brighten up a loft conversion. The more daylight there is in a room, the more spacious it will feel. If it can come in from more than one direction, the shadows and quality of light will feel harmonious. Easily the best source of daylight comes from roof

Views out of windows are often as important as the light that they let into the room. The Loft Company

lights, which are generally easy to fit in a typical roofspace. The sky is many times brighter than the landscape and scenery that you see through a window in a wall and so windows that look up will let in maximum light. Daylight streaming in from above also creates a pleasant feel to a room.

Windows also offer an opportunity to look out of the building into its surroundings and enjoy any pleasant views. If the views are unattractive, or reduce privacy to an unacceptably low level, some creative placing of the windows will be needed to let in light without making the occupants feel uncomfortable. Large areas of glazing in a roof or wall, apart from affecting the style and appearance

outside, will also make a room seem more spacious, especially if the sills are very low. If you are faced with a room or corridor that feels cramped, extra glazing or concentrating the glazing in full height strips will reduce claustrophobia.

Similarly there are many benefits to allowing plenty of sunlight into a house, although these can sometimes be offset by the overheating and glare that is caused by the sun's rays. In the right place at the right time, sunlight entering into a room will make people feel happier and probably help them to be healthier as well. If properly controlled, it can even help to reduce fuel bills. Sunlight falling onto a desk or kitchen worktop, however, produces glare that can at least cause headaches and prevent them from being used comfortably until the clouds block it off or a blind is drawn. Anyone who is unlucky enough to have a badly sited south-facing conservatory will tell you that the heat gain that is generated from the sun makes it unbearable to sit in for most of the summer.

Finishes, Colour and Materials

Regardless of how the conversion is constructed, the treatment of the interior is an important part of the design.

Small swatches and samples can be very deceptive. The intensity of a colour should be multiplied many times in your mind when looking at them. What appears to be a subtle shade of rose white on a little square in your hand can turn into bright pink when spread across a whole wall. As long as you bear this limitation in mind a sample board can be helpful in selecting materials and finishes, and is particularly helpful when comparing different finishes, such as ironmongery and a natural finish to a door, or a painted architrave with the wall it will be set into.

Some materials could be described as 'self-finished', which look good just left once they are in place, without any need to treat them for appearance or weatherproofing – the most obvious examples being brick, stone, and glass.

In exceptional circumstances, paint can be used to make a bold statement, at a relatively low price, by painting interior or exterior walls in bright colours. This can be difficult to achieve, however, without the end result looking cheap and garish.

Dark colours tend to make a room feel more cramped and small, so should be confined to the floor only in a typical loft conversion, which will have sections of ceiling that are already lower than we are used to in a normal room. Conversely, light colours help to make a room feel larger and are particularly effective in doing this when combined with plenty of natural light.

Circulation Spaces

The design of the staircase and the space that encloses it is possibly more important than most

Strong use of colour can have a striking effect.
Julian Owen Associates Architects

Daylight always helps make a circulation space more pleasant to move through.
Julian Owen Associates Architects

ABOVE: **Another example of a rooflight helping to add headroom.** Attic Designs Ltd

RIGHT: **This rooflight makes the staircase feel less cramped, partly because of the extra daylight, and partly because it adds more headroom.** Julian Owen Associates Architects

of the rooms, in terms of its impact on the design of the inside of a house. It is part of a three-dimensional space that is used many times a day. A good staircase has plenty of daylight and celebrates the double height space that it occupies. Although it is often not possible, it is a good idea to create plenty of space around the staircase where you can. Rooflights or windows increase the daylight levels for a staircase and landings and help to convey a feeling of spaciousness.

Features

Otherwise characterless spaces can be made special by the careful placing of features. In many rooms, fireplaces can be used to provide a focal point but these are not easy to integrate into the average loft and the hard truth is that the real focal points of many modern living spaces are the television, computer and hi-fi. Because the planning possibilities of a loft space are often limited their locations should be considered before the plans are finalized, and such items may usefully be integrated into some built-in furniture.

HOW TO BE GREEN

'Sustainable' is the current buzzword in the construction industry for what used to be called 'green' or 'environmentally friendly' building. It means that when any building work is designed and carried out the impact that is made on the environment is considered. This is an issue that has rightly been increasing in importance over recent years. Our homes are amongst the worst offenders, responsible for about 25 per cent of all carbon dioxide emissions in the UK. It is a potentially vast subject and if you are interested in pursuing this ideal, it is well worth getting one of the many books that describe in depth how to be as green as possible when building. Below are some suggestions, with a cautionary note that some of them conflict, and there are not always clear-cut answers as to the best way to achieve an environment-friendly house.

Use Less Energy

When you embark on a building project of any

kind, the decisions that you take will have an effect for decades or more into the future. Adding extra insulation over and above the minimum required by the Building Regulations will give an immediate saving in the energy needed to heat the house, which will last for the life of the building. The law of diminishing returns applies to insulation, however, and as the thickness of insulation to the structure increases, the relative benefits reduce. Another place to increase the insulation is around the hot-water storage cylinder, if you have one. Also stopping up the draughts around the doors, windows and floors will help an older house reduce heat loss.

Position windows to ensure that good natural light reaches all areas, but remember that consideration also needs to be given to the external appearance of the building. Bear in mind that windows, even when triple glazed, allow far more heat loss than well-insulated walls, floors and roofs.

There are ways of recovering heat energy that may otherwise be lost, by using a heat exchanger. A condensing boiler uses this principle by extracting some of the heat from the exhaust gas before it is vented to the outside. Mechanical ventilation systems can also follow the same principle.

Ensuring that the boiler is energy efficient, and that all the main radiators in the house have thermostatic radiator valves (TRVs) will help to reduce your fuel bills. TRVs allow the room temperatures to be set much lower in some rooms, such as bedrooms, without the need for sophisticated and expensive programme controls. When rooms are heated to different temperatures, doors should be kept closed.

Another concept relevant to building projects is called 'embodied energy'. This is the energy that is used to produce a material, get it to the site and finally to destroy or recycle it when the building is redundant. Unfortunately, there is yet to be agreement on the way in which embodied energy is measured and how it is compared with more obvious energy usage by a building. For example, the wood for a timber joist may come from abroad, and not be reusable for construction when the building is demolished. How does this compare with a steel beam, which has to be mined, then manufactured at great energy cost, but is lighter to transport than a timber beam of equivalent strength and can be reused?

Generate your Own Energy

Most people do not have much option as to how energy is supplied to their house – with a few exceptions most have a choice of mains electricity, and either mains gas or stored fuel such as oil, gas or coal. It is prohibitively expensive for most people to remove their reliance on external power altogether, but it is possible to use alternative methods to gather some energy from other sources.

Passive solar gain – or heat that builds up when the sun gets through windows and is trapped behind it – is an easy way to collect natural, free energy, although the increased areas of glazing will lose more heat in winter and risk overheating in summer. The glass should face within 25 degrees of due south and ideally have some kind of overhang above it to screen out the summer sun, which is at a much higher angle than in winter.

A more sophisticated method of using the sun's heat is to fit solar collectors on to any roof that faces in a southerly direction. In their simplest form these are radiators, painted black, under a glass or clear plastic sheet. Heat builds up in the panels as the sun shines, and the water that is piped through them is used to contribute heat to top up the main heating and hot water system. This is relatively easy to do, but requires some alterations to the heating system.

It is possible to generate your own electricity using the sun's rays with photovoltaic technology. Unfortunately, at the time of writing, the cost of fitting this type of solar panel is so high that you will have to wait many years for them to recoup their costs with the money they save on your fuel bills. However, demand for them is increasing year by year so there is a good chance that the price will eventually come down to a realistic level for domestic projects.

Wind power is another possibility, although again, not really economic at the moment unless you are in an exposed countryside location. Burning wood or inert waste products, such as blocks of compressed newspaper, is also worth considering as a way of heating rooms and hot water, particularly if these fuels are readily available.

Reduce Pollution

Pollution can result from the contents of your drains and waste bin, but also the materials that are incorporated into your home. The former can partly be dealt with by your lifestyle, rather than how the house is built – for example by separating out rubbish that can be recycled. The pollution caused by waste water can be dealt with in several ways, depending on how keen you are to follow through a green lifestyle. Surface water – that is water that enters the drains from rain falling on the roof – can be diverted into a chamber or sump buried under the ground, then pumped up and used for watering the garden or even flushing the toilets. It can even be treated and used for drinking water. Surface water could also be piped to a soakaway rather than the main drains, reducing the quantity of water passing through the sewage treatment plants.

'Grey' water that comes from baths, wash basins and washing machines can also be recycled with the right technology. The ultimate move is to do away with the worst source of pollution and use a composting toilet – it does not use water or flush and eventually provides fertilizer for the garden. These are surprisingly effective and odourless when installed correctly. However, many of these systems require extra water storage tanks in the loft, which may rule them out if the conversion leaves little to spare.

Building materials can cause pollution when they are being manufactured, when they are in part of a building or when they have to be disposed of at the end of the life of the building. Throughout the life of some materials small amounts of gases believed to be harmful to health by environmentalists are released into the atmosphere. Natural products, such as sheep's wool insulation, not only cause little pollution in their manufacture but can also be recycled. The disadvantage is that these products need to be a lot thicker than the more efficient insulation types that are less environmentally

friendly, and will reduce the headroom once installed along the line of the rafters.

Use Recycled and Recyclable Materials

In addition to recycling the waste produced by living in a house, you can also use materials for building work that are either provided by recycling or can in themselves be recycled.

There are many materials that can be recycled, such as timber for windows, doors, steel used for structural support, slates, tiles and bricks – provided that the latter have been laid in a soft lime mortar that can easily be cleaned off (modern hard cement mortars stick firmly to bricks, making them difficult to reclaim).

MAXIMIZING SPACE

One aspect of loft conversions that make them different from other types of house alteration is that part or all of the ceilings of the new rooms are sloping. Before the conversion has been carried out, this can make it difficult to visualize how the furniture will fit in the spaces that have been created. Standing in the existing loft space can help, but you have to use quite bit of imagination to picture how it can be divided up and used.

The first step is to identify how much of the area of the finished conversion will have full headroom. Over about 1.8m is adequate for most people. If this space is in the wrong place for a staircase, or is not big enough to justify the cost of converting it, the roof will have to be extended to provide more space.

The following examples illustrate the principles that have to be applied when planning out a loft conversion. They have been chosen because they represent the worst case for common situations.

The hipped roof shown has slopes on all four sides, so the area that has headroom is concentrated in the middle of the roof. This is often inconvenient for the positioning of the staircase and the area created may also be too small. The lack of an existing full-height wall also makes it harder to find a comfortable location for the bed. There are a

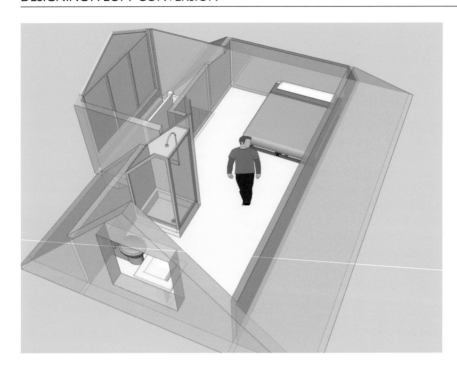

The basic requirements for a conversion are space for a proper staircase, room to fit the required furniture and enough head height to move around in the space. This conversion has room for a bed, but it will only be accessible from one side. Julian Owen Associates Architects

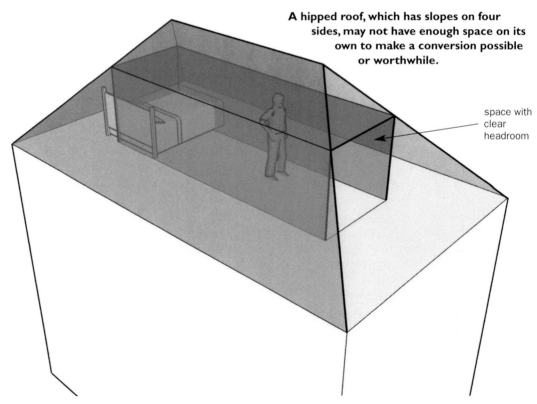

A hipped roof, which has slopes on four sides, may not have enough space on its own to make a conversion possible or worthwhile.

space with clear headroom

couple of options that will increase the size of the roof.

The hip can be removed and replaced by a gable end. This extends the area with headroom, and provides a full-height wall. This may be a good place to put the new staircase, a large window or even make space for French windows and a Juliet balcony. Hipped roofs usually have a purlin halfway up their rafters, propped off internal walls, and some steelwork will be needed to replace the purlin that will have to be removed to make this configuration possible.

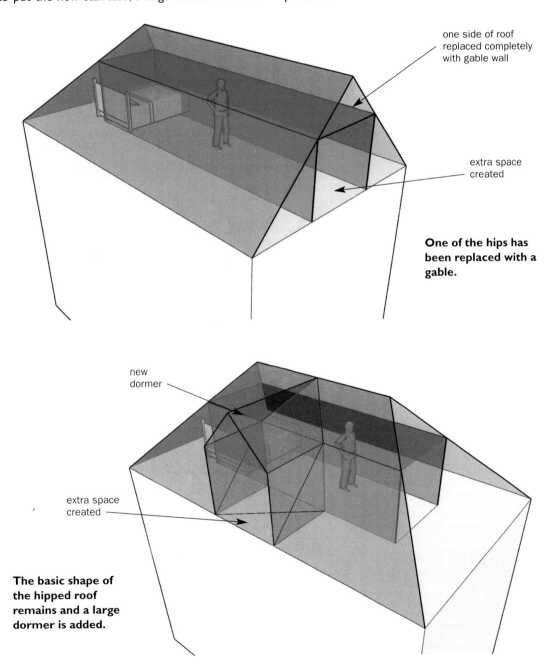

one side of roof replaced completely with gable wall

extra space created

One of the hips has been replaced with a gable.

new dormer

extra space created

The basic shape of the hipped roof remains and a large dormer is added.

A smaller dormer added above the purlin line of the main roof.

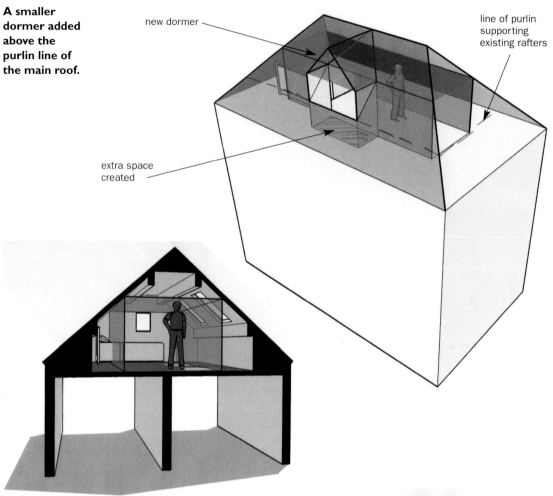

new dormer

line of purlin supporting existing rafters

extra space created

A gable roof may have enough space on its own. If not, the addition of dormers is a simple way to increase the floor area that has clear headroom.

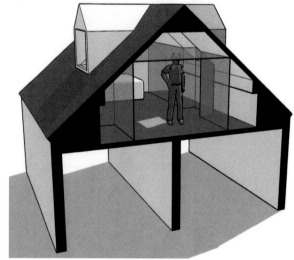

Adding a dormer to the side of a roof is a relatively straightforward way of increasing the headroom. A large dormer can easily provide space to fit in a staircase and this approach is common in a typical semi-detached house when the new staircase is fitted over the existing one between ground and first floor. Even a large dormer is unlikely to be large enough to fit in a double bed, however, because as it gets wider, the ridge of the dormer roof gets higher and would eventually be above the ridge of the main roof.

It is easier (and cheaper) to build a smaller dormer window, above the line of the main purlins. This adds a relatively small amount of space, but in a fairly cramped roof void this can be valuable, especially if several dormers are built. Because the purlin is usually in the middle third of the rafter, it may be too high for the window to count as an escape window under the Building Regulations (see Chapter 5 for a full explanation of the implications of this limitation).

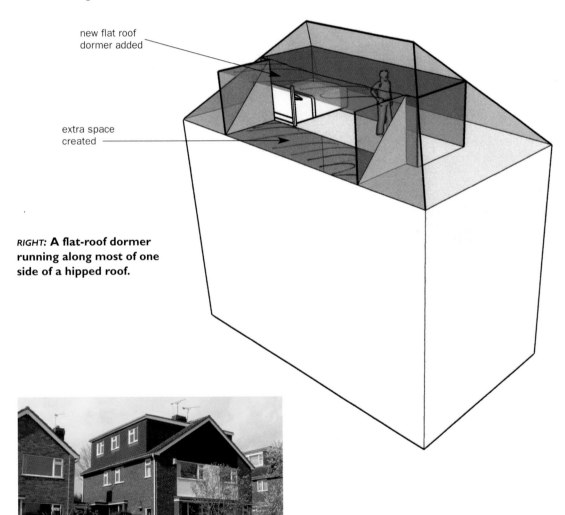

new flat roof dormer added

extra space created

RIGHT: A flat-roof dormer running along most of one side of a hipped roof.

LEFT: The flat-roof dormer is a common feature of 1970s room-in-the-roof design.
Attic Designs Ltd

Although it is less satisfying architecturally, a very effective way of creating a lot of new space is to add a flat roof dormer along one side of the roof. This is usually done to the rear-facing roof so it will not spoil the front elevation of the house and may not need planning approval.

RIGHT, AND BELOW RIGHT: **This room has been squeezed in to a tiny section of roof that has only a strip of about 700mm wide along one side with headroom. However, it still makes a usable study bedroom. Note that the rooflight is positioned to allow the door to open fully, which otherwise would jam against the ceiling.**

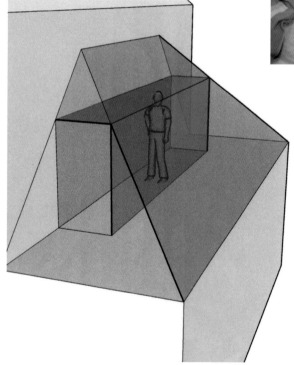

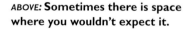
ABOVE: **Sometimes there is space where you wouldn't expect it.**

Many two-storey houses have single-storey additions sometimes called 'outshots' or 'lean-tos' at the rear, perhaps over the utility rooms. It is sometime possible to make use of the roof void above these spaces. In order to do so, you need a corridor that has clear headroom. It can be made to work even when this corridor is quite narrow. The example shown here has only 700mm, but with a clever use of the extra headroom made possible by the insertion of a rooflight, it has been possible to create just enough space to open a door into it. Although there is not a lot of space to stand up in, the floor area is sufficient to fit in a desk, storage cupboards and a bed. This kind of space is particularly suitable for younger children to whom the room seems much larger as they don't require as much headroom.

STAIRCASE PLANNING

Having established the configuration of space that it will be possible to create at the loft level, the next major decision is to decide where the

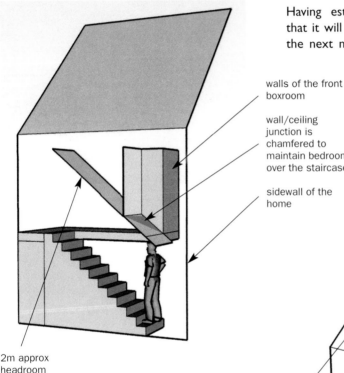

walls of the front boxroom

wall/ceiling junction is chamfered to maintain bedroom over the staircase

sidewall of the home

2m approx headroom is needed above the steps

ABOVE: **Designing a new staircase – Stage 1. A typical staircase arrangement in a standard semi-detached house.**

BELOW: **Designing a new staircase – Stage 2. A new staircase is added over the existing to access the loft.**

headroom is required over new staircase – higher than existing roof

new staircase

landing

winders raise height of staircase over the one below and maintain headroom

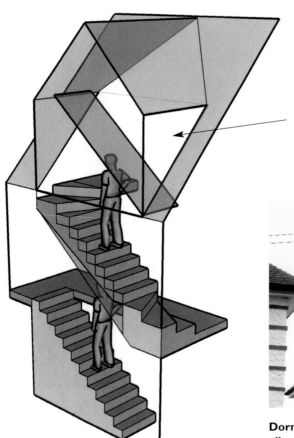

LEFT: **Designing a new staircase – Stage 3. A dormer is needed to maintain headroom above the new staircase.**

addition of new dormer allows headroom for new staircase and space to turn and face into the main roofspace

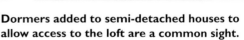

Dormers added to semi-detached houses to allow access to the loft are a common sight.

Attic Designs Ltd and Julian Owen Associates Architects

staircase will be located. At this point it is essential to think in three dimensions. A common mistake is to locate the staircase in plan and only then realize that there is no clear headroom above it. Another arrangement that it is tricky to visualize is where the staircase is winding around as it ascends upwards. The Building Regulations have some fairly strict requirements about the headroom necessary to build a staircase, so apart from working out how it will fit into the house plan, it must also penetrate the roof void in such a way that there is 2m headroom above the steps and particularly at the top. This 2m rule is relaxed in the regulations for part of the staircase in certain conditions but it is not a good idea to work to the absolute minimum headroom clearances, because it is rarely possible either to carry out a measured survey to sufficient accuracy, or guarantee that it will be built without a bit of tolerance during the design work.

Typical Staircase Layouts

New Stairs above Existing

The drawing below illustrates a very common arrangement of a staircase running from the ground to the first floor of, say, a 1930s semi-detached house. The existing staircase is often on the outside side wall, with a box room or similar fitted in over the top, the corner of which is chamfered to maximize the room size without losing headroom below.

When a new staircase is built, to maintain headroom over the existing staircase it is usually necessary to sacrifice some or all of the box room to allow the new stair to turn using winders, or wedge-shaped steps. The underside of the new staircase is built to be just high enough to comply with Building Regulations. However, the new stairs

also need headroom and if they are built on an outside wall, this will in fact be the lowest point of the roof and impossible to form without extending it.

A typical solution to the need for headroom over a staircase in this location is to build a new dormer on the side roof of the house (see previous pages). This creates plenty of headroom and also allows the staircase to turn 90 degrees so that anyone climbing up is facing the right way to access the main roofspace. The dormer also allows in light, which helps to alleviate the negative effect on the existing staircase, which will feel a lot more cramped with the new one built directly above it. A window is also fairly important to avoid a blank dormer wall looking over the side of the house.

New Corridor and Staircase

Sometimes it is not possible to fit a new staircase in the area above the existing one, perhaps due to planning restrictions or because of the extra cost of building a new dormer. If the roof void is large

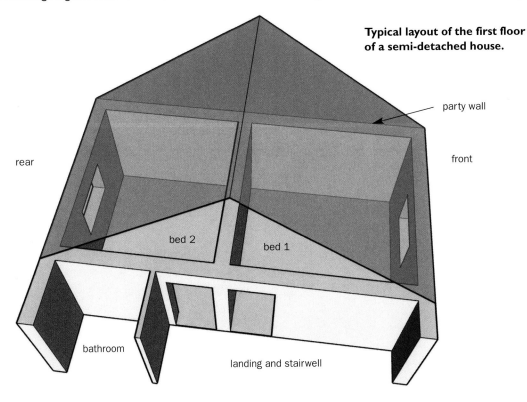

Typical layout of the first floor of a semi-detached house.

party wall

rear

front

bed 2

bed 1

bathroom

landing and stairwell

**A corridor is created
and the new staircase
placed at the end of it.**

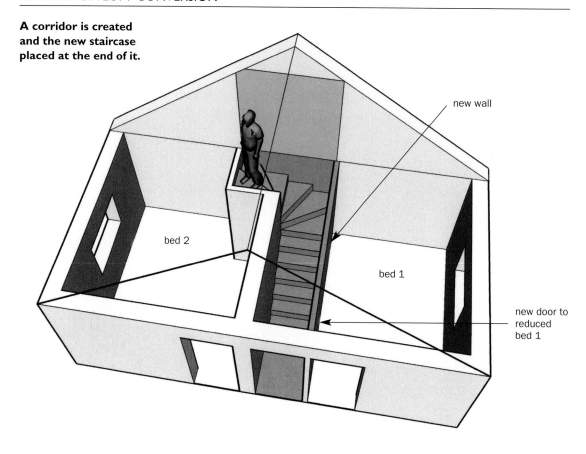

new wall

bed 2

bed 1

new door to
reduced
bed 1

enough there is an alternative location that is nearly as popular as the previous example. A corridor is divided off from the largest bedroom and used for the new staircase. This option is not particularly space efficient because it takes floor area away from important rooms on the first floor, as opposed to using the 'free' space above the existing staircase. It also takes floor area away from the loft, which is even more precious. Sometimes the lost space has to be made up by constructing a dormer at the rear of the house.

In a 'Two Up, Two Down' Terraced House
Another classic loft conversion in a tight situation occurs when more room is needed in a terraced house where the original floor plan consists of a combined kitchen/dining room and a front living room on the ground floor, with two bedrooms

Winders are the wedge-shaped treads that minimize the space needed for a staircase.
Attic Designs Ltd

94

Typical existing floor layout of a two-up, two-down terraced house.

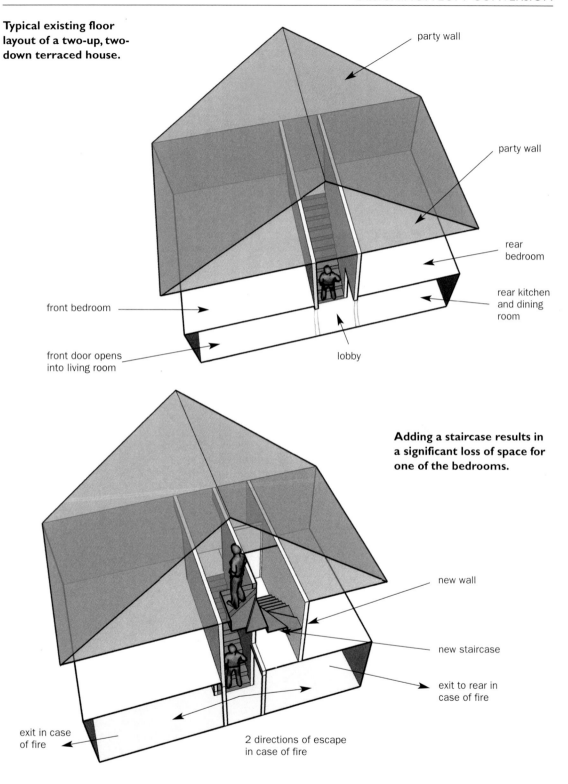

party wall

party wall

rear bedroom

rear kitchen and dining room

front bedroom

front door opens into living room

lobby

Adding a staircase results in a significant loss of space for one of the bedrooms.

new wall

new staircase

exit to rear in case of fire

exit in case of fire

2 directions of escape in case of fire

upstairs. The front and rear doors open directly into the rooms and the bathroom is added as an extension on the ground floor at the back in order to avoid losing one of the first floor bedrooms. The staircase in this traditional Victorian and Edwardian floor plan is designed to use the minimum floor area possible and so it is positioned in the centre of the building with a very small lobby at the bottom. The disadvantage of this arrangement is that the only way to add a staircase economically is to take a slice out of one of the fairly small bedrooms. Often the space that remains is too small for a bedroom and gets redesignated as a bathroom.

The trick is to make the staircase take as little as possible out of the roofspace as it turns around 180 degrees and allows access to the new room above. The limited area with headroom in the loft usually means that there is just enough space to fit a single bedroom and a few pieces of furniture. It is not shown on the drawing, but there is also usually a door at the bottom of the staircase rather than the top, again to avoid reducing the available space upstairs. The Building Regulations require that there is escape in two directions once the bottom of the staircase is reached on the ground floor. This is so that if there is a fire in the living room or kitchen there is always an escape route in the opposite direction. This requirement means that if the staircase is so tight that there are winders at the bottom, opening out into only one ground floor room, it may be difficult to achieve a satisfactory conversion. There are some ideas on how to deal with this problem in the section of the book on the Building Regulations (Chapter 5).

WINDOWS AND GLAZING

After the actual space created and the staircase, the third most important practical aspect of the

OPPOSITE: **If possible, it is a good idea to introduce natural light into the stairwell, or avoid cutting across an existing window with the new staircase.** Attic Designs Ltd

If there is space, the newly-altered staircase can become a dramatic feature of the house. Attic Designs Ltd

design of a loft conversion is the location of the windows into the new rooms.

Rooflights

Rooflights, which are sometimes referred to as skylights, are a major asset to the design of the interior of a house. They provide a quality of light to loft conversions that helps to create a spacious airy feel to a room. In a normal room most of the light that comes through the window is reflected off the surrounding landscape, which will reduce its brightness, while a window that faces upwards is filled with sky, which is many times brighter. The effect can be further enhanced by adding rooflights on more than one side of the room. This increases the level of light, but also changes the character of the shadows and generally helps to create a feeling of wellbeing. This is the reason that so many artists

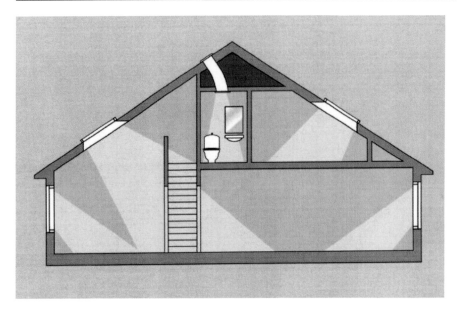

LEFT: **Rooflights provide more light from the sky than normal windows.** The Velux Company Ltd

BELOW: **The amount of light coming through the roof windows is far greater than the larger conventional window in this picture.** Julian Owen Associates Architects

prefer an attic room because they can get maximum benefit from whatever natural daylight is available.

The construction of a rooflight is relatively complex in comparison to a normal window and it is rare for them to be purpose made especially for a house. There are many types and varieties of prefabricated rooflights available, designed for easy installation. Some can be fitted without having to climb outside onto the roof. The standard type are hinged at the centre, but there are versions that hinge at the top. A variant of the latter has a mechanism that automatically lifts the window open to allow someone to climb through it on to the roof, for example in the event of a fire.

Local authority planning departments take a dim view of modern rooflights in conservation areas or on listed buildings because they are much larger and more sophisticated in their construction than those that were used before the middle of the twentieth century. The old-fashioned rooflights were made of cast iron with screw-threaded winches to open them and were much smaller than their contemporary descendants. It would contravene current Building Regulations to use traditional construction methods because they lose heat through the single glazing as well as the metal frame. There is also a significant problem with condensation on the inside of the frame. Consequently window manufacturers have developed rooflights that look very similar to the old ones, but have double glazing and are thermally broken – this means that the metal surround does not penetrate all the way from the outside to the inside.

There are some creative uses of rooflights – for example, ones that can be folded out into temporary balconies, or others designed to be used in rows or combinations to create a large section of glazing out of the ceiling. Apart from letting in plenty of daylight, these features have the added benefit of reducing the cramped feeling that can result from the relatively low roof in a converted loft.

A potential disadvantage of using lots of rooflights is that, although sunlight is often a welcome visitor in the room, sometimes there can be too much, either because of the resultant glare

Rooflights are fairly discreet features when seen from the outside. Julian Owen Associates Architects

that can make reading or watching TV almost impossible, or due to the heat gain that results. It is essential to ensure that a blind is provided and these can be purchased as part of the window kit in a range of colours. Some of them are specifically designed to cut out the sun. Where the windows are inaccessible, perhaps because they are at high level, the opening mechanism and the drawing of the blinds can be motorized and controlled from switches. If the rooflight is easily accessible from the outside it can be a security weak point. The better designed rooflights have a secure locking system, but for extra security motorized shutters can be built into the outside construction.

Dormer Windows

An important function of a dormer is to allow more space with clear headroom and enlarge the useable space in the loft. Extra light and ventilation can be provided by adding a window into the front face of the dormer, which also usually offers a better view out of the building than a rooflight would if it were in the same location. For these reasons, most dormers are initially located as part of the design of the inside of the loft. However, it is also important to take account of the effect it will have on the design of roof from the outside.

Dormer Styles

This gabled dormer has been clad in lead. The roof is large and has a reasonably steep pitch, so the dormer ridge is lower than the main ridge. The front of the dormer is fairly close to the line of the gutter, which, along with the sill height, suggests that the floor level is lower than the eaves.

Julian Owen Associates Architects

This dormer is on a relatively low roof and it has been necessary to take its ridge height up to the same level as the main ridge. This lack of height means that the window and front dormer wall cannot get any wider, unless the roof pitch is made more shallow or the sill level is dropped.

Attic Designs Ltd

In some instances, particularly where headroom is needed to make a staircase possible, the largest possible dormer is created, stretching from the top wall of the side of the house to the main ridge. In this example, to reduce the impact of the large volume added on to the side of the house the walls have been tiled to match the existing building as well as the roof. This dormer could not have been made any larger without looking odd or even ugly.

The Loft Company

The roof of this dormer has been hipped to match in with the house style. However, a full hip was not possible because it would have cut across the line of the window. Note the slightly awkward location of the vent pipe, which probably had to be moved to keep it away from the openable window – a building regulation requirement.

Attic Life

Here the walls have been tiled to reduce the visual impact of the roof extension. Note the window that is smaller than the ideal; this is because of the building regulation that restricts the size of windows facing on to a boundary to reduce the risk of fire spreading from one house to another. Attic Designs Ltd

This is a classic example of what is sometimes referred to as a 'dustpan' or 'shed' dormer. There is not enough height to allow a gabled dormer to fit with a window this large and it was felt that a flat roof would be out of keeping with the existing pitched roof, so this is a compromise. The tiles on the dormer roof have been laid at an unnaturally low pitch and as a result there is significant risk of the wind lifting them off, so special fixings are needed to prevent this. Julian Owen Associates Architects

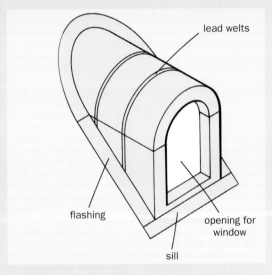

lead welts

flashing

opening for window

sill

An arched dormer roof formed from lead.

Arched dormers have been used for this roof to cleverly get around the problem of the main ridge being very low. They have been clad in the neutral grey of lead to remain in keeping with the building style. However, the spacing of the dormers does not relate well to the windows below.
Julian Owen Associates Architects

LEFT: The dormers added to this house have been designed to closely match the style and materials of the house and located symmetrically to blend in with the elevation below them. Attic Life

Creating Outside Space

With the right size and pitch of roof, it is possible to squeeze some extra outside space for the house in the form of a balcony. These can be a great asset, reducing the feeling of enclosure that many loft conversions can suffer from, as well as making the best of a view, if there is one. If a balcony would allow significant overlooking of neighbours, it may not be possible to get planning approval on privacy grounds. Because you are creating a flat surface outside the building, which will collect water when it rains, the balcony must be properly drained and fully waterproofed to prevent water seeping through to the rooms below.

Even though this balcony is a tiny area, the skilful insertion of outside space and French windows makes the rooms inside feel more spacious. Absolute Lofts

This large roof offered the opportunity to fit in a stylish addition to the house design as well as provide a usable balcony area.
Julian Owen Associates Architects

This ingeniously designed component acts as a roof window in bad weather but can be opened out to form a temporary balcony when the sun shines. The Velux Company Ltd

Three large rooflights, with a temporary balcony for use in good weather.
Attic Designs Ltd

This house is sited on the side of a steep slope with a panoramic view, which has been fully exploited by the new balcony and loft conversion. To avoid detracting from the traditional style of the house a modern glass handrail has been used, which is almost invisible from the ground. Attic Life

Modern window design can allow balconies to be created where they would otherwise be difficult to build. The Velux Company Ltd

The use of three rooflights transforms an otherwise unusable section of the converted roofspace. Attic Designs Ltd

The designer of this conversion spotted an opportunity to extend the first floor and at the same time fit in a spacious balcony nestled between three roof pitches.
Julian Owen Associates Architects

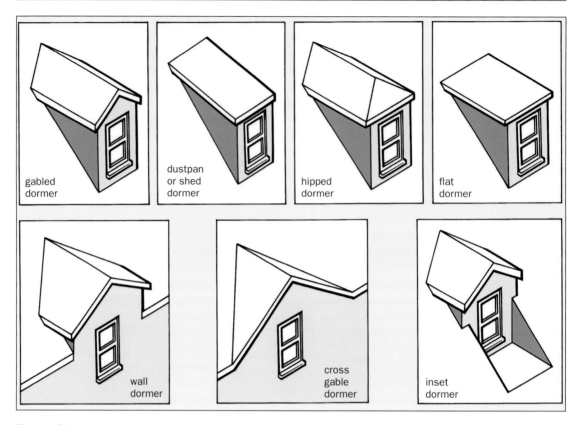

Types of dormer shape.

Designing a Gabled Dormer

1. Work out the approximate dimensions of the largest dormer that will fit with reasonable window sill height and a pitch that matches the main roof. Sometimes it becomes apparent that only a very narrow dormer is possible given these constraints, so an alternative design for the roof has to be considered, for example using a flat roof.

2. Locate the windows in plan to give the most useful space in the new rooms.

3. If the maximum size is larger than needed, select a width based on factors such as the dimensions of a standard window frame and the clearances needed in the room or over the staircase.

4. Draw the chosen dormer on an elevation of the house, to see how it will relate to the existing design. If an elevation is visible from a distance, for example the front of a house, it is more important to get this relationship right.

5. Choose the materials to suit the rest of the house. Sometimes a contrast in the choice of finishes can have a striking effect, but if the dormers are small compared to the main house and not very frequent, the best strategy is to match the existing materials.

These attic trusses have been designed in two sections, with top 'caps' to be added once they are in position. Julian Owen Associates Architects

Attic trusses are a great way to easily build new loft space, provided that the roof shape is very simple. Julian Owen Associates Architects

RIGHT: **This mansard roof is a typical example of a new roof being added to a property in the centre of a city. The new tiled surfaces prevent the extra floor detracting from the design of the façade of the building, which would be difficult to match with modern materials, and also create the illusion that the building is lower in height.** Julian Owen Associates Architects

EXTREME SOLUTIONS

Sometimes, however skilled the architect, it is impossible to find enough headroom, or enough headroom in the right places, to make the conversion of the loft viable. Some older roofs have such a complicated structural design that it makes them difficult to alter without causing major structural weaknesses. In a few unusual situations it may be worth considering the removal and replacement of part or all of this type of roof structure. In financial terms, this sort of work can only be justified if there is no way of extending the existing floors of the house, and if the land values in the area are significantly higher than average.

If the house is in a row of identical neighbours, altering the roof height sufficiently to create more space may be forbidden by planning rules. If the roof is to be replaced it helps if the shape is simple – ideally a rectangle in plan – and the span is not too great. Such circumstances are ideal for attic

trusses to be used. These are a variation on the standard modern fink trussed rafter, but instead of the short pieces of timber that interrupt the roof-space, they have a hole in the middle, created especially for use as living space. If the roof design requires the intersection of two or more double-pitched sections, attic trusses become less viable and it may be simpler and cheaper to construct an entirely new traditional roof construction, although this route is usually more expensive. If it is possible to raise the walls above the existing eaves line before the new roof structure is created, this will contribute significantly to the usable space available in the completed rooms. A 'halfway house' between raising the walls and a simple roof pitch is the mansard roof, which actually has two roof pitches on each side. One is almost vertical, for example 85 degrees, and the other is a more conventional pitch, such as 35 degrees. This has the benefit of forming a large area with clear headroom, in effect adding a complete new floor to the

An attic space lends itself best of all for use as a bedroom. Attic Designs Ltd

This dormer roof provides extra space as well as a view across the surroundings. Attic Designs Ltd

The quality of light in a roof space helps you to relax as you wake or prepare for sleep. Attic Life

ABOVE: **This bedroom has the benefit of a view through one window and a high level of light from a rooflight.** Attic Life

LEFT: **The roof window has been positioned to provide a bedside shelf as well as extra headroom to one side of this bed.** Attic Life

Here the roof space is large enough to accommodate some French windows that maximize the view. Absolute Lofts

A room-in-the-roof is an ideal space for children to play. The Velux Company Ltd

house, whilst reducing the visual impact, because the 'walls' are clad in tiles and do not appear as imposing as a continuation upwards of the existing wall would be.

USES FOR A CONVERTED LOFT SPACE

Bedrooms

The most obvious use for a loft conversion is to provide extra bedrooms. Sometimes a bedroom has to be lost to allow the staircase to get up there and, in these cases, to be worthwhile the size of the new room created should be considerably more than the one that is removed. Sometimes it is hard to gauge the headroom that will be available by studying the plans before construction starts, but it is worth taking the time to do this if the idea is to create enough space for a double bed. The plans may show enough floor area for a double bed to be fitted in, but you also have to account for the sloping roof. It is not uncommon for a loft conversion to be completed before the couple who are going to sleep in it realize that there is not enough headroom either side of the bed to stand up in, requiring them to roll off the end of the bed before they can stand up. For this reason, the new room is often more suited to a twin bedroom, that is two single beds, which each have space on one side to get out of bed without banging your head.

Loft conversions are particularly suited to bedrooms for young children, partly because they are a more exciting space than the usual full-height rooms and often have interesting views across the neighbourhood. But also younger children can make use of more of the room than their parents, because they can stand up in the spaces close to the eaves, which are out of bounds to fully grown adults.

Another benefit of using the space for bedrooms is the quality of light achieved by the use of rooflights, which create a particularly restful feeling not provided by a standard window in a wall. On the other hand, roof windows can have the reverse effect in heavy rain, which can be very noisy, particularly during a night-time storm.

In a house with two or more storeys, attic rooms may also be quieter, being further away from the hurly burly of the main living areas on the ground floor.

Bathrooms

A potential drawback of adding an extra floor to an existing house is that the main bathroom will not be at the same level as the new bedrooms. It is an unwanted hazard to have to navigate stairs to get to the toilet in the middle of the night. If at all possible, it is a good idea to fit a bathroom somewhere in the loft space. If there is only one bedroom and space is at a premium, a very small

As well as ensuring a high level of natural daylight, this rooflight also provides just enough headroom for the wash basins, allowing an efficient use of the rest of the space. Attic Life

When this lady climbs out of the bath, she will have to be careful not to bump her head on the sloping roof above. Note the use of a mirror to make the room seem larger than it really is. The Velux Company Ltd

It is a good idea to form an en suite bathroom off a bedroom in the roof space. Attic Life

The shower is the hardest element of a bathroom to locate in a roof space because it needs the most headroom. Attic Life

The quality of light in a bathroom in the roof space can be used to dramatic effect, especially if there is plenty of space available. The Velux Company Ltd

LEFT: Toilets and wash basins do not need full height space above them except where people have to stand. Attic Life.

RIGHT: The relatively cramped space for the shower has been offset by the use of good quality finishes and fittings.
Julian Owen Associates Architects

BELOW: To be practical as a living room, the loft space needs to be a quite large.
The Velux Company Ltd

If there is space to fit a kitchen as well as a bedroom and a bathroom, it is possible to create a self-contained area of the house. The Velux Company Ltd

en suite will be adequate. It surprising how much can be fitted into a relatively tiny bathroom. The lack of headroom can be absorbed into the areas above fittings that do not need it. For example, the cistern of a WC can be fitted into the slope of the roof and still be perfectly usable, provided that the pan is carefully located so that there is adequate headroom to stand up in front of it.

In a similar way, whereas the front of a wash-basin obviously needs full height above it, the back of the sink does not. The hardest appliance to accommodate in a room-in-the-roof bathroom is a shower. Usually the tray cannot be inset in the floor and so there is a step up into it, and 2m head-room above the tray is barely adequate for the shower-head position. These limitations mean that the shower location can often compete with the door or bedroom area for the premium space that has good headroom.

As with bedrooms the quality of light available from rooflights can be a big benefit for a bathroom. Strong natural daylight is excellent for getting a good impression of the effect of make-up on the face, without the colour distortions caused by artificial lighting.

Living Spaces

If the intention is that new rooms are to be used for main living spaces this needs thinking through quite carefully at the planning stage. The floor is likely to be timber boarding on softwood joists and so will only have a limited capacity to reduce any noise that could penetrate down to the bedrooms below at night. If there will be people moving between the ground floor and the new second floor past the bedrooms on the first floor, this will also cause disturbance. Assuming that these problems are not applicable or can be dealt with, the roofspace makes an excellent place for a living room, study or playroom. Larger lofts are sometimes converted for use by someone living a partially separate life from the main household, for example an au pair or older child. They are generally unsuitable for elderly dependent relatives due to the need to climb one or more sets of stairs.

More unusual uses of loft spaces include for an observatory by an amateur astronomer (because of the opportunity to point a telescope straight up to the sky), for elaborate train set layouts, for home cinema and for an artist's studio (making good use of the large amount of natural daylight that is available).

The top light from a roof window makes for a nice working environment, particularly for artists.
The Velux Company Ltd

A playroom is a good use of the space, provided that there is not a problem with noise transmitting down to the rooms below. The Velux Company Ltd

An open plan layout for a self-contained living/dining area. Julian Owen Associates Architects

Here a sophisticated interior design has been created to make the most of the light and shape of the room. The Velux Company Ltd

CHAPTER 5

Preparing and Submitting Applications to the Local Authority

PLANNING PERMISSION

Unless they are in an area of special control, such as a conservation area, householders are allowed to make minor alterations and additions to their homes without seeking planning approval. The list of these 'permitted development rights' is lengthy and you should always consult the local authority rather than simply assuming that they will apply to your house. The rights can be used on a one-time-only basis, and are applied to all work carried out since 1948 (when the current planning legislation was enacted). So if an extension has been added to a house by previous owners since 1948 the permitted development rights for extensions and alterations may have been used up and planning permission may be required for even modest additions. The permitted development rules were significantly amended by the government in October 2008, so most of the methods of calculating how much you can add to the house without needing planning permission used before this date are obsolete.

The practical effect of these rules is that many loft conversions will not need express planning approval, saving eight weeks in the design stage of the project. The thinking behind permitted development rights is that alterations to houses should be allowed with minimum fuss provided that they do no significant harm to the occupants of neighbouring houses. A key consideration here is to prevent any windows being created that lead to the overlooking of private areas such as back gardens or living rooms. This is why there is a requirement

---

Permitted Development Rules for Loft Conversions

You can convert your loft without needing planning approval assuming that there are no special planning controls and provided that you follow these rules:

- The increase in volume should be no greater than 40 cubic metres for terraced houses.
- The increase in volume should be no greater than 50 cubic metres for detached and semi-detached houses.
- No extension should be beyond the plane of the existing roof slope of the principal elevation that fronts the highway.
- No extension should be higher than the highest part of the roof (usually the ridge).
- Materials must closely match the existing house.
- There must not be any verandas, balconies or raised platforms added.
- Side-facing windows should be obscure-glazed; any opening to be 1.7m above the floor.
- Roof extensions, apart from hip to gable ones, should be set back, as far as practicable, at least 20cm from the eaves.

You do not need planning approval to re-cover or maintain the roof, or add skylights in most cases.

Solar panels are encouraged by the UK government's planning rules.

Julian Owen Associates Architects

verified that planning approval is not required for your conversion, however confident you are of your case. All that is needed is a short letter to the planning department along with the drawings and a location plan. Many local authorities have special forms, called 'householder enquiry forms' or something similar to make the process easier.

If it is required, it is vital to ensure that planning approval is obtained. Should the local authority find out work has gone ahead without it they will require you to submit an application retrospectively. If this is unsuccessful, the work will have to be demolished and the house restored to its former condition. Ignorance of the planning rules is no defence if this happens, so it is up to you to ensure that whoever is responsible in your design and construction team either obtains a letter from

for side windows to have obscured glass or to be above eye level. Balconies are not included as a permitted development right for the same reason. The restrictions regarding alterations to the front of the roof are to avoid radical alterations being made to the appearance of the street without some form of control. Limitations are placed on the volume that can be added without planning approval because a very large increase in the habitable area of a house can have undesirable side effects, such as a requirement for an extra car-parking space.

Remember, if your proposal does not come within these limits it does not mean that you cannot carry out the work, just that you will have to submit an application and get formal approval. Some aspects of these rules are actually open to interpretation and it is essential to make sure that the local authority have been consulted and have

---

Solar Panels

- You can fit solar panels to your roof in an area where there are no special controls provided that the panels are not above the ridgeline and project no more than 200mm from the roof.
- If your property is a listed building, installation of solar panels is likely to require an application for listed building consent, even where planning permission is not needed.
- If your property is in a conservation area, or in a World Heritage Site, planning consent is required when panels are to be fitted on the principal elevation (usually this means front or side elevation) and they are visible from the highway. The panels should be sited, within reason, to minimize the effect on the appearance of the building and the effect on the amenity of the area. When they are no longer needed the planners will expect them to be removed as soon as possible.

These permitted development rights apply to houses. If you live in a flat and are considering fitting solar panels you are advised to contact your local planning authority for guidance.

the local authority stating that approval is not needed or confirms that an application has been made and approved for the work. It is not sufficient to accept the word of your builder that the proper procedures have been followed – ensure that you have copies of all the relevant documents in your possession and put them with the house records. If planning approval has been obtained, the minimum you need is a complete copy of the approval notice and a copy of the approved drawings. That way you can check that what is being built is correct. Unfortunately, there have been many instances of conversions being carried out either without any approval, or to a different design to that shown in the approved drawings. In these cases a lot of worry and stress has resulted for the homeowners, who have occasionally also incurred considerable expense having the conversion altered to comply with the wishes of the planning committee.

So the best situation is for your loft conversion to be covered by permitted development rights, avoiding the necessity of obtaining planning approval. But if you have to do it, getting planning approval is the part of the project over which you have least control. You are in the hands of the local authority, and the procedure will move at its own pace, regardless of your anxiety to move forward as quickly as possible. The planning authority may consult other people and organizations, who will get the opportunity to try to influence the outcome of the application. A decision is supposed to be reached within eight weeks of the application being registered, but the complexities of reconciling all the competing interests and the high workload of the planning officers mean that often it takes much longer. If your proposal is particularly unusual or ignores planning restrictions, despite your best efforts you may get a refusal and have to go to appeal, which may in turn also be rejected.

There are many things that you can do to make your encounter with the planning system less stressful, but you should never assume that getting planning approval is going to be automatic, and always allow a contingency in the programme for the process to overrun.

Planning approval must be in place before any significant building work starts, and you must build in accordance with the approved drawings and comply with any conditions. The conditions are listed on the approval document immediately after the decision and allow the planners to add requirements that are not covered by the drawings that have been submitted. This is why you should always make sure you have a copy of the whole approval document. Some typical conditions require certain windows to be in obscured glass, or that the make of any new materials has to be approved in writing by the planners before work starts, or even larger-scale detailed drawings of features such as new windows are required. The local authority make an extra charge each time you apply for the approval of a planning condition, so if possible, you should apply for the discharge of all of them in one go.

Giving Your Application the Best Chance of Approval

If you are unsure of your chances of success, or you particularly want your application to have a smooth passage through the planning process, there is plenty that you can do to help it along.

In areas of special control, such as conservation areas, the planners may place some strict limitations on the external appearance of the conversion. For example, it is common for this type of rooflight to be insisted upon. It is relatively small and has restrictions on how it can be opened, but it looks a bit like an old-fashioned rooflight, such as those made in Victorian times. The Velux Company Ltd

Ensure that you employ a good architect or designer and that they produce a well-presented set of drawings. They are especially useful if the application will go before the planning committee, who are not as used as the planning officers to reading building plans.

Regardless of whether or not you believe that your application will get approval, an early step in the approval process is to get some feedback on the principal elements of your scheme from the planning department. Find out the status and authority of the planning officer that you are dealing with and whether they will deal with the application when it is submitted. In most cases it is likely to be a junior officer, who may handle the paperwork, make the site visits, and so on, while the decision on whether to recommend approval will be made by someone more senior. It is not unknown for applications that are initially encouraged during these early discussions to be refused. Often the reason is that the officer involved has been overruled, or there are some aspects of the proposal that were not obvious until either a full set of drawings was produced or a site visit was made.

If you have an early meeting with a planner, make sure that you are quite clear on the comments made during the discussion and if possible get confirmation in writing. Occasionally planners can give ambiguous advice that an optimistic applicant might wrongly interpret as positive support.

Some local authorities have stopped providing preliminary advice because of limited resources and government targets that encourage them to process applications quickly – regardless of whether it is an approval or rejection. Others may make a charge for an early indication of the likelihood of success. A few planning authorities, under severe pressure, may refuse even to discuss the application by telephone and you will only know if they have any concerns when the rejection notice arrives in the post.

You should also find out whether the decision will be put before the planning committee or be dealt with under delegated powers. The latter allow the officers, usually in consultation with a small representative group of councillors, to make decisions. This is to your advantage if the planners are generally sympathetic, but not so good if they are not. If you feel that your views are not receiving just consideration, or that you deserve more support than you are getting, you could approach some local councillors. The best person to approach is the chair of the planning committee, because this person will have the most influence, but it is well worth talking to others and trying to build a consensus of support for your proposals. In theory, councillors are not allowed to interfere in the progress or process of consideration of an application, or try to influence the actions of the planning officers until the planning committee meeting. Ultimately the planning committee can override its own planning department and approve an application that has been recommended for rejection, but this is rare. However, you may get more attention paid to your relatively minor part of the case load of a planning officer if it is known that councillors are taking an interest. Parish or town councils can also be approached, although their support or opposition is unlikely to be decisive unless the decision is very evenly balanced.

If the planning officer raises objections to your proposals ensure that they make their argument quite clear and specific and relate it back to the agreed planning policy for the authority. For example, if the roof is 'too high' do they mean 1m too high or 3m too high? Why is it too high? Is it because all the houses in your row are the same height, or because it will overshadow a neighbour's garden? This information can then be used either to demonstrate that making the roof lower will not materially affect the application, or to redesign it lower so that it is more likely to be approved. If you are told that the design is not 'in keeping', be aware that this phrase is sometimes used by planners who do not like something but are not really able to work out why, particularly in areas that are a mix of different building ages styles and design. What is it not 'in keeping' with?

Before the application is submitted and at as early a stage in the design process as possible, you should consult all the affected neighbours. Take the drawings to them in person and explain what you

Before. The planners are mainly concerned with the visual impact of the alterations on the appearance of the house and its effect on its surroundings. Attic Designs Ltd

After. This new dormer may be covered by permitted development rights, but if it does need planning permission, because it is on the rear of the property it will be assessed mainly on how it affects the neighbours. Attic Designs Ltd

plan to do and why. If possible have a few compromises up your sleeve to offer if they object. If you are not able to reach agreement take note of them and raise them with the planning officer yourself, at the same time explaining why you think they are unreasonable. Objections from neighbours should not carry any weight when the application is considered unless they raise legitimate concerns. In practice, an application that has strong objections from the neighbours is more likely to be refused than one that they support or are neutral about.

About seven days before the relevant planning committee meets, the officers will prepare a written report making a recommendation. You should ask for a copy of this report before the meeting. Some local authorities issue them as a matter of course with the decision notice, but if you suspect consent may be refused, it is useful if you can obtain a copy of the report before the decision is made. If the application is to be put before the committee, as opposed to being decided under delegated powers, you may be allowed the opportunity to address the planning committee immediately before the application is considered. Only do this if you are good at public speaking or can hire a professional on your behalf. A poor or dull presentation might work to your disadvantage. Objectors may also be granted an opportunity to put their views forward.

If you expect a refusal but do not wish to go to appeal, it may be better to withdraw the application and resubmit at it at a later date to allow more time for negotiations and lobbying. If an application is resubmitted within a year you do not have to pay another planning fee to the council.

Making a Planning Application

Having completed the initial consultation process, you should be ready to submit your application. The documentation has to be accurate, and everything should be carefully checked before submitting.

Types of Planning Application
Almost all applications for alterations to private houses are for detailed approval, otherwise known as 'full' planning approval, and are made up of a set of drawings describing the external appearance of the proposal and plans of the internal layout. The alternative is an outline application, which can be made up of nothing more than a set of completed forms and an Ordnance Survey map with the site outlined in red. An outline application is not appropriate for a loft conversion project, so you should be making an application for full planning permission.

The traditional method for making an application is to copy all the relevant documents and put them in the post. A recent innovation is the Planning Portal, a website that makes it possible to make a planning application on line via the internet, using PDF files. The Planning Portal (www.planning-portal.gov.uk) is also an excellent source of background information about all aspects of making planning applications.

Checklist for a Detailed Planning Application (by Post)

- Covering letter.
- Four sets of the completed application form.
- One certificate of ownership.
- One certificate of notification (if you do not own the site).
- One certificate of agricultural holding.
- Four copies of an Ordnance Survey location plan.
- Four copies of the plans and elevations.
- Four copies of a site plan.
- A cheque for the planning fee.

If in a conservation area, typically also:

- Six rather than four copies of the drawings.
- Design access statement.
- Application for conservation area consent if significant demolition is involved.

The Drawings
The drawings will be the main focus of attention as the application is considered, and should be well presented and competently drawn. Poor presentation will harm the chances of approval and inaccuracies may invalidate the approval unless someone spots them before the application is considered. However far you have progressed with the design, the drawings should contain as much information as necessary to obtain the approval, and no more. Everything that is on the approved drawings is part of the permission, and any changes require consent. This means, for example, that if you state that the roof is to be 'clay pantiles' but when you come to build it is too expensive and you use concrete

instead, you will need to seek permission to use an alternative material. In fact, unless you are in an area of special control such as a conservation area, the planners may include a condition on the approval that materials are to be approved at a later date.

A set of design drawings for a typical loft conversion will normally comprise two or three sheets of A3 paper with 1:100 scale line drawings, each clearly marked with the name of the project and given a unique number. It might appear to be just a small package of drawings, but your architect will have spent a lot of time developing the proposals and a lot of the design will have been thought about in far greater detail than implied by the scale of the drawings. It is essential to ensure that the project can be built as indicated, to avoid having to make a further application to get approval for modifications due to changes in the construction detail or alterations needed to obtain Building Regulations approval.

Extra Information
Sometimes, especially if the building is prominent or in an area of special control, such as a conservation area, the planners will ask for additional information. They may even ask for computer models, photomontages or actual card models. If the house is in a conservation area or near to a listed building, design and access statements are required to accompany any planning application for alterations to private houses – that is, written documents describing the design approach and how the surroundings have been taken into account.

Ordnance Survey and Accuracy
As part of the set of drawings, a section of an Ordnance Survey (OS) map must be included showing the location of the site and its relationship with surrounding buildings, usually at 1:1,250 scale. The area of the site is outlined on the plan in red pen, and any areas next to the site that you own or have an interest in must be edged in blue. It is essential that this map is accurate. Usually the land registry map or deeds will show where it is, but if you have not yet purchased the property you should ensure that the vendor confirms the

Some typical drawings of the sort that would form part of a planning application. Julian Owen Associates Architects

Ground Floor   First Floor   Roof Space

exact location of the boundaries. Apart from showing the planners clearly where the site is, this drawing also defines the area that is part of the application.

OS maps can be obtained through local authorities, or OS plan agencies. To photocopy an OS map without permission is a breach of copyright rules, and since your planning application is a matter of public record, it is unwise to ignore this restriction. You can usually obtain a plan from your architect, provided that the practice holds a licence from the OS to copy them.

If any part of the site included in the red line is owned by someone else, a notice has to be served on them advising them about the application. If you fail to do this it can invalidate any approval received. Some councils consider apparently minor infringements, such as a gutter overhanging the neighbour's land, require a notice to be served.

Filling in the Planning Form

Each item on the planning application form is explained below.

Name and address of applicant You are the applicant, in a normal situation. You don't have to

own the land to submit the application. Anyone can submit an application in respect of someone else's property if they wish, as long as they tell them about it (*see* Planning Certificates below).

Name and Address of Agent If an architect or designer has prepared the drawings for you, it is usual for them to act as your agent. This means that any correspondence or queries go through them in the first instance.

Full postal address of the application site Sometimes a property may not have a proper postal address, in which case it must be described as accurately as possible. As long as there is an OS map indicating the exact boundaries, this will be acceptable.

Description of proposed development The planners are mainly interested in the use and extent of whatever is being proposed.

Type of application Loft conversions require full permission.

Outline applications Not relevant for a loft conversion.

Site area This only has to be approximate, measured off the OS map. There are 10,000 square metres in a hectare.

Newtown
District Council

DEVELOPMENT DEPARTMENT
COUNCIL OFFICES
LETSBY AVENUE
NEWTOWN

APPLICATION FOR
PLANNING PERMISSION

Application No...........................
Fee Paid £ ....Rec. ....

YOU ARE ADVISED TO READ THE ACCOMPANYING NOTES BEFORE COMPLETING THIS FORM.

Four copies of this form completed in BLOCK CAPITALS, the appropriate fee and completed Certificates under Article 7 must be submitted to the above address. Cheques should be crossed and made payable to Newtown Borough Council.

1.	NAME AND ADDRESS OF APPLICANT	2.	NAME AND ADDRESS OF AGENT

1. NAME AND ADDRESS OF APPLICANT

Mr P Smith
999 Letsby Avenue
Denton   Essex

Post Code **NO2 IAB** Tel. No. **0143 99199**

2. NAME AND ADDRESS OF AGENT
(If form completed by agent)

Julian Owen Associates
276 Queens Road, Beeston
Nottingham
Post Code **NG9 2BD** Tel. No. **0115 9229831**
(Personal contact name **J. Owen**)

3. FULL POSTAL ADDRESS OF THE APPLICATION SITE

999 Letsby Avenue, Denton, Essex NO2 IAB

4. DESCRIPTION OF PROPOSED DEVELOPMENT

LOFT CONVERSION WITH 4 new dormer windows

5. TYPE OF APPLICATION - PLEASE TICK APPROPRIATE BOX

A ☐ Change of Use not involving building work

B ☑ New Building Works (Which may also include a change of use) Alterations & Extensions.

If box ticked, is application (i) FULL ☑
(ii) OUTLINE ☐

C ☐ Mining, Engineering or Other Operations

D ☐ Approval of Reserved Matters
Ref. of Outline permission ....
Date granted ....

E ☐ Removal/Variation of a Condition
Ref. of previous relevant permission
....
Date granted ....

F ☐ Renewal of Temporary Permission
Ref. of previous temporary permission
....
Date granted ....

Planning application form. This form is a typical example of the kind of form that a council will require to be completed and submitted with the planning application. Alternatively, the application form can be filled in online and the drawings submitted in the form of computer files in PDF format.

If you ticked 5B(ii) please answer this question   **NOT APPLICABLE**

6.   OUTLINE APPLICATIONS

A   Please tick the items which are
reserved for further consideration   Siting ☐   Design ☐   ☐ Means of Access

               ☐ External Appearance   ☐ Landscaping

---

7.   SITE AREA

Please state area of application site ......**120**.......................... Sq. m/~~hectares~~

---

8.   EXISTING USES

Please state existing or, if vacant, the last use(s) of the site or building ..**PRIVATE RESIDENCE**.................

Please tick the appropriate box

9.   DRAINAGE   Mains sewer   Soakaway   Other

A   Disposal of surface water will be to: -   ☐   ☑   ☐

B   Disposal of foul sewage will be to: -   Mains sewer   Cesspit   Septic tank   Other

                                     ☑   ☐   ☐   ☐

---

10.   TREES

Does the proposal involve the felling of any trees?   Yes ☐   No ☑
If the answer is YES, indicate the position on plan

---

11.   ACCESS TO ROADS

Do you intend to form a new vehicular or pedestrian
access to a public road, or alter an existing one?   Yes ☐   No ☑

---

12.   RIGHTS OF WAY

Will the proposed development affect any public
rights of way?   Yes ☐   No ☑

---

13.   INDICATE GROSS FLOORSPACE FOR NON-RESIDENTIAL DEVELOPMENT

	Existing	Proposed	
Industrial	.... m²	.... m²	**NOT APPLICABLE**
Office	.... m²	.... m²	
Retail	.... m²	.... m²	
Warehousing	.... m²	.... m²	
Ancillary Storage	.... m²	.... m²	
Total gross floorspace	.... m²	.... m²	

14.   HAZARDOUS SUBSTANCES

Does the proposal involve the use or storage of a hazardous substance?   Yes ☐   No ☐

If YES state the type and quantity ....

---

15.   Please complete

I attach plans
and I attach the completed Article 7 Certificate and the Agricultural Holdings Certificate
and I enclose the appropriate fee of £ **150 — 00** ... (see Fee List)
Signed .... ~~Applicant~~/Agent   Date **02.02.10**..........

Existing uses This will tell them if you are trying to change the use of the land.

Drainage This is so that the likely extra impact on the sewers can be assessed, if there is any.

Trees Probably not applicable to a loft conversion.

Access to roads Probably not applicable to a loft conversion.

Rights of way Probably not applicable to a loft conversion.

Indicate gross floorspace for non-residential development This does not apply to your application. For other kinds of development, the planning departments need more information to assess the impact of the development. Some local authorities send out separate forms to householders for this reason.

Signature A planning application must be complete and signed before it will be accepted and logged, and a cheque for the planning fee must also be sent. If there is anything missing, there will be a delay of one or two weeks while they notify you to supply whatever has been forgotten.

Planning Certificates

Along with the actual application form, you also have to submit certificates relating to the ownership and use of the land:

Part I – Land Ownership, Certificate A You must be absolutely clear who owns all the land that forms the application, and only fill this certificate in if you are quite certain that it is you.

Part I – Land Ownership, Certificate B If the land belongs to someone else, you must send a notice to them when you submit, formally notifying them of what you are doing. This is to prevent unscrupulous people from getting an approval before buying land without the owner knowing. Intentional failure to notify an owner, or a deliberate mis-statement about who owns the land, is a serious offence and may also invalidate the planning application. If you don't know who the owner is, a notice has to be put in the local paper.

One Certificate A, B, C, or D, must be completed, together with the Agricultural Holdings Certificate with this application form

CERTIFICATE OF OWNERSHIP - CERTIFICATE A

Town and Country Planning (General Development Procedure) Order 1995 Certificate under Article 7

I certify/The applicant certifies that on the day 21 days before the date of this application nobody except myself/ the applicant was the owner *(owner is a person with a freehold interest or leasehold interest with at least 7 years left to run)* of any part of the land or building to which the application relates.

Signed - Applicant:	Or signed - Agent:	Date (DD/MM/YYYY):
	Julie Chen	02.02.2010

CERTIFICATE OF OWNERSHIP - CERTIFICATE B

Town and Country Planning (General Development Procedure) Order 1995 Certificate under Article 7

I certify/ The applicant certifies that I have/the applicant has given the requisite notice to everyone else (as listed below) who, on the day 21 days before the date of this application, was the owner *(owner is a person with a freehold interest or leasehold interest with at least 7 years left to run)* of any part of the land or building to which this application relates.

Name of Owner	Address	Date Notice Served
	NOT APPLICABLE	

Signed - Applicant:	Or signed - Agent:	Date (DD/MM/YYYY):

Ownership Certificate.

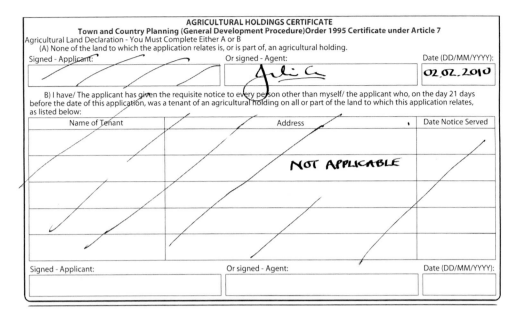

AGRICULTURAL HOLDINGS CERTIFICATE
Town and Country Planning (General Development Procedure)Order 1995 Certificate under Article 7
Agricultural Land Declaration - You Must Complete Either A or B
(A) None of the land to which the application relates is, or is part of, an agricultural holding.

Signed - Applicant:	Or signed - Agent:	Date (DD/MM/YYYY):
	Julie C	02.02.2010

B) I have/ The applicant has given the requisite notice to every person other than myself/ the applicant who, on the day 21 days before the date of this application, was a tenant of an agricultural holding on all or part of the land to which this application relates, as listed below:

Name of Tenant	Address	Date Notice Served
	NOT APPLICABLE	

Signed - Applicant:	Or signed - Agent:	Date (DD/MM/YYYY):

Agricultural Holdings Certificate.

Part II Agricultural Holdings Certificate This is to ensure that tenant farmers and others are notified of the application. Surprisingly, if a tenant is not farming the land, for example rents the property on a limited lease, there is no obligation to notify them, unless the lease is greater than seven years.

If you have had discussions with a planning officer, make sure that they are named in a covering letter, and also refer to any correspondence that may have taken place. If you do not and your case is allocated to another person who is unaware of your previous negotiations, they may not be taken into account.

What Happens Once an Application is Submitted?

Acknowledgement

Assuming that the application has all the necessary drawings, documents and payment in place, an administration officer will log the date and time that the application is received and allocate it to a planning officer.

Consultations

Once the allocated officer has received the application, letters of notification will be sent to neighbours and other interested parties inviting comments, usually within twenty-one days.

Keeping in Touch

If you have already had a pre-application meeting or contact with the planning department, allow three to four weeks for consultations to take place before you make further contact. There may be nothing further to discuss until comments are received back from the parties being consulted.

Representations

Once you do contact the planning officer, if you then find there are unanticipated problems, arrange a meeting as soon as possible. Planning departments have targets for the time it should take to get a decision made, and they will want to either get a problem sorted out, or reject the application very quickly if they don't believe that there is any possibility of a compromise.

Officer's Report
Once an officer, in conjunction with the senior planner, has decided on a recommendation a report will be prepared, usually recommending approval with conditions or a refusal. In uncontroversial situations, the councillors may delegate the decision, which means that it is made by the planning staff rather than the committee.

Local Councillors
In any situation where there have been several objections, or the approval may have important implications (for example if it is in a prominent location), the decision may be put to the planning committee for debate.

Planning Committee Meetings
Planning committee meetings are open to the public and are often attended by interested parties, and journalists as observers. The officers will make their case, in a written report sent out in advance, and with a verbal summary before the application is discussed by members of the planning committee. Some committees allow short presentations from objectors and applicant. It can be more effective if you can persuade a councillor to speak in support of your application on your behalf.

Decision
Usually a written confirmation of the decision is sent out to the applicant and others who have made written comments within a few days.

Conditions
You may feel ready to relax about the planning approval now, but be aware that the list of conditions that are included as part of the approval notice are integral to the permission. Some of these are fairly routine, for example preventing work from starting before the brick and tile samples have been approved by the Council. Others may be more onerous and can cause more expense or may be less acceptable to you. An example may be an express requirement to accommodate more cars on the site, or for someone who plans to work from home, a restriction on any ancillary business use. Other conditions

that could add to the cost but are unlikely to affect a loft conversion are mining and contaminated land reports, or archaeological investigations. If you think a condition is unreasonable, or unenforceable, you can appeal against it in a similar way to appealing against refusal of planning consent.

Appeals
If the application is refused, you may decide to resubmit an amended application if you can accommodate the modifications, or lodge an appeal. If you are going to appeal, it is essential to get some professional advice, either from your architect or a planning consultant. Appeals are decided by a government-appointed inspector who is from outside the area, and can be in writing only, at a private hearing, or in public. An excellent booklet on how the appeal process works is published by the planning inspectorate and is available from your local planning office.

Summary
At the end of the planning process, you should have a document in your possession that gives you planning approval to carry out the alterations to your house and convert your loft. If you wish to make any minor changes they can be agreed by the local authority as amendments to the application. If you have any major variations, for example, significant changes to the size of a dormer window, or an increase in the overall height of the roof, you will have to submit a fresh application. If you are fortunate, the process from submission of the application to getting approval should take about eight weeks, but if you have serious problems it could take twice as long. In most cases there is a condition stipulating that work must start on site within three years, after which time the permission expires.

BUILDING REGULATIONS

Once you have obtained planning permission, the next key task is to obtain approval under the Building Regulations. All loft conversions must have approval under the Building Regulations and there are no exemptions, assuming that a habitable room is being created. Although the same department of the local authority usually gives the approval, this is a separate exercise from obtaining planning permission. Granting of planning approval does not imply that a design will get Building Regulations approval, and vice versa. If you have been using a professional to prepare your plans, they will be very familiar with the current regulations and will have ensured that your planning drawings also comply with the regulations. However, as with planning approval, it is the owner's responsibility to ensure that Building Regulations approval is obtained, and you should accept nothing less than a certificate approving the work at the end of the project, known as a completion certificate. It is perfectly acceptable for you to ring your local building control office if you have any questions or doubts regarding the work being carried out to your home.

What are the Building Regulations?

The Building Regulations have been created to ensure that all significant building work complies with some minimum standards of construction. This protects the people who are to use or live in a building, for example, by checking that the structure is sound. But they also serve the interests of the general community, for example by ensuring the need for burning fossil fuels is kept to a minimum. The main regulations, passed by parliament, state that a building must comply with these requirements, and guidance on how this might be achieved is given in a set of booklets called 'Approved Documents' (ADs).

The Approved Documents are regularly updated, which means that designers and builders have to ensure that they keep abreast of changes. If you can find other ways of complying with the law, which could be summed up as 'it has to be built properly', you do not necessarily have to do what the Approved Documents stipulate. However, proving this to a sceptical building control officer is quite difficult, so it is far easier to simply comply with the written standards in the ADs.

Getting Building Regulations approval is quite different to the highly subjective planning approval

Building control officers monitor the construction of the building and certify that it has been done correctly at the end of the project. Julian Owen Associates Architects

process. Whether or not a building complies is mostly a matter of fact rather than opinion. Building control officers are usually very pragmatic people, and will agree changes and improvements on site if necessary.

The ultimate responsibility for compliance with the regulations lies with the developer, that is you. It can be delegated to a main contractor or site manager, but the buck stops with the homeowner. So you must make sure that it is written into your contract with a builder that it is their responsibility to liaise with building control and ensure that all the regulations are complied with.

Although there is no escape from the approval process for a loft conversion, there are certain building works that do not need to have building control approval. These are summarized in the table.

> ### Less Obvious Work that is Likely to Require Building Regulations Approval
>
> - Fitting new windows in new openings or replacing existing windows.
> - Fitting out a bathroom where the appliances are in new locations.
> - Creating a new opening in a wall (if it is structural).
> - Fitting a new boiler, even if the radiators are not altered.
> - Installing cavity insulation.
> - Replacing a flat roof with a new pitched roof.
> - Converting a garage to a room, even if there are no structural alterations.
> - Changing the use of a building, for example converting two flats into a single house.
> - Replacing the covering of a pitched roof with a different material.
> - Altering or installing a new electrical ring main.

Full Plans Approval

There are three ways of getting approval under the regulations and completing work to a house. The safest procedure, 'full plans approval', involves two stages. Drawings and specifications describing the basic construction of the building are prepared and submitted with a fee. After about three weeks a building control officer writes to whoever has submitted the plans, asking for any amendments or extra information. Once this is provided satisfactorily, full plans approval is granted, in the form of an approval notice, along with a set of plans stamped 'Approved'. Quite often, approval will be conditional on further information being provided, which is not currently available, for example roof truss calculations that will only be provided by a supplier once an order is placed, long after construction has started.

The approval process usually takes between five and eight weeks to come through after submission, and you can then start work on site after giving a couple of days' notice. You can start work fairly confident that the house will comply with all the major requirements of the regulations, and have some drawings that can be used as a basis for its construction. However, Building Regulations drawings are not sufficient to get accurate tenders from contractors to build the whole conversion – only the basic construction is covered.

Assuming the drawings and specifications are followed and any changes are agreed with the building control officer beforehand, you can maintain this confidence throughout the project. The building control officer will make periodic inspections at key points in the build programme. On completion you will get a certificate that states that the house has been built to the regulations, something that will be essential if you intend to sell the property later. A fee is paid when the plans are submitted, about 25 per cent of the total, with the balance being paid once work starts.

Building Notice

If the conversion is very simple and straightforward, it is possible to use the building notice procedure. A simple form is completed, forty-eight hours before work starts, along with a fee. No detailed drawings or specifications are required. This route is not suitable for any projects other than the most simple and straightforward, where an experienced builder is carrying out the work, for a number of reasons. If anything is built that does not comply with the regulations, it will probably not be noticed until later on, requiring work to be taken down and rebuilt. You or your builder will carry the risk of delay and extra cost if this happens. If you want an architect to certify the structure, it will be difficult to find an architect who is prepared to take the risk. The fee to serve a building notice is the same as for the full plans approval route, but instead of being paid in two stages, it is all due when the notice is sent.

Regularisation Certificate

A lot of work is carried out to private houses and on commercial buildings without seeking the necessary Building Regulations approval. This is illegal. Often it happens due to ignorance, and occasionally it is because the client or contractor wishes to avoid the extra cost. If the regulations are avoided wilfully and the case is serious, the local authority can prosecute and the offender will be fined many thousands of pounds. What is more likely is that on discovery you will have to ask for Building Regulations approval to be applied retrospectively. You do this by applying for a Regularisation Certificate. If you are in this unfortunate situation you will be required to uncover any work that has been concealed as a result of the work being finished in order to demonstrate that it complies with all regulations. This opening up could cause extensive damage, for example if the floorboards have to be lifted or plasterboard taken down.

The commonest reason that Regularisation Certificates are applied for is when a house is being sold, and the purchaser's solicitor discovers that work has been carried out recently and asks to see a copy of the Building Regulations approval. Where approval has not been obtained, inevitably the sale falls through and the vendor has to correct the omission before the house can again be offered for sale.

Types of Building Control Service

At one time, all Building Regulations applications were dealt with by the local authority responsible for the area where the building work was being carried out. The current system allows private companies, using 'approved inspectors', and even other local authorities to provide a building control service. So any organizations that have suitable expertise, staff and insurance cover can qualify to provide it. Most local authorities offer a plans approval service for projects outside their area, leaving the inspection stage to others. The benefits of this arrangement are mainly to large developers, builders and architects, who may form a mutually beneficial relationship with one of their local authorities.

For loft conversions it is generally better to make use of whichever local authority covers the area in which you are building, unless your builder has an ongoing relationship with an approved inspector. The local officers are a very useful source of information at an early stage, with an intimate knowledge of things such as ground conditions. Building control officers have always been amongst the most helpful officials in the building industry, and they are keener than ever to help now that they have competition.

Scotland

The procedure covered in this book mainly relates to the Building Regulations as they apply in England and Wales. Scotland has significant differences. North of the border, work cannot start until a building warrant has been issued (you can start before plans approval has been granted in England and Wales if you wish). The Scots also base the size of the fee on the size of the house, whereas in England and Wales the fee is a flat rate unless the project is very large. In Scotland, a house cannot be occupied unless a habitation certificate has been issued at the end of the project. In Northern Ireland the rules are very similar to England and Wales.

The Scottish regulations are based on a move away from stipulating constructions and details that comply with the regulations to a more flexible system based on guidance contained in technical handbooks, one for non-domestic buildings and one for houses. The handbook has six sections, covering structure, fire, environment, safety, noise and energy, and is accompanied by a procedural handbook and a certification handbook. Approval can be a obtained from an 'approved certifier', who issues certificates to the local authority as evidence that the regulations have been complied with. The whole system is administered and monitored by the Scottish Building Standards Agency.

Approved Documents (ADs)

At the centre of the Building Regulations for England and Wales approval process is a set of documents that methodically go through each aspect of building construction and give detailed advice on how to meet the requirements. Copies can be ordered from most bookshops or are available online, free, and anyone who is contemplating carrying out the building work themselves should ensure that they have a set before starting.

Even a well-prepared set of plans will not cover every regulation that applies. Many of the regula-

The Approved Documents of the building regulations. Julian Owen Associates Architects

tions are assumed to apply, or may be included using phrases such as 'drains to be laid in accordance with Approved Document H of the Building Regulations'. The purpose of the full plans approval

is to identify compliance with the major aspects of the construction, not list every last paragraph from the Approved Documents. Consequently, no one should work on your project unless they have a basic knowledge of the Approved Documents. Much of the guidance covers non-domestic buildings and is irrelevant, but most of the ADs have something in them that affect loft conversions.

One strange anomaly is that most of the Building Regulations do not apply to the construction of external works beyond the immediate area of the house.

Making a Building Regulations Application

Drawings and Specifications
If you are using an architect to prepare a tender package as well as to obtain Building Regulations approval, the same set of drawings and specifications may be used for both. If you have asked for 'Building Regulations only' this is probably what you will get – just enough information to get full plans approval and no more. These drawings do not need to be particularly detailed, and will not tackle any of the detailed construction problems, which will have to be sorted out on site. Usually

---

The Approved Documents of the Building Regulations

- A Structure
- B Fire Safety
- C Site Preparation and Resistance to Moisture
- D Toxic Substances
- E Resistance to Passage of Sound
- F Ventilation
- G Hygiene
- H Drainage and Waste Disposal
- J Combustion Appliances and Fuel Storage
- K Protection From Falling, Collision and Impact
- L Conservation of Fuel and Power
- M Access and Facilities for Disabled People
- N Glazing – Safety in Relation to Impact, Opening and Cleaning
- P Electrical Safety

Note: there is no Document I or O

What to Include for a Full Plans Building Regulations Application

- Covering letter.
- Completed application form.
- Two copies of location plan (usually the same one as used for planning application).
- Two sets of drawings, including plans, elevations and sections at 1:50 scale.
- Two sets of specifications, which may be a separate document or written on the drawings.
- Two sets of structural calculations.
- A cheque for the full plans approval application fee (amount will vary between authorities).

Drawings like this, often with the specifications written on them as well, are typical of the kind required for a Building Regulations Application. Julian Owen Associates Architects

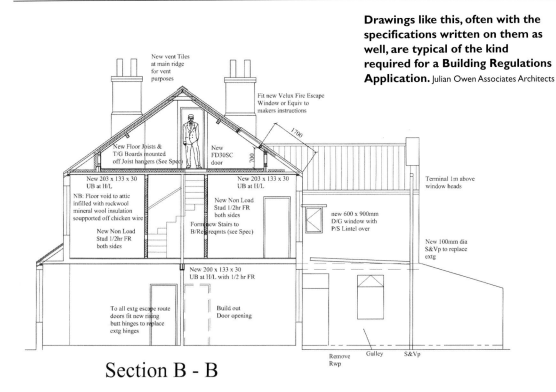

New vent Tiles at main ridge for vent purposes

Fit new Velux Fire Escape Window or Equiv to makers instructions

1700

700

New Floor Joists & T/G Boards mounted off Joist hangers (See Spec)

New FD30SC door

New 203 x 133 x 30 UB at H/L

New 203 x 133 x 30 UB at H/L

Terminal 1m above window heads

NB: Floor void to attic infilled with rockwool mineral wool insulation soupported off chicken wire

New Non Load Stud 1/2hr FR both sides

new 600 x 900mm D/G window with P/S Lintel over

New Non Load Stud 1/2hr FR both sides

Form new Stairs to B/Reg reqmts (see Spec)

New 100mm dia S&Vp to replace extg

New 200 x 133 x 30 UB at H/L with 1/2 hr FR

To all extg escape route doors fit new rising butt hinges to replace extg hinges

Build out Door opening

Remove Rwp

Gulley

S&Vp

Section B - B

1:50 scale is acceptable, even for a section through the building. This does not really tell you much about the construction other than the broad principles, which is all the building control officer is looking for at this stage.

Some local authorities insist on an OS location plan before they will log a full plans application, on the grounds that they need the property to be accurately identified. However, this is not a strict requirement in the same way as for a planning application. Hopefully, given the correct address, a building control officer is sufficiently experienced to spot an extension under construction. Many local authorities check Building Regulations drawings against the drawings that have received planning approval, and will pick up any changes that need further consideration by the planning process. But there is no obligation for them to do this, so someone on your team should review any alterations to ensure that there are no conflicts.

Filling in the Form

The application form is short, and only requires basic information about the project. The questions to pay special attention to are (numbers refer to those used on the form:

5. You should always agree to conditional approval. The alternative is that the application will be refused unless everything of concern has been approved, even though the information may not be available because it is going to be provided later. However, it is very important that this information is submitted and approved before the relevant work is carried out.

6. Likewise it is sensible to agree to an extension of time to the prescribed period. Like their planning colleagues, building control officers are under pressure to deal with applications promptly, so if they run out of time and you won't agree to extend it, they may issue a rejection notice.

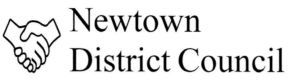

Newtown
District Council

Building Regulations

Full Plans application

DEVELOPMENT DEPARTMENT
COUNCIL OFFICES
LETSBY AVENUE
NEWTOWN

Application No.................................
Fee Paid £ ....Rec. ....

Receipt No. . . . .

Notice of intention to erect, extend, or alter a building, execute works or install fittings or make a material change of use of an existing building.
I/We hereby give notice of intention to carry out the work set out herein in accordance with the accompanying plans.

Signed . . . . *Julian* . . . . Date . **05.05.10** . . . .

1.	NAME AND ADDRESS OF APPLICANT	2.	NAME AND ADDRESS OF AGENT (if applicable)

Mr. P. Smith, 999 Letsby Avenue, Denton, Essex

**Julian Owen Associates
276 Queens Road
Beeston, Nottingham**

Post Code **NO2 1AB**. Tel. No. **0143 99199**

Post Code **NG9 2BD** . . . . . Tel. No. **0115 9229831**
(Personal contact name **Julian Owen** .)

3.   FULL POSTAL ADDRESS OF THE APPLICATION SITE

999 Letsby Avenue, Denton, Essex NO2 1AB

4.   DESCRIPTION OF PROPOSED DEVELOPMENT

LOFT Conversion

5.	CONDITIONS Do you consent to the plans being passed subject to conditions where appropriate?	YES/NO
6.	EXTENSION OF TIME If it is not possible to give a determination within the prescribed period do you consent to an extension of time?	YES/NO
7.	Is the building to be put to a Designated Use for the purpose of the Fire Precautions Act?	YES/NO
8.	Do you wish to receive a Completion Certificate on completion of the work?	YES/NO
9.	Is a new vehicular crossing over the footway required?	YES/NO
10.	Means of water supply	**MAINS**
11.	Details and dates of any additions made to the property since 1948 (this includes garage, conservatory, etc.).	**See drawings**
12.	State whether building is private, Council or ex Council	**Private**
13.	Amount of fee enclosed herewith	£ **150**
14.	Fee payable for inspection of work	£ **375**
15.	Estimated total cost of work	£ **25,000**
16.	Floor area of proposal Sq. m	**30 sq m**

This form must be accompanied by two sets of plans and the appropriate fee.
Where Part B (Fire Safety) applies a further two sets of plans are required.

A Full Plans application form.

7. A house is not covered by most of the fire regulations, which are separate from the Building Regulations.

8. It is essential that a completion certificate is requested at this point. If it is not, there will be no obligation for one to be issued, and it is a vital document if the house is to be sold on.

16. If the project is larger than average, the fee will be calculated in a different way.

Unlike the fee for a planning application, VAT is payable on the Building Regulations fee – make sure that when you write the cheque it has been included.

Working with Building Control Officers

After a full plans application has been submitted, the building control officer will usually have some questions, or require extra information before it is approved. Because there is no prescribed level of information, similar applications to different local authorities or even different officers will elicit a different set of queries. If there is a good working relationship between the designer and the building control officer, this checking process can be invaluable to both sides, and helps to ensure that any areas that may be a potential problem are picked up and dealt with at an early stage. Likewise, a competent officer inspecting a site provides an extra pair of eyes working on your behalf.

Site Inspections
The building control officer must be informed two days before work starts on site, and the inspection fee paid (or the notice fee if you are courageous enough to do it that way). There will then be a series of inspections at those points in the building programme that are most critical, which officially require at least one day's notice. Building control officers generally start work early and carry out office administration duties up until around 10am, after which they will set off to carry out their inspections. Provided a builder can telephone before this time, a site meeting can usually be set up the same day, thus avoiding having builders

Building control officers are interested in the construction of, rather than the appearance of, the converted loft. Julian Owen Associates Architects

standing around waiting for a visit before they can carry on with their work.

The building control officer only has to ensure that the Building Regulations are being complied with, and is not there to provide a site inspection service to you or monitor the progress of the builder. A helpful building control officer will make informal comments off the record, but many do not have the time to get involved with quality-control issues. For example, if a brick wall is structurally satisfactory, its appearance is not their concern, nor that it is patchy because the pallets of brickwork have not been mixed up after delivery. Likewise, if the specification or design has been changed, as long as it still complies, you should not rely on a building control officer to point this out for you.

What Can Go Wrong?

If you make a full plans application, the likelihood of something going wrong is greatly reduced, and the problems are not usually complex. Occasionally something proposed, or even built, does not meet with the approval of the building control officer.

Failure at Full Plans Stage

If something is wrong on the plans, the list of queries issued halfway through the approval process will pick it up, and it can be easily corrected – assuming that the necessary changes do not affect the planning approval. A rejection of a full plans application is not as bad as it sounds, since if you resubmit with amendments straight away, most of the checking will have already been done and the approval can come through in a matter of days.

Failure to Comply on Site

If you or your contractor build something that does not follow the approved drawings and specifications, or that was not covered by them, and the building control officer decides that it is significantly contrary to the Building Regulations, your only realistic option is to demolish it and rebuild. Sometimes, if the infringement is relatively minor, you may be able negotiate a compromise, but the building control officer has powers to refuse to approve the work if you try to ignore any direction to correct a contravention. There is an appeals process, where you essentially ask for the government to decide you are right, or if you are wrong that the rules should be relaxed in your case. Such a course of action could result in extra cost and delay to the programme.

Speeding up the Process

The ideal progression is to wait for planning approval, then have a Building Regulations package prepared, then a tender package, and then appoint a contractor. This all takes time, but is the safest way to proceed and will greatly reduce the risks. But if there is an unavoidable rush, several things can be done to get on to site more quickly. You can ask your designer to start work on the Building Regulations before planning approval is granted.

The disadvantage of this is that any changes that result from the input of the planning system will require the more detailed Building Regulations drawings to be amended, at extra cost. Legally you cannot start work before you have planning approval.

Another way to save time is to start on site immediately after the Building Regulations application for full plans approval has been lodged, which is fine if you are totally confident that any work affected by the first few weeks of building will definitely comply. You are unlikely to get your architect or builder to guarantee this, however, because the consequences of being wrong can be very expensive. It will be your risk. But this is still a better option than the high-risk route of serving a building notice, without any drawings at all, because the checking process will eventually catch up with the building work and any problems discovered at that point may come as a nasty shock.

A compromise is to wait until the initial queries come back before starting to build, which will indicate the areas that are questionable. If none of the queries involves the early stages of construction, you will know it is safe to start on site. Unfortunately, it is not unusual for a letter from Building Control to state that checking of structural calculations by the local authority is still underway and any questions regarding these may come later. There would be an obvious risk in carrying out any work covered by the structural calculations before approval is in place.

Summary

To get approval under the Building Regulations you just have to comply with the minimum requirements of the Approved Documents, and nothing more. Aspects of the work not covered by the regulations do not need to get approval. So work like decorations, fittings and fixtures and most of the electrical work are of no direct interest to building control officers and will not be checked by them. A Building Regulations package alone is not sufficient on its own to describe fully the building that is going to be built. Many more decisions, often affecting the budget, have to be made either by a designer producing a proper tender package, or by you or the contractor or the subcontractor or the builders on site.

KEY BUILDING REGULATIONS AFFECTING LOFT CONVERSIONS

It is not the aim of this section of the book to comprehensively describe all the relevant regulations that apply to loft conversions. If this level of detail is sought there are other publications that cover the regulations in detail, not least the Approved Documents themselves. Instead, the key regulations that have the most significant impact on the design and construction of a loft conversion are listed, along with a brief explanation.

The Building Regulations are sometimes regarded with irritation by people who are carrying out a loft conversion. The requirements can affect other parts of the house, requiring more work upgrading it than expected and when the rules are applied properly it can sometimes cause design problems. But it cannot be stressed too strongly how important it is to ensure that the regulations are followed and that whoever carries out the work notifies the local authority to ensure that the work is inspected by a building control officer and Building Regulations approval is obtained. The regulations that relate to fire resistance and escape are particularly important. They have been developed in consultation with the fire brigade to reduce the number of deaths that result from house fires. Especially if you are above first-floor level you are less likely to be aware of a fire starting on the ground floor and will need more time to escape. If it is dark and the power has failed the staircase must be easy and safe to run down. A loft space which does not comply with these rules is a potential death trap.

Approved Document A: Structure

Approved Document A is about making sure that the building will stay up and bear the loads and stresses that are put upon the structure comfortably. To demonstrate that this will happen, calculations will have to be prepared, and the usual

Document A sets out the requirements for structural design, for example, any new purlins or rafters. Julian Owen Associates Architects

person to do this is the structural engineer. These calculations will be related to things such as adequacy of the size of beams, the strength of the floor and the effect of cutting out sections of the roof structure to form dormer windows. Once these calculations have been submitted, they are checked by another qualified engineer who works on behalf of the local authority.

Approved Document B: Fire Safety

Different regulations apply to loft conversions depending on how high they are from ground level. If you are converting the loft space of a bungalow or single-storey outbuilding many of the fire regulations do not apply. Likewise, if there is more than one route from the loft to escape down, the regulations are not as exacting. If you are converting a loft to a house that already has two floors above ground level, that is you are adding a third floor, more onerous regulations apply and it is a good idea to obtain professional advice in these cases.

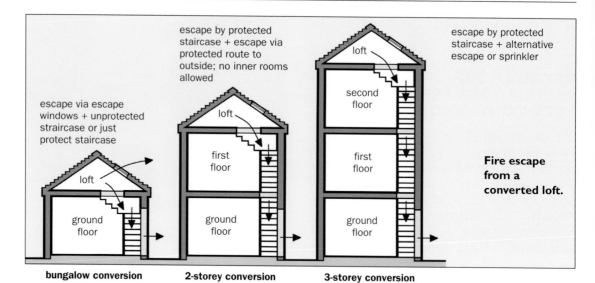

escape via escape windows + unprotected straircase or just protect staircase

escape by protected staircase + escape via protected route to outside; no inner rooms allowed

escape by protected staircase + alternative escape or sprinkler

loft

ground floor

loft

first floor

ground floor

loft

second floor

first floor

ground floor

Fire escape from a converted loft.

bungalow conversion   **2-storey conversion**   **3-storey conversion**

LEFT: **If a roof window is top hung like this one, it is easier to climb out of it, but it must not be too high to comply with the regulations that would deem it to be an escape window required in a bungalow conversion.** The Velux Company

Escape from a Loft Conversion Added to a Two-Storey House

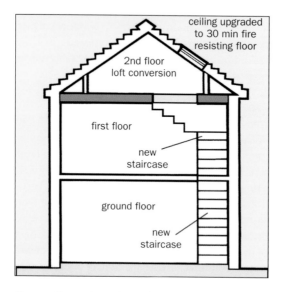

ceiling upgraded to 30 min fire resisting floor

2nd floor loft conversion

first floor

new staircase

ground floor

new staircase

Converting a two-storey house.

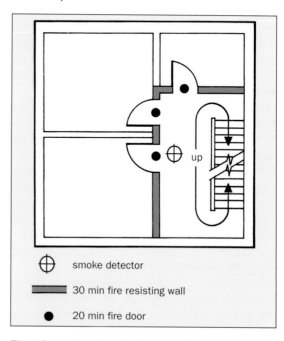

up

⊕ smoke detector

▬ 30 min fire resisting wall

● 20 min fire door

First-floor plan for a loft conversion of a two-storey house.

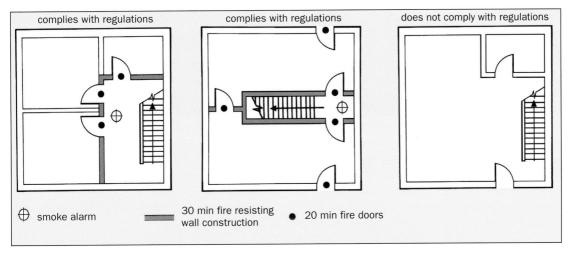

complies with regulations   complies with regulations   does not comply with regulations

⊕ smoke alarm   ▬▬ 30 min fire resisting wall construction   ● 20 min fire doors

Fire escape for a loft conversion of a two-storey house – alternative ground-floor plans.

If a fire starts in the house it must be possible to escape from the loft space safely. For a bungalow the regulations are satisfied as long as it is fairly easy to climb out of the windows. If a conversion is added to a two-storey house, a protected escape route must be created from the loft down the stairs and all the way to the outside of the building. The walls around this escape route usually have to last for at least 30 minutes and the doors for 20 minutes before the fire and smoke starts to get past them. In other words, anyone in the loft will be guaranteed at least 20 minutes within which to realize that there is a fire and escape from the building without being exposed to flames or smoke at a life-threatening level. New construction can easily be made to comply with these requirements using standard stud partitions with 12.5mm plasterboard, or ordinary masonry walls. Older wall constructions, such as existing lath and plaster walls, are unlikely to achieve the required 30 minutes durability and will have to be upgraded by covering with plasterboard.

New fire-resisting doors are readily available. The existing doors all along the escape route have to be replaced or upgraded to resist fire for 20 minutes, a standard referred to in the regulations as FD20 or E20. 'FD' stands for fire door and is a UK standard, and 'E' stands for Europe, but there is no real difference between the two. In the UK the differences between a 20 minute fire-resisting door and a 30 minute version are considered so subtle that it is easier and more cost-effective for manufacturers only to make the latter. FD20 doors are not readily available. Some door types, especially the older panelled ones, are difficult or impossible to upgrade and have to be replaced. Hinges have to be steel and special seals that expand when they get hot may be needed (known as intumescent seals). The ceiling between the loft and the rooms below also has to be upgraded to provide 30 minutes of fire resistance. This means that for 30 minutes it has to remain strong enough to stand on, stay intact and insulate the rooms above from the heat. For a small loft conversion it is possible to get this requirement relaxed and expert help is advisable if this is necessary.

If the intention is to comply with the regulations by providing a single escape staircase with a fire-protected route all the way down and directly to the outside, all the bedrooms in the loft have to open directly on to the stairwell and it must be possible to get from the bottom of the ground-floor staircase to an outside door without going into another room.

A common problem with this approach to complying with the regulations is that in some houses the bottom of the staircase on the ground floor opens into a room, rather than a hallway leading to an outside door. There are several ways of dealing with this. Many older houses, particularly those that started their life as the 'two up, two down' variety, have the staircase in the centre of the building to save space, with the front door opening into the front room. It may be impractical to create a protected corridor from the bottom of the stairs to the front or back door because the room that it passes through is too small or windows will be lost. The regulations allow an alternative solution, which is to provide two escape routes in different directions and through different rooms. However, to comply with the regulations with this approach the bottom of the staircase must be enclosed in the fire-protected walls and have fire doors leading from the stairs into the rooms.

In some modern house layouts the bottom of the staircase opens directly on to a living room, with no hope of arranging an alternative direction of escape. In these circumstances, the regulations can be complied with by adding a fire door at the top of the staircase on the first floor, ensuring that the ceiling between ground and first floors is fire protected, and that there is also an escape window at first-floor level. To be classified as an 'escape window' the window must comply with the regulations (see section below on bungalows). The open-plan ground floor must also have a sprinkler system added. The idea is that in the event of a fire people can get to first-floor level safely and then escape through a window.

If it is not possible to upgrade the lower floors of the house to form a protected escape route, there are still two options available although they are comparatively radical. One is to provide a new, separate fire exit, for example in the form of an external steel staircase. This must not pass by any windows into the lower floors unless they are fire protected with Georgian wired glass or blocked up. The second option is to provide a highly sophisticated fire detection and alarm system. A normal off-the-shelf arrangement of smoke alarms is not adequate and specialist help is required to persuade the building control officer to approve such a system.

Smoke alarms are required on every floor; usually one in the hallway and one on each landing are sufficient although it is advisable to have them fitted throughout the house at the same time. Ordinary battery-operated smoke alarms are inadequate for the regulations because they can fail unless regularly maintained. Also they will only sound once the smoke has reached them, so if someone is asleep in the loft they may not hear a ground-floor alarm two floors away. The regulations require mains-operated alarms, on a separate circuit but linked together so that if one goes off the others will also be activated.

Escape from a Loft Conversion
Added to a Bungalow
The requirements for conversion of a bungalow's

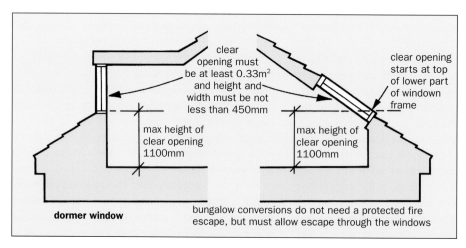

dormer window

bungalow conversions do not need a protected fire escape, but must allow escape through the windows

clear opening must be at least 0.33m² and height and width must be not less than 450mm

clear opening starts at top of lower part of window frame

max height of clear opening 1100mm

max height of clear opening 1100mm

Escape windows to loft conversions of a bungalow.

loft are less onerous than for a two-storey house because it is easier to escape out of the loft windows, which are only at first-floor height. The simplest method of providing escape is to open the rooms off a new staircase up from the ground-floor hall, which does not have to be a fire-protected exit, and ensure that the new windows to the loft comply with the regulation requirements for escape windows.

If it is not possible to fit escape windows to the loft, perhaps because of planning restrictions that prevent windows from overlooking neighbours, the alternative is to upgrade the staircase to 30 minutes' fire resistance and have an exit to the outside or in two directions. If even this is not practical, it may be possible to provide a separate external escape staircase and upgrade the ground-floor ceiling to provide 30 minutes' fire protection, which is also permitted by the regulations.

Escape from a Loft Conversion Added to a House with Three Storeys

Complying with the regulations to escape from a house with any existing second floor or higher can get more complicated. The most straightforward way is to upgrade the staircase to be a protected route, either with an exit to the outside, or in two directions on the ground floor, or allow escape from the first floor with similar provisions to the two-storey house scenario described above. If the existing stair cannot be upgraded, one option is to provide an advanced fire detection and alarm system, although this has to be in conjunction with either a separate fire escape stair or the installation of a sprinkler system throughout the whole house.

Resistance to the Spread of Fire

Another important aspect of the regulations in relation to fire that may be important for some loft conversions is preventing a fire in one house spreading to its neighbours. The thinking behind this is that if a house is on fire, the most likely route for it to spread is through windows or flammable walls close to the boundary with another house. If the wall of a house is more than 1m away from the boundary, there are some fairly complex

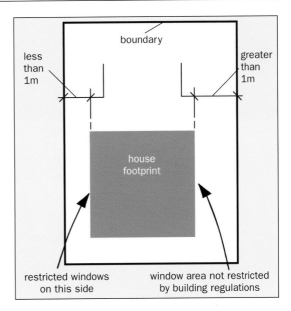

The building regulations restrict the area of glass allowed when a wall is close to a boundary.

rules that are used to calculate the size of windows and doors that will be allowed to face the boundary. Fortunately these are unlikely to come into play with a normal loft conversion.

However, the regulations assume that if a wall is closer than 1m, the chances of fire spreading are greatly increased and there are quite strict limits on the area of windows and doors that can be placed in that wall. The windows and doors are deemed to be 'unprotected areas' because they are more vulnerable to fire passing through them. Wall constructions that have less than 30 minutes' fire resistance and walls that are clad in flammable materials such as timber boarding are also considered unprotected areas. The most likely feature that may be affected by these regulations is a dormer window. If it has a window or timber boarding close to the boundary the exact distance should be determined and the regulations consulted to see if they will be permissible. The rules are not entirely straightforward, but effectively limit the size of a window or area of boarding to no more than 1sq m, and any such areas have to be at least 4m apart from each other.

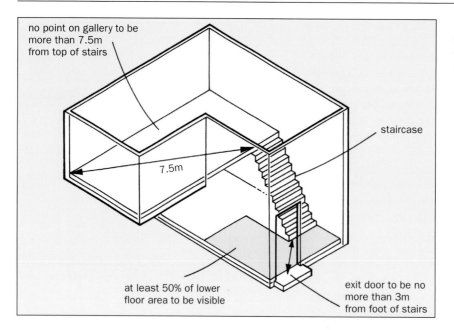

no point on gallery to be
more than 7.5m
from top of stairs

**Escape from a
gallery floor
without an
alternative exit.**

staircase

7.5m

at least 50% of lower
floor area to be visible

exit door to be no
more than 3m
from foot of stairs

Gallery Floors

Occasionally a loft is not quite big enough to provide a separate room, but can be incorporated into
the room below by creating a gallery or mezzanine
area. The gallery level is completely open to the
room and part of the main room becomes 'double
height', with a staircase up to the gallery leading
directly off it. With any building apart from a bungalow conversion, if the gallery was walled off from
the room it would be a separate space and the regulations would not allow the only means of escape
to be through the room below. This is because if
the fire started in the lower room there would be
no way of easily escaping. However, the regulations
recognize that if the two areas are effectively part
of the same space, any fire would become quickly
apparent to anyone on the gallery (often used as a
sleeping area), who could then quickly escape. So,
provided the rules indicated on the drawing shown
above are followed, it should be possible to turn a
loft space into a gallery.

The fire regulations are probably the most complex issue that has to be tackled in the conversion
of a loft. In anything but the simplest of cases, it is
advisable to seek professional guidance before
embarking on the project.

Approved Document E: Resistance to the Passage of Sound

These rules require that adequate sound insulation
is provided between the new rooms created and
between new and existing. The requirements for
floor construction can usually be met by incorporating 100mm of mineral wool insulation into the
gaps between the floor joists. Masonry walls, particularly brick, will probably comply if they are
lined with plasterboard or covered with two-coat
plaster finish. Stud walls can be made to comply
either by doubling up the plasterboard on each
side, or if there is only a single layer, by adding
25mm or so of mineral wool into the gaps
between the studs.

Approved Document F: Ventilation

Mechanical ventilation to bathroom and toilet area
is necessary, with a pull-cord switch, and a fifteen-
minute overrun if there is no window. 'Trickle
vents' are the openable grilles that are fitted to the
top of most modern windows, which provide background ventilation without the need to open the
window itself and are required by this section of
the regulations for all rooms that do not have

Fresh air ventilation through windows.

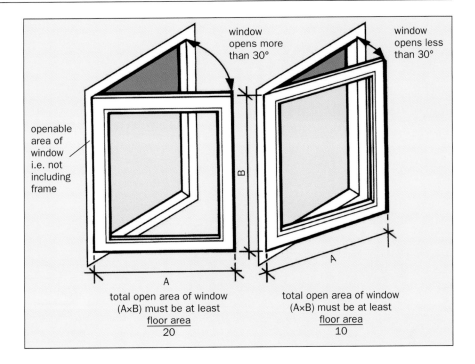

openable area of window i.e. not including frame

window opens more than 30°

window opens less than 30°

B

A

A

total open area of window
(A×B) must be at least
$$\frac{\text{floor area}}{20}$$

total open area of window
(A×B) must be at least
$$\frac{\text{floor area}}{10}$$

mechanical ventilation. There is also a requirement that every room that does not have a method of artificial ventilation has a window or windows that can be opened. These windows must have an area of one-twentieth of the floor area of the room or one-tenth if the opening of the window is restricted.

The other aspect of the ventilation requirements applies to the ventilation of the voids in the roof. How this is achieved is dealt with in detail in Chapter 6. In principle, warm, moist air from inside the building percolates through the construction and eventually passes beyond the insulation. At this point, in cold weather, the air cools rapidly and water condenses. If not dealt with, this would build up and eventually cause rot and rust. This can be avoided if there is sufficient air circulation to evaporate this condensate and carry it out of the building, so the regulations require that there are gaps at the eaves and ridge of the roof and that there is a clear path for the air to circulate between them. An alternative to this is to replace the impervious roofing felt under the tiles with a permeable modern plastic sheet that allows the air and moisture to pass directly through it.

Approved Document K: Protection from Falling, Collision and Impact

Very occasionally the restrictions placed by the regulations on staircase design can make a loft

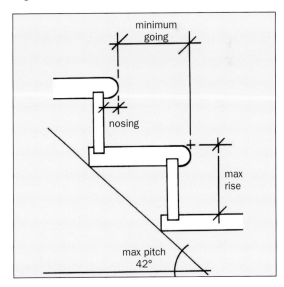

minimum going

nosing

max rise

max pitch 42°

Pitch, rise and going of a staircase.

if there is not sufficient space to provide 2m clear headroom across a new staircase to the roofspace, the reduced headroom shown here will be allowed under the building regulations

1.8m

1.9m

half of stair width

There are some strict rules in the building regulations regarding the design of staircases.
The Loft Company

Reduced headroom allowed to the side of a new staircase to a loft.

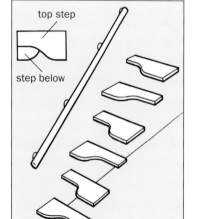

top step

step below

LEFT: **An alternating tread staircase.**

RIGHT: **Clearance of headroom above a staircase.**

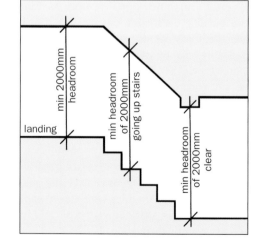

min 2000mm headroom

min headroom of 2000mm going up stairs

landing

min headroom of 2000mm clear

Keeping stairwells clear of door swings and obstructions.

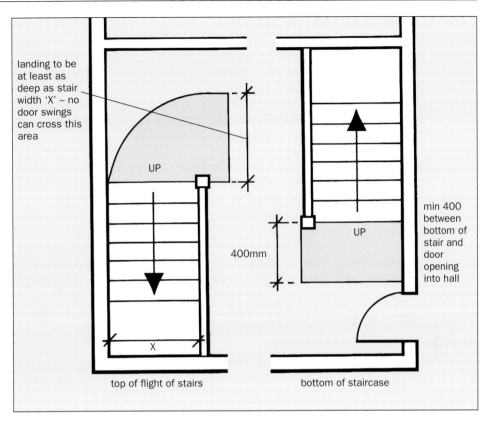

landing to be at least as deep as stair width 'X' – no door swings can cross this area

UP

400mm

min 400 between bottom of stair and door opening into hall

UP

X

top of flight of stairs

bottom of staircase

conversion impossible to achieve. More often they make the conversion tricky, requiring accurate measurement of the existing spaces and careful design. Usually the designer is trying to keep the staircase as compact as possible, because it takes space away from the areas of the loft with good headroom as well as from the floor below.

The staircase must not be too steep. There is an absolute limit on the height of the each step up or 'riser' on the staircase, and a minimum length for the spacing between each riser, known as the 'going'. The rules say that the riser shall be between 155mm and 220mm, which can be used with any going between 245mm and 260mm. There is also a provision that twice the rise plus the going should be between 550mm and 700mm (2R + G = 550 to 700mm). In addition there is a maximum angle or 'pitch' allowed for the whole staircase and minimum headroom of 2m required in most cases.

Where the staircase steps go around a corner, with triangular treads known as 'winders', the turn must not be too tight and cramped.

A special exemption to these otherwise strict rules has been created for loft conversions, known as an 'alternating tread' stair. This is steeper than a normal staircase, but it saves space by providing the length of going needed only on one side of each step. To go up the stairs you always have to start with the same foot (either left or right) and go up placing a foot on the side that has the right size of tread. It is allowed in private houses because the assumption is that the occupants will come to know how to use the staircase and will not get it wrong, even in the middle of night when they are half asleep. Someone unfamiliar with it would be at risk of falling, especially in the dark. It is not recommended where the elderly or partially infirm may need to use it.

The headroom requirements are designed to allow everyone except the unusually tall to walk up the stairs without bumping their head. The requirement that applies to new staircases in all houses for at least 2m above the run of the staircase is again relaxed slightly for a loft conversion in recognition of how difficult it can be to achieve.

A regulation that can affect the planning and design of the staircase reduces the risk of accidents by prohibiting doors that open onto the landing areas at the top and bottom of flights of steps. A door opening into the area at the bottom or top of a staircase must be at least 400mm away from the last riser. If the door opens into the room rather than out into the circulation area, this rule does not apply. Similarly, a landing has to be kept clear of any doors opening onto it or any other obstruction.

Approved Document J: Combustion Appliances and Fuel Storage

Loft spaces are very often penetrated by vertical service pipes, such as soil vent pipes (SVPs), which allow air into the drainage system, and chimneys and other flues that exhaust hot fumes from fires and boilers. The latter are subject to regulations principally because they are hot, creating a risk of fire, and because they give off poisonous fumes that must be kept away from occupants.

Because of the heat generated by the hot gases passing through a chimney when it is in use, the regulations require the structure of the floors to be kept away from them as much as possible. The two options for floor structure are shown below and opposite. The flue or chimney penetrates the roof covering and the gases are exhausted into the open air. If there are air currents or the air is cold and so tends to sink, the fumes may take a while to be removed from the space surrounding the roof, so the regulations control how close opening windows are to the top of the chimney. There are also provisions for avoiding the foul smell that comes out of the top of an SVP although these are actually covered in another Approved Document (H).

BELOW: **Building floors near a chimney – joists parallel.**

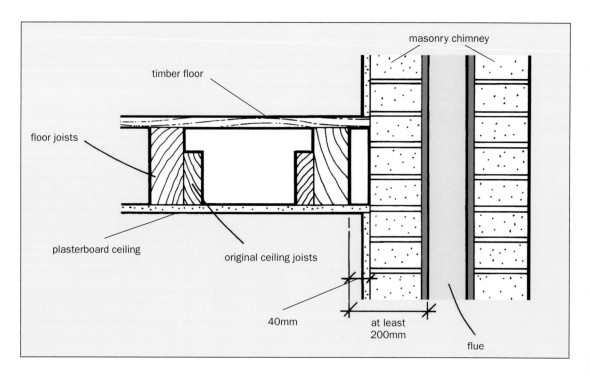

RIGHT: **Building floors near a chimney – joists built into wall.**

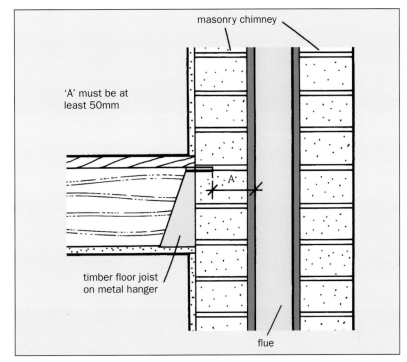

masonry chimney

'A' must be at least 50mm

A

timber floor joist on metal hanger

flue

BELOW: **Rooflight positions in relation to chimneys and soil vent pipes.**

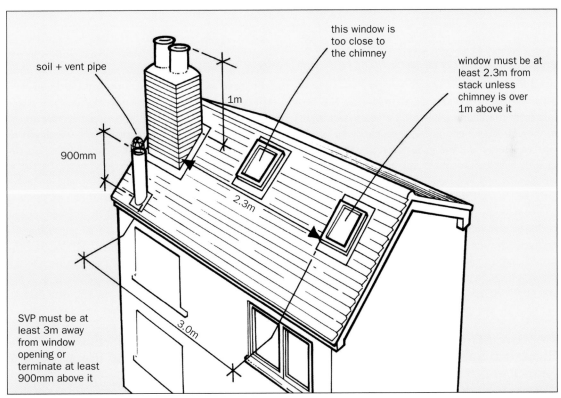

soil + vent pipe

this window is too close to the chimney

window must be at least 2.3m from stack unless chimney is over 1m above it

1m

900mm

2.3m

SVP must be at least 3m away from window opening or terminate at least 900mm above it

3.0m

The regulations controlling loss of heat through the roof and sides of a loft conversion can be quite complex. There are minimum figures for the thickness of insulation and also limits on how much glass can be used. Room Maker Loft Conversions

Approved Document L: Conservation of Fuel and Power

This document is designed to minimize the heat loss from the building, partly to save the occupants money on their heating bills, and partly to reduce wasted energy and the generation of extra carbon dioxide in the atmosphere, the main culprit causing global warming. How the insulation is incorporated into the construction is dealt with in more detail in Chapter 6, but 100mm of high-value insulation between the rafters with 30mm or 40mm fitted underneath them is a typical specification that will satisfy the requirements at the time of writing. However, the provisions that reduce energy usage are now revised every three years or so and are increasingly stringent.

Approved Document P: Electrical Safety

Electrical work is not something amateurs should take on, except for the simplest of tasks. The regu-

lations reflect this sensible advice and will not approve the electrical work necessary to fit out a loft space without thorough testing. Qualified electricians can certify their own work, but if it is put in by an experienced DIY enthusiast it has to be checked during construction and certified by someone with proven competence. Under no circumstances should an amateur attempt to put in an electrical circuit. The regulations quote British Standards and other accepted authorities applying to the electrical work as well as stating specific requirements, many of which are aimed at electricians and do not have a major bearing on the design of a loft conversion. For the non-technical it can all be summed by saying 'it must be safe'. If you are creating a lot of extra rooms you may have to provide some light fittings that will take only an energy-efficient light bulb.

The section of the regulations that governs the height of switches and sockets does not apply to loft conversions.

CHAPTER 6

The Detailed Construction of Loft Conversions

There are three key stages to constructing a loft conversion: the structural alterations, the main construction, and finishing off the interior. If you use a builder to do all the work for you, the last stage will be the one that you are most involved in but it is useful to have an understanding of the principles governing the first two. If you are planning a DIY project this section will help you to work out how the conversion is likely to be built, but is no substitute for the design expertise of an architect and structural engineer, who will ensure that these general techniques are applied to the specific building work needed for your project.

ADAPTING THE TWO MAIN TYPES OF ROOF STRUCTURE

Trussed Rafter Roofs

It is harder to convert a trussed rafter roof than a traditional construction. This is partly because the pitch of a modern roof tends to be more shallow, to save money on materials, but mainly because of the structural timbers that criss-cross throughout the roofspace. Because trussed rafters are designed to use timber to its maximum efficiency (again to reduce the initial cost), all these timbers are essential to hold up the roof. Each one plays an important, precisely calculated role and if they are cut through the roof is immediately weakened. Because they are spaced at approximately 600mm centres, the roof cannot be converted into usable living space unless all of the intrusive structure is removed.

ABOVE: **Trussed rafters.** Julian Owen Associates Architects

BELOW: **A trussed rafter roof under construction.** Julian Owen Associates Architects

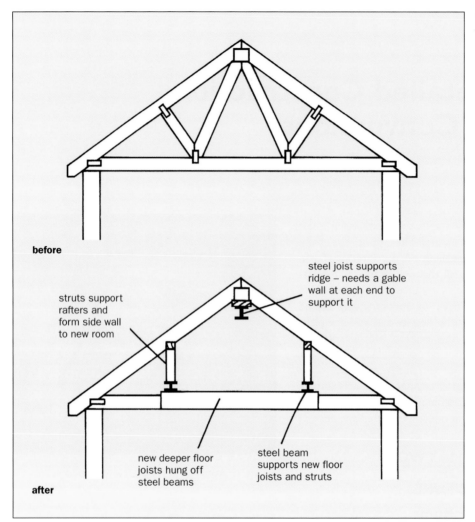

Converting a trussed rafter roof.

before

after

steel joist supports ridge – needs a gable wall at each end to support it

struts support rafters and form side wall to new room

new deeper floor joists hung off steel beams

steel beam supports new floor joists and struts

There are two ways that this may be achieved. One is to insert steel joists running the full length of the roof, which carry out the same role as the parts of the truss that are being removed. There usually needs to be a structural gable wall at each end of the roof for the steels to bear on to support their weight. The remaining rafters are then supported off the steel, either resting directly on them as purlins, or on props if the steels are at floor level. The joint between the tops of each pair of rafters also has to be reinforced, either with another steel beam, or with a horizontal length of timber known as a 'collar'. There is a logistical problem with this method of conversion in that the steel joists have to be somehow manhandled into the space and positioned correctly. This is difficult to do without removing a large area of the roof tiles and battens. One way around this problem is to make the beams in shorter sections and bolt them together on site. Complex calculations by a structural engineer are needed and a lot of manoeuvring on site results. If a truss needs a lot of new steel beams to support it in this way, it can be cheaper to replace the whole roof.

Provided that the span of the roof is no greater than 7m or 8m there is an alternative method of conversion, which relies on telescopic beams

Constructing a Trussed Rafter Roof

Feet of trussed rafters exposed ready for work to begin. Telebeam

Beams are inserted from the eaves. Telebeam

New beams are ready to take the loads so the wooden struts can be removed. Telebeam

Sections of the truss are trimmed back.
Telebeam

Insulation is laid between the new floor joists to provide sound and fire protection.
Telebeam

The finished conversion, after boarding out and decoration. Telebeam

A typical gable roof with purlins, before conversion. The purlin on the right is supported by a strut that is built off an internal structural wall. The horizontal timber in the bottom centre is a ceiling binder, which rests on an internal wall and the gable at the end, and supports the floor joists. Julian Owen Associates Architects

A typical hipped roof with purlins and struts. The purlins have no gable wall to support them, so more support is needed from struts, in this case built off the ceiling binder in a 'V' formation. Attic Designs Ltd

designed especially for the purpose. These are inserted across the span at floor level, by removing three courses of tiles immediately above the eaves. Vertical timber struts can be used to support the remaining rafters, propped off the strong new floor structure that is created. This type of system can be fitted quickly, leaving the roofspace ready for conversion either as a DIY project or by a professional builder.

Traditionally Constructed Roofs

As described in Chapter 2, traditional or cut roofs come in many different forms but the general principles of altering the structure are the same. The rafters are usually supported by purlins, which in turn take support from the supporting walls. Any timber or section of timber that is removed will leave a structural gap that must be filled by a new structure that helps to make the roofspace more appropriate for its new use as a room. Fortunately the structural design of most traditional roofs is not as highly refined as those made from trussed rafters. Before the modern Building Regulations came into existence, traditional roofs were often completely improvised on site. The builder would

use a mixture of experience and oversizing the timber sections to create a strong, reliable roof structure. When engineers design modern cut roofs, they still allow 'safety factors' in their calculations, which also results in the beams and joists being larger than the absolute minimum necessary to do the job. This means that there is usually plenty of tolerance when the roof is altered. For example, it may be possible to move the location of the supporting purlin a fair distance without significantly reducing its effect and openings for windows may be able to be created using trimmers, without any additional support or propping from structural walls.

If the roof has no timbers interrupting the central area, and the height of the purlins is such that they will not interrupt any new windows, it may be possible to convert the roof without alterations to the roof structure (although the floor will probably still need to be strengthened). But most roofs will need the addition of some steelwork. With a gable roof the steel beams can be supported at each end by an external wall, in the same way as for the trussed rafter conversion above. However, if the roof is hipped this is not possible and support for

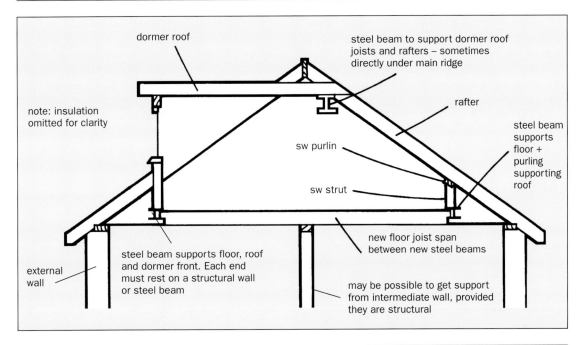

dormer roof

steel beam to support dormer roof joists and rafters – sometimes directly under main ridge

rafter

note: insulation omitted for clarity

steel beam supports floor + purling supporting roof

sw purlin

sw strut

new floor joist span between new steel beams

external wall

steel beam supports floor, roof and dormer front. Each end must rest on a structural wall or steel beam

may be possible to get support from intermediate wall, provided they are structural

ABOVE: **Converting a traditional roof – structure.**

BELOW: **This purlin is supported by a stud wall that is built off the floor joists, which in turn are supported by the steel beam at floor level on the left of the picture.**

Julian Owen Associates Architects

Standard Classifications for Timber Exposure

- Under cover with dry conditions. This covers timber inside houses, protected from the weather, for example on the first floor and walls, or a pitched roof. The only risk is from insect attack, because unless the building becomes derelict, the moisture level in the timber never rises to a level that will allow wet rot or other fungi to flourish.
- Internal location, but with a risk of getting wet occasionally, for example timber on the ground floor or in a flat roof.
- External location, above ground, with frequent wetting due to the weather, for example external decking, balustrades and fence boarding.
- Direct contact with soil or fresh water, for example timber used for fence posts and lock gates.
- In or close to seawater. These are the most extreme conditions that timber can be subjected to and this category includes jetties and sea defences. There is a risk of attack from creatures above and below the waterline.

any existing timbers that may be removed has to be taken off the structural walls. This is usually done by spanning steel beams at floor level, above the line of the ceiling below, and using them as support for timber props that in turn support a purlin and the new floor. Most hipped roofs are built with structural internal walls to support the original roof design, which can usually play the same role for the new beams.

PRESERVATIVE

The softwood likely to be used for the construction of the new parts of the roof structure is potentially vulnerable to attack from insects or rot if it is exposed to damp for a prolonged period. The modern way to reduce the risk of decay is to treat the timbers with preservative. The conditions in which timber will be used will determine the level of preservative treatment required.

Because preservatives, which are pesticides, are very potent chemicals and are potentially damaging to human health, the UK has some strict rules about where and in what circumstances they can be used. A favourite treatment of builders for many years was chromated copper arsenate (CCA) because it is effective and easy to apply. In the UK this is now banned in all residential and domestic locations and where humans or animals are likely to come into direct contact with it. This type of preservative is also being phased out of use by some other countries. Timber treated with CCA is considered hazardous waste, although there is no evidence to suggest that it is harmful where it is already in place.

It is possible to apply preservative treatment on site, but the most reliable way is to do it in a factory, either using a chamber that creates a vacuum, forcing the chemicals to migrate into the structure, or by dipping. There are various levels of penetration of the preservative into the timber that can be achieved depending on how inhospitable the future environment of the timber is going to be, and how long it will be necessary for the wood to last. The vacuum high-pressure process is the most effective and aims to penetrate as deeply as possible into the wood. Double vacuum low-pressure processes (sometimes referred to as 'Vac Vac') do not penetrate so far and are used for locations where there is less likelihood of attack, generally above ground, for example trussed rafters. Water-based emulsion products are used with combinations of insecticides and fungicides, mixed according to the final use.

If new or existing timber that has been preservative treated is cut during the building work, the exposed ends should be re-treated on site.

STRUCTURAL DETAILS

For anything but the simplest, smallest loft conversion, the advice of a structural engineer will be invaluable. Even in the rare situations where the building control officer will allow sizes to be 'guesstimated' by an amateur, an engineer will be able to prevent unnecessary oversizing or suggest more elegant solutions. For a more cramped situation, such advice can make the difference between a very successful conversion and one that is merely adequate and does not make the best use of the available space.

Beams and Main Structural Elements

Almost as important as the overall structural design of the alterations is the selection of the individual beams, how they connect and how they link to the structure of the existing building.

Steel Beams

Steel joists, with their characteristic 'I' section, are most commonly used for converting the structure of a loft because they are relatively strong for their size and will take high loads in a way that ordinary timber cannot. The top and bottom of the beam are called flanges and are actually what take most of the structural load that runs through a beam. In a typical situation, the beam tends to sag fractionally when loaded, which means the top flange is compressed slightly and the bottom flange is stretched slightly (or in tension). The web that joins the two is under a lot less load and this is why it is possible to drill holes of limited size and frequency into it.

Types of steel beam.

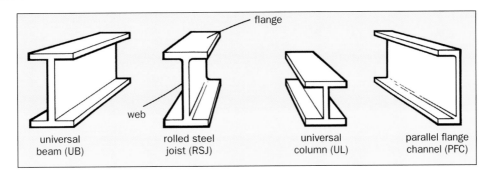

There are several types of steel beams for use in different situations. The rolled steel joist (RSJ) is the most widely known but probably the least used type of steel beam. The flange thickens towards the middle so there is not a right angle between it and the web. This means that it is harder to sit a square-shaped section of timber into it. The universal beam (UB) has square corners that are much better suited for this purpose, so these beams have effectively replaced RSJs.

Both UBs and RSJs have the familiar 'I' section and tend to be greater in height than width because this is the most efficient structural shape for such a beam. However, sometimes the height of a beam can be a disadvantage, for example when you wish to conceal it in the depth of the floor. In these cases a variant on the UB, called a universal column (UC), is used. The height of a UC is the same as its width, which is the best structural shape for a column because all the loads are running straight down through it and it will resist the buckling that could result from this. When the UC is used as a beam, it has the advantage of being shallower that an equivalent 'I' beam and can be concealed in the depth of a floor more easily. Another frequently used beam type is the steel channel (parallel flange channel or PFC). This is often used where there is restricted space and allows a timber section or the ends of timber joists to sit easily within its 'C' shape.

Purlins

Purlins are the horizontal beams that stretch along the roof and help to support the rafters above them and sometimes the floor joists below. Most loft conversions have to deal with existing purlins

in an inconvenient position, or with ones that need to be cut to allow a window to be inserted or have floor joists that are of inadequate depth to support the extra loads imposed on them by the new use as a room. Usually the answer to these problems is to use one of the steel beams described above. Sometimes alternatives to steel are used, however, either because the beams will be visible after the work has been completed or for operational reasons – for example it may not be possible to crane up a steel beam, while a timber alternative may be lifted up by the builder's team.

Assuming that a simple timber joist is not available with a sufficient depth to take the loads, there is a variety of modern substitutes for the steel 'I' beam. Some, such as Parallam, are made from reconstituted timber. It is made of waste wood chippings that have been mixed with a strong adhesive

Purlins are a common feature of a traditionally constructed roof. Julian Owen Associates Architects

151

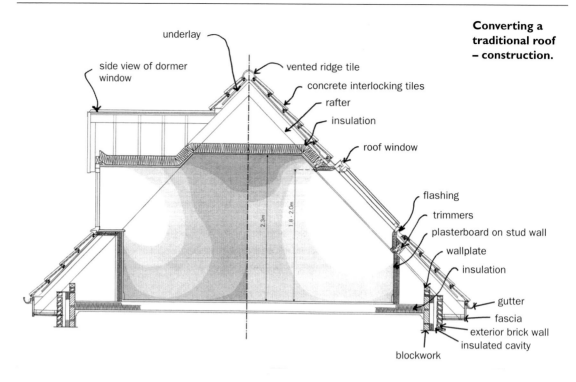

Converting a traditional roof – construction.

underlay

side view of dormer window

vented ridge tile

concrete interlocking tiles

rafter

insulation

roof window

flashing

trimmers

plasterboard on stud wall

wallplate

insulation

gutter

fascia

exterior brick wall

insulated cavity

blockwork

2.3m

1.8 - 2.0m

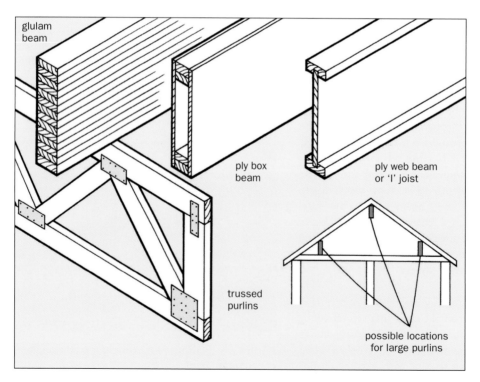

Alternatives to steel purlins.

glulam beam

ply box beam

ply web beam or 'I' joist

trussed purlins

possible locations for large purlins

to form a new beam. The result is a much stronger beam than its natural timber equivalent. Glulam beams are made up of strips of timber, again held together with strong glue. These beams have the added benefit that they can be formed into curved shapes if required. Composite beams are made up by combining ordinary softwood with plywood panels and have the advantage of being very light for their span. This reduces the loads on the rest of structure and makes them relatively easy to lift into place. Within reason they can be drilled, fixed to and painted like ordinary timber and are often used to form the actual wall of the room along the

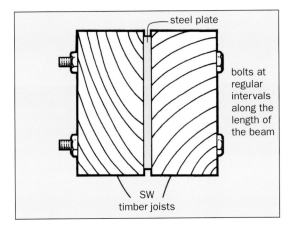

A section through a flitch beam.

A flitch beam hides the steel element of its construction behind the timber.

Julian Owen Associates Architects

eaves. If used at higher level, their increased depth in comparison with steel may be a disadvantage as they will reduce headroom.

There is another hybrid that can be used that combines the benefits of timber with some of the strength of steel, called a flitch beam. These are formed by bolting two softwood joists together as a sandwich with a steel plate in the middle. The bolts ensure that timber and steel work together as a single structural beam, which looks a lot better than a plain steel joist but has more strength than an ordinary timber joist. Sometimes it is not possible to tell where a flitch beam has been used without careful inspection. A flitch beam can be used to reinforce and strengthen an existing timber beam.

Collar Roofs

Another element of roof structure that can get in the way of the free space needed to create a room is the collar. This is a horizontal beam that is often fixed to the middle third of the rafters on each side of the roof. Sometimes there is just one collar in the whole roof structure, sometimes there are several (for example, on every third rafter). The collar is a tie beam that helps to prevent roof sagging and roof spread and is in tension. Timber is very strong when under tension, because it would literally have to be ripped apart to fail, so collars tend to look deceptively thin and weedy. As a result it is tempting to conclude the collar is not performing a structural role and remove it without bothering to replace it. This is a mistake; almost every part of a roof structure is doing something

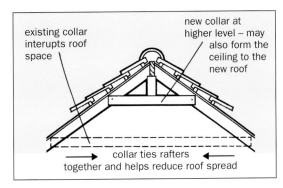

Roof collars.

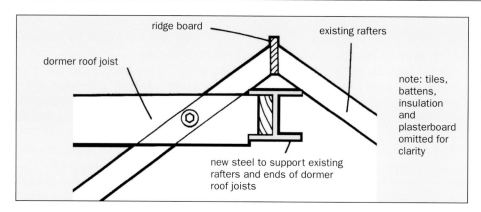

ridge board

existing rafters

dormer roof joist

note: tiles, battens, insulation and plasterboard omitted for clarity

new steel to support existing rafters and ends of dormer roof joists

Supporting timbers with a ridge beam where there is a large dormer.

useful, otherwise the original builder would not have bothered to fit them.

Occasionally a roof develops a problem with the feet of the rafters slipping outwards and pushing out the tops of the external walls supporting them, and this is stabilized by nailing collars onto the rafters. This might be the situation in cases where the timber used for the collar is newer than the rest of the roof.

The loss of collars can be compensated for by fitting new purlins to support the rafters, or fitting new collars at a higher level to allow headroom to walk under them. Another option is to fit a ridge beam, for example in the form of a UB directly beneath the ridge, which can also act as a support for a dormer roof if necessary.

Supporting and Connecting New Beams
Complete lengths of new purlins are not easy to manoeuvre into place in the limited space usually available in a loft, and where this is impossible without removing the roof they can be brought up in sections and bolted together, although this will mean they have to be slightly bigger.

The beams have to pick up the loads from the floor and roof and transmit them back to the existing structure. Where they rest on a wall they concentrate the load they are carrying on to that

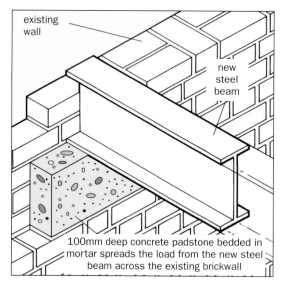

existing wall

new steel beam

100mm deep concrete padstone bedded in mortar spreads the load from the new steel beam across the existing brickwall

Supporting the end of a steel beam using a concrete padstone. Julian Owen Associates Architects

ABOVE: **Here a wall has been removed to open out a section of the loft. Two steel purlins have been fitted to replace the wall, bearing onto a concrete padstone that spreads the load across the bricks of the side wall.** Julian Owen Associates Architects

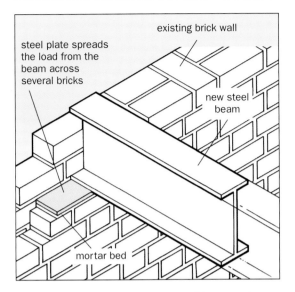

steel plate spreads the load from the beam across several bricks

existing brick wall

new steel beam

mortar bed

Supporting the end of a new steel beam using a steel plate. Julian Owen Associates Architects

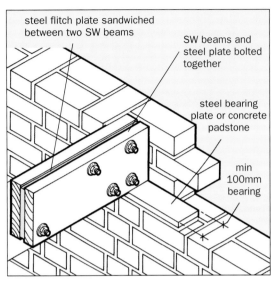

steel flitch plate sandwiched between two SW beams

SW beams and steel plate bolted together

steel bearing plate or concrete padstone

min 100mm bearing

Supporting the end of a new flitch beam using a steel plate. Julian Owen Associates Architects

one single point. The bricks or blocks of the wall are designed to take moderate loads comfortably, but there is a risk of the extra weight in one small area crushing and deforming the wall underneath it. So a beam of any significant size, for example spanning further than across a door opening, without any extra support, may cause some structural defect to develop. The way around this problem is to spread the load along a strip of wall using a

material that is strong enough not to be crushed. This is usually done with either blue engineering bricks or a concrete or steel padstone.

In the course of the work, beams may also have to be connected together. The simplest way to do this is to use joist hangers, galvanized steel straps that fix to one beam and allow the other to hang from it, possibly at a lower level. This is a connection commonly used to hang a new floor at a lower

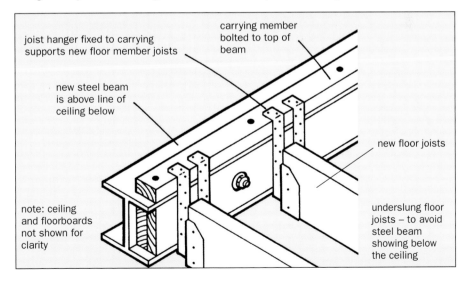

joist hanger fixed to carrying supports new floor member joists

carrying member bolted to top of beam

new steel beam is above line of ceiling below

new floor joists

note: ceiling and floorboards not shown for clarity

underslung floor joists – to avoid steel beam showing below the ceiling

Underslung floor joists, to avoid the steel beam showing below the line of the ceiling.

level than the beam supporting it close to the eaves. To hang a softwood joist off a UB an extra timber is bolted to the top of the steel. This provides an easy fixing for the joist hanger.

Trimming Rafters and Floor Joists

Part of the process of converting a loft will involve creating holes and an opening in the existing roof and floor. Assuming that you wish to keep as much of the existing timber structure of the loft intact as possible, the rafters and floor joists that are on either side of any new opening will have to be strengthened. If a hole has to be very large then a full structural design will be needed, possibly involving new steel beams built off the existing structural walls. For most openings it is possible to upgrade the existing structure by adding new timber beams of a similar size parallel to the existing beams.

Opening for a rooflight, showing the trimmers and doubled-up rafters. Julian Owen Associates Architects

RIGHT: **Rules of thumb for cutting openings in rafters.**

BELOW: **Forming a new opening in an existing roof.**

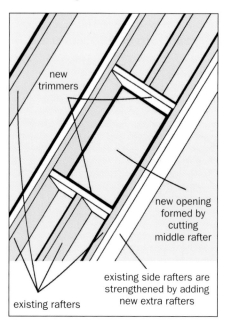

new trimmers

new opening formed by cutting middle rafter

existing side rafters are strengthened by adding new extra rafters

existing rafters

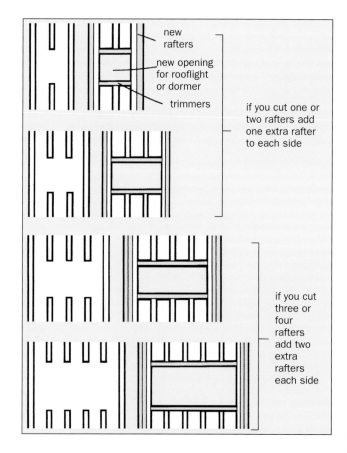

new rafters

new opening for rooflight or dormer

trimmers

if you cut one or two rafters add one extra rafter to each side

if you cut three or four rafters add two extra rafters each side

Creating an opening in an existing floor using trimmers and double joists.

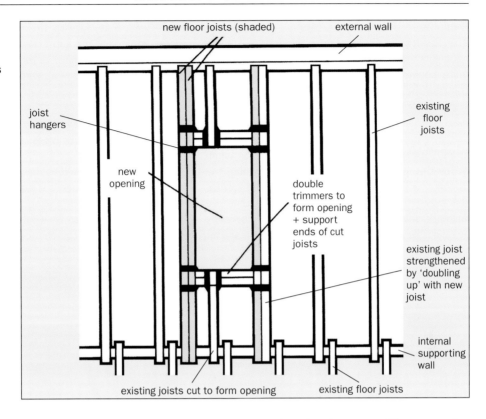

new floor joists (shaded)

external wall

joist hangers

existing floor joists

new opening

double trimmers to form opening + support ends of cut joists

existing joist strengthened by 'doubling up' with new joist

internal supporting wall

existing joists cut to form opening

existing floor joists

Once the required opening in the roof has been positioned, the ends of the rafters are cut, with temporary support to the ends as necessary. The trimmers are fixed in place across the ends of the cut rafters, transferring the load on to the remaining rafters either side. The number and size of the extra timbers depends on the size of the opening. Builders use some rules of thumb to estimate the extent of the strengthening work needed, adding extra new rafters as the size of the opening increases. It should be noted that as with all such estimates, they rely on the experience of the person using them to ensure that they are appropriate and cannot be used slavishly as a guide to all situations. If you intend to carry out this work yourself and are unsure, get professional help.

A similar strategy can be used to create openings in the floor for a loft hatch or small staircase access hole, although the rules of thumb are not applicable in the same way as for a roof. The existing floor joists will almost certainly be inadequate to bear the extra loads imposed by using the loft

for a room rather than for storage. This means that the whole floor will have to be upgraded with new, stronger floor joists. But the principle of forming a small opening is the same. If a large opening is needed, extra support will have to be designed in, probably by using steel beams.

Rooflights, Dormers and Roof Covering

One of the most important elements of a loft conversion is the introduction of natural light into the new rooms and spaces. There are several ways to adapt the roof structure and construction to create windows, the two simplest and most common being rooflights and dormer roofs.

The Building Regulations affect the way that windows are designed and built in a loft conversion. The key restriction is that too many windows may lead to unacceptable heat loss. Their size and position may also be controlled by planning legislation, even to the level of requiring obscured glass in windows that may overlook neighbours.

157

Rooflights

The easiest way to create a window is to use rooflights that follow the line of the roof. There are quite sophisticated proprietary systems available to make the job as easy as possible, in some cases without having to climb outside onto the roof itself, with all the work being carried out from a safe position standing inside. It is often carried out as a DIY project although it is not a job to be taken on by the inexperienced. Aside from forming the opening by cutting back and trimming the rafters, the other most crucial job is ensuring that the flashings around the roof window are correctly installed. 'Flashings' are the strips of sheet material, often lead, that lap into the surrounding tiles or slates and cover the gap between the edge of the roof frame and the roof covering. The objective is to allow a little movement, while covering and sealing the gap completely so that no rain can get through. Manufacturers have recognized how important it is to get this potentially tricky detail right. Most of these types of window can be bought with a complete flashing kit integrated into the frame and designed to make it a simple as possible to install. Although it is just about possible for one person to fit such a window, it is advisable for at least two people to lift it into place because the assembled kit of a large window is heavy.

Rooflights being fitted to the front elevation of a house. Attic Designs Ltd

Fitting a rooflight. The Velux Company Ltd

Dormer Roofs

Dormer roofs can make a dramatic difference to the space, with clear headroom that is available to a new room (*see* Chapter 4). They are a more drastic alteration than the roof window and it is essential to climb out onto the roof to build them, so their construction is best left to the professionals, particularly when the roof is on a house with two or more floors. The structural design and construction detailing is also more sophisticated than for a roof window. The existing building has to accommodate a complete new structure, including the loads that result from a new roof. There are also many more junctions between different materials that need to be covered and protected with flashing, usually lead or a similar malleable metal.

159

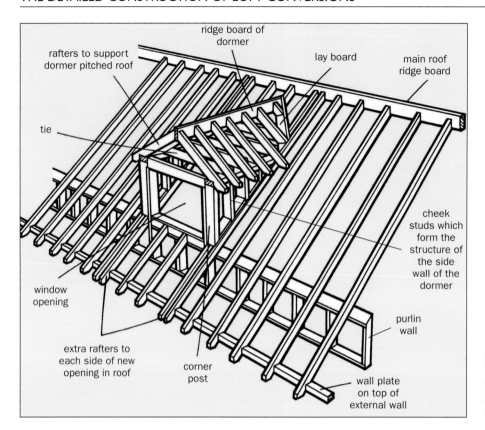

Typical structure of a small pitched roof dormer.

ridge board of dormer

rafters to support dormer pitched roof

lay board

main roof ridge board

tie

cheek studs which form the structure of the side wall of the dormer

window opening

purlin wall

extra rafters to each side of new opening in roof

corner post

wall plate on top of external wall

BELOW, LEFT: **Typical structure of a small flat-roof dormer.**

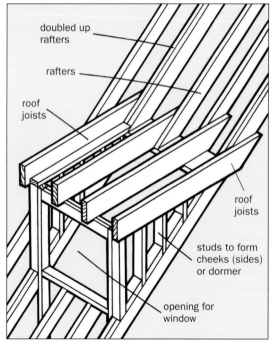

doubled up rafters

rafters

roof joists

roof joists

studs to form cheeks (sides) or dormer

opening for window

After increasing the number of rafters either side of the opening, the walls of the dormer are built up with timber studs that provide a space for insulation between them. The roof over the dormer is typically pitched or flat, or occasionally monopitched, and an opening is formed in the wall facing out from the roof. Any existing purlins that interrupt the space formed by the new dormer have to be removed and the appropriate structural alterations put in place to compensate.

If a double-pitched roof is created, the junction between these two pitches and the main roof is called a 'valley' and is a point on the finished roof that is at risk of water leaking into the inside. The junction can be protected either by a lead or a pre-formed glass reinforced plastic (GRP) tray, cut to fit. The most expensive way of detailing this junction, which is generally agreed to look the best, is to use valley tiles. These are especially made tiles that match the main roof and are shaped to fit the junction between the roof surfaces and give the

Constucting a Dormer Roof

The construction sequence of a dormer roof. Julian Owen Associates Architects

Flashings being positioned to protect the junctions between the walls and roof of a dormer. Julian Owen Associates Architects

be necessary to introduce some steel beams to support the masonry on each side, or 'cheek' of the dormer. The studs support foil-backed plasterboard on the inside. The foil acts to reduce the amount of warm, moist air that can find its way into the construction and reduces the chances of condensation forming. The external side of the studs usually has a plywood sheathing that gives it strength and rigidity. Over this is a sheet of material that allows moist air to pass out through it, but also keeps out any water, called a breather membrane. The most common facings for the outside of the studs are tiles on battens, lead, render and timber boarding. Occasionally the front wall of a dormer can be built directly off the outside wall. In these cases, assuming that the side walls are difficult to build in brick, there will be a change of finish from brick to lead or a similar cladding. The junctions between the walls of the dormer and the main roof covering have to be protected with flashing, usually strips of lead. It is important that these are fitted expertly because, apart from performing the crucial role of preventing rain from getting inside, they are often visible and form part of the design.

appearance of a seamless join. This is really only going to be worth doing if you are replacing the tiles of the whole roof to the house, otherwise a break between new and existing, covered by a dark grey strip, will look better.

Insulation is needed in the roof void. If the dormer ceiling is to be flat there is usually space to use the cheaper mineral wool insulation or equivalent. If the line of the ceiling follows the line of the roof, a higher grade of insulation will be necessary, similar to that used for the sloping ceiling of the main roof. Either way, there has to be a way of preventing condensation forming in space above the dormer ceiling.

The walls are usually formed from timber studs built off doubled up rafters. It is possible to form the side walls from brick, but assuming that the floor of the new roofspace room is timber, it will

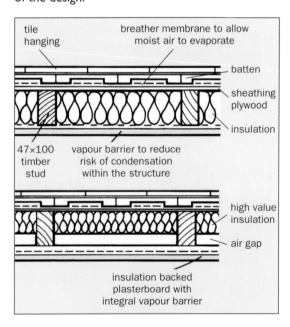

Two alternative constructions for a dormer wall. B is more energy efficient.

Section through a dormer window, showing the construction.

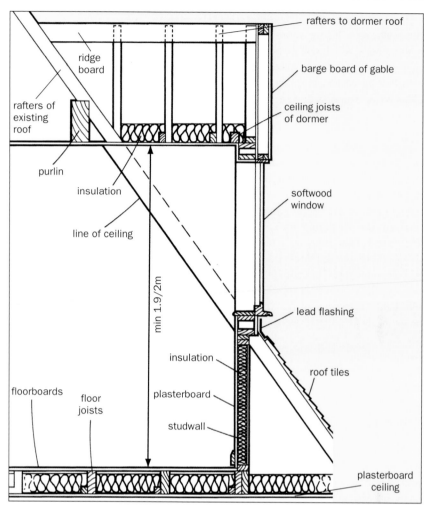

rafters to dormer roof

ridge board

barge board of gable

rafters of existing roof

ceiling joists of dormer

purlin

softwood window

insulation

line of ceiling

min 1.9/2m

lead flashing

insulation

roof tiles

floorboards

floor joists

plasterboard

studwall

plasterboard ceiling

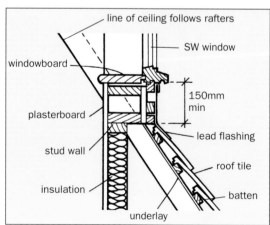

line of ceiling follows rafters

SW window

windowboard

150mm min

plasterboard

lead flashing

stud wall

roof tile

insulation

batten

underlay

Section through the sill of a dormer window.

A dormer with a hipped roof being built onto a small existing roof. Room Maker Loft Conversions

There is not much space within the thickness of the walls, so a higher value insulation material is needed here, which will be more expensive. If possible, it is a good idea to allow enough space to get a high level of insulation into the walls because, being more exposed, dormer roofs can lose heat in winter and leave the space immediately inside them cooler than the rest of the roofspace.

Another detail that is important to get right is the flashing at the base of the window. There is sometimes a conflict between the location and design of a dormer window with a double-pitched roof, in that it has to sit comfortably on the main roof, but the sill should preferably not be too low. This means that there is a temptation to reduce the gap between the underside of the window and the existing roof. This should be resisted if at all possible because the sill should be well clear of the tiles below it to prevent rot, and the flashing has to be properly fitted to prevent leaks.

Roof Covering

As part of the initial inspection of the roof, an estimate should have been made of the remaining life of the roof covering. The most likely coverings are slate, clay tiles and concrete tiles. An assessment should also have been made to check that the covering of the roof is appropriate to the roof pitch. For example, clay or concrete rosemary tiles should not be laid at a pitch lower than 35 degrees, but interlocking concrete tiles can, in theory be laid as shallow as 12.5 degrees (although this is not advisable). If the roof covering has very little life left it is sensible to replace it whilst the rest of the conversion work is underway. This is partly because it is a lot cheaper than getting a builder back and erecting another scaffold only a short while after the conversion is completed. Furthermore, an experienced builder will not want to start working on a roof that has a covering in poor condition. The slates or tiles with failed fixings will start to slip off as soon as any hammering or sawing starts on the rafters and purlins. Also if the tiles themselves are in poor condition, trying to cut or flash into them will be difficult without causing damage.

If the roof covering is to be replaced you will have to decide whether to use the same product

If the roof covering is replaced, the battens and felt will probably have to be renewed as well. Julian Owen Associates Architects

An advantage of re-roofing the house is that the covering to the dormer will match the rest of the main roof. Julian Owen Associates Architects

or to use a different one. This may be decided on cost – the difference in price between cheap concrete tiles and traditional clay rosemarys runs into many thousands of pounds on an average roof. Concrete tiles do not look as good as the natural alternatives, however, and sometimes the appearance of a building can be improved by swapping slate for tile. In any case, the new material has to be suitable for the roof. The roof pitch may be inappropriate, for example concrete tiles on a 25-degree roof cannot be changed to plain tiles because the pitch is too shallow. Another problem that arises with modern houses that use concrete interlocking tiles is that they are much lighter than their traditional equivalents and if replaced with plain clay tiles the roof structure will also have to be upgraded to prevent the rafters from sagging under the extra weight.

Floor Construction

Before conversion work starts, what is to become the floor of the new rooms is usually inadequate for the job. The original builders of the house would not have seen the need to go to the unnecessary expense of providing joists strong enough to act as a floor to a bedroom or other room. The assumption would have been that the softwood joists would have to support just the ceiling and the relatively limited loads imposed by old suitcases and other stored items. The structure may feel fairly sturdy as you walk around the loft before it is converted but unless you are very lucky, the building control officer will not find joists acceptable for use as the floor to a room. You may only plan to furnish the new room with a bed and a desk, but the design of the new space has to allow for all future eventualities, including book-laden shelves and heavy pieces of furniture.

There are several ways of ensuring that the new floor construction will be satisfactory. One is to remove the entire floor and ceiling and start again with an entirely new structure. This has the benefit of being the most straightforward and is worth considering if the house in question is being gutted to the extent that damage to the floors immediately below the loft will not be a concern. A more likely situation is that the effects on the other

Herringbone strutting is a way of strengthening a floor so that it will span further without bending. Julian Owen Associates Architects

rooms in the house are to be minimized and keeping their ceilings intact is important for keeping the cost of the whole project realistic.

It is possible to leave the existing ceiling joists in place along with the ceiling below and construct a new floor above it. This will avoid the need for a new ceiling and allow the new floor joists to run wherever it is easiest to put them. The disadvantage is that the floor of the new room will be a lot higher than the top of the original joists, possibly as much as 195mm. This is fine if there is a nice steep, wide roof and plenty of headroom to achieve the required floor area. Unfortunately, headroom is a precious commodity in most loft conversions and a few centimetres can make the difference between a simple, viable conversion and a more expensive one. The most common solution to this dilemma is to interleave the new joists between the existing ones, using the new to support the old and keep the ceiling intact. If this is done with sufficient expertise, it reduces the need for steel beams and minimizes the lost headroom.

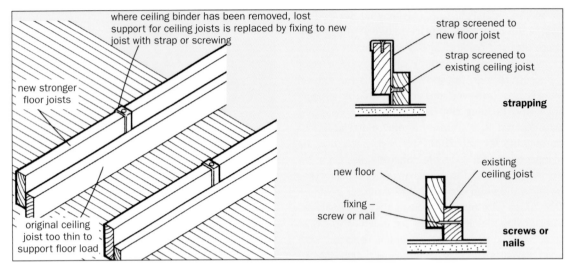

where ceiling binder has been removed, lost support for ceiling joists is replaced by fixing to new joist with strap or screwing

new stronger floor joists

original ceiling joist too thin to support floor load

strap screened to new floor joist

strap screened to existing ceiling joist

strapping

new floor

existing ceiling joist

fixing – screw or nail

screws or nails

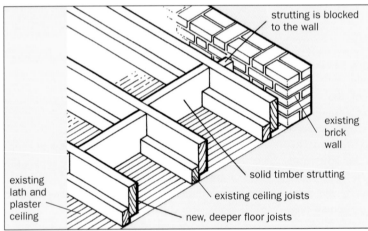

strutting is blocked to the wall

existing brick wall

solid timber strutting

existing ceiling joists

new, deeper floor joists

existing lath and plaster ceiling

ABOVE: **Replacing a ceiling binder and strengthening a ceiling so that it can take floor loads.** Julian Owen Associates Architects

LEFT: **Interleaving new floor joists between the existing with solid timber strutting.** Julian Owen Associates Architects

BELOW: **Section through a typical converted floor.** Julian Owen Associates Architects

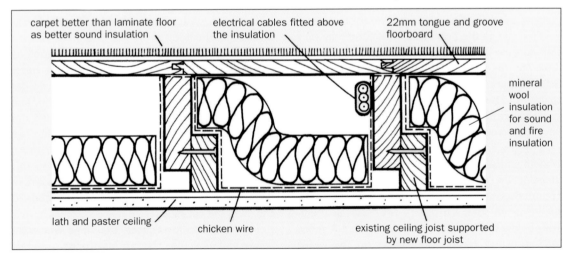

carpet better than laminate floor as better sound insulation

electrical cables fitted above the insulation

22mm tongue and groove floorboard

mineral wool insulation for sound and fire insulation

lath and paster ceiling

chicken wire

existing ceiling joist supported by new floor joist

Achieving fire resistance with existing lath and plaster ceilings and existing floorboards.

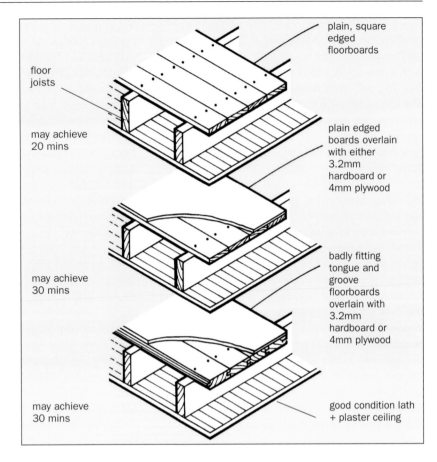

floor joists

plain, square edged floorboards

may achieve 20 mins

plain edged boards overlain with either 3.2mm hardboard or 4mm plywood

may achieve 30 mins

badly fitting tongue and groove floorboards overlain with 3.2mm hardboard or 4mm plywood

may achieve 30 mins

good condition lath + plaster ceiling

The ceiling joists of many older roofs are supported by binders at the middle of their span. These are larger timber beams that run across the joists at 90 degrees. Their purpose is to prevent the ceiling joists from sagging, but they are usually much higher than the ideal new floor level and therefore need to be removed. The new, stronger joists can be used to make up for this loss of support, by fixing new and old together along the line of the old binder, using either nails or galvanized steel straps. Where the span is significant, extra strength can be given to both ceiling and floor joists by building in 'blocking' from extra sections of timber (see diagram).

Assuming that the structural requirements for the converted loft can be resolved, there are also two other crucial requirements the floor has to meet apart from supporting all the extra loads that will be placed on it. If the loft being converted is above two or more existing floors, in other words in any cases apart from a bungalow, the Building Regulations are likely to require fire insulation between the new rooms and the existing space underneath them (see Chapter 5). As well as preventing the spread of a fire from below, the floor should also reduce the transmission of noise. Apart from this being a reasonable expectation for the occupants of the rooms, a basic level of sound insulation is now included in the Building Regulations. If the rooms below are under separate ownership the requirements for fire and sound resistance of floors are more onerous, but this is an unusual situation and so it is assumed for the purposes of the following details that the whole house is owned by one family.

The level of fire resistance required by the regulations is typically 30 minutes – that is, it would take a fire below the roofspace 30 minutes to burn through the floor and destroy it. This is relatively easy to achieve if the whole floor is being replaced with a new construction. However, it is more likely that you will want to minimize the disruption to the spaces below the loft and will want to avoid removing and replacing the ceilings of the existing rooms. This means that any improvements in the new floor will have to be implemented from above. It also means that how effective the work is will be partly dependent on the construction of the existing ceiling, how well it was built originally and its current state of repair.

It is usually fairly easy to make an assessment of a modern, plasterboard ceiling, which will comprise either 9.5mm or 12.5mm plasterboard nailed to the ceiling joists. The necessary fire resistance can probably be achieved by filling the spaces between the new joists with mineral wool insulation suspended on chicken wire and putting a good-quality board over the top. The older, lath and plaster type ceilings need a little more thought. If they are very old, they could be in very poor condition, in which case it is wise to bite the bullet and replace them completely. Where the floor is strong enough and there is already some boarding across the floor in the attic, it may be possible to avoid removing it, provided that some insulation can be put in position between the joists. If the structure is in reasonable condition there are several ways to achieve 30 minutes of fire resistance (see diagram p. 165).

Sound resistance is provided by placing mineral wool between the joists, which also helps to provide fire resistance. However, modern hi-fi equipment, digital televisions and other sources of entertainment produce high levels of noise and it is arguable that the minimum requirement for sound insulation in the Building Regulations is inadequate for modern living. One way to improve the sound resistance, to the benefit of occupants of the rooms above and below, is to introduce rubber strips on to the tops of the floor joists. The floorboards are then fixed into these strips rather than directly into the floor joists. A major route for sound transmission is through the plasterboard ceiling, into the joists and via the floorboards, but the rubber strip interrupts this flow, significantly reducing the transmission of sound through the structure. It is recommended that the floor of the new roofspace is covered with a good-quality carpet rather than a hard surface, which would amplify the noise of feet clumping on the floor.

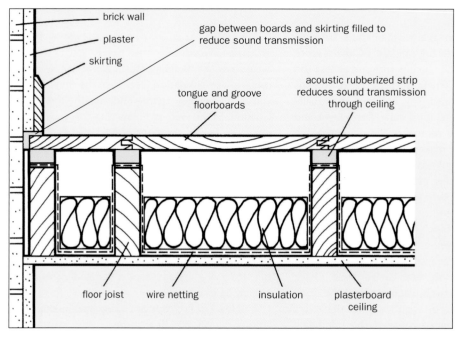

How to improve the sound insulation of a timber floor.

Insulation and Ventilation

In a typical loft before conversion the insulation, if there is any, is usually mineral wool laid between the ceiling joists. The latest Building Regulations require that a further level of insulation is laid over the joists, and at right angles to them. This is because although it is relatively cheap, mineral wool is not the most efficient form of insulation and it needs to be quite thick (250mm or more) to achieve modern standards. If it is in good condition, there is no harm in reusing it between the joists of the upgraded floor, since it will help achieve the noise and fire insulation needed. However, it is likely to be unsuitable to relocate to a position between the rafters, where the line of maximum insulation has to be to keep the heat loss from the attic rooms at a minimum. Headroom is often at a premium in a roofspace and from this point of view the thinner the section of construction that is made up by the roof covering, structure, insulation and lining, the more room will be available inside. With a rigid, high-insulation board, it is possible to achieve the Building Regulations minimum by filling some of the space between the rafters and boarding over with a second sheet to a total depth of about 130mm–140mm. It is best to place the second layer of insulation board over the rafters because timber is not as good at insulating and would otherwise reduce the effectiveness of the insulation between the boards.

A relative recent innovation is multifoil. This is more like a sheet of material than a board and it is made up of many layers, such as reflective foil and a sheet a bit like bubble wrap. The advantage of multifoil is that it is very thin and therefore increases headroom. When it was originally put on the market, the manufacturers claimed that the multifoil alone achieved Building Regulations requirements and for a while building control officers accepted this claim and certified its use as adequate to obtain approval. However, subsequent testing led to approval being withdrawn and at the time of writing multifoils have to have additional insulation board to be accepted. This combination still helps the headroom, but not to such a great extent.

A problem that can be caused by insulating a sloping roof in this way arises when warm, moist air percolates through the structure from the inside. As it passes through the insulation towards the colder section of the construction, immediately below the battens, this air cools. As it cools, the moisture condenses and can appear as water

Multifoil is a recent innovation, but at the time of writing the regulations will not accept these unless there is also a certain amount of traditional insulation board between the rafters. Julian Owen Associates Architects

A breathable membrane used in place of traditional felt is a lighter colour and much thinner. Julian Owen Associates Architects

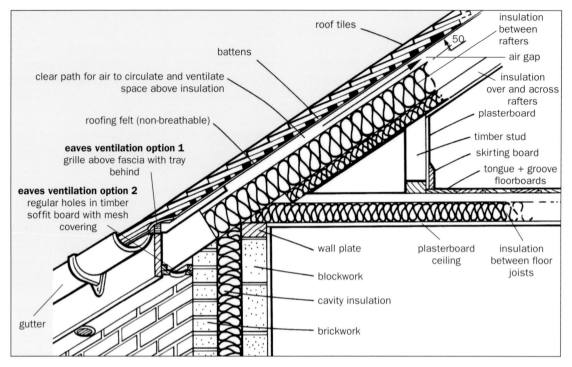

ABOVE: Roof insulation with non-breathable felt and ventilation path.

BELOW: Roof insulation using a breather membrane in place of roofing felt.

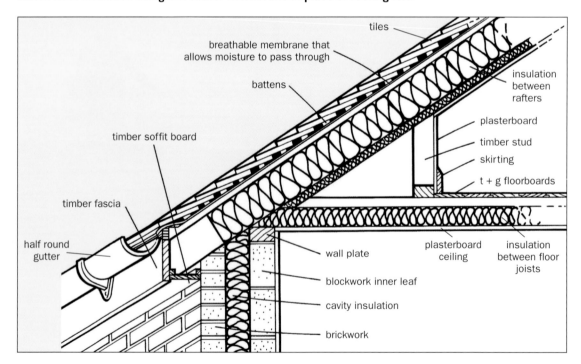

Ventilation to the void above the insulation is essential if normal roofing felt has been used under the battens.

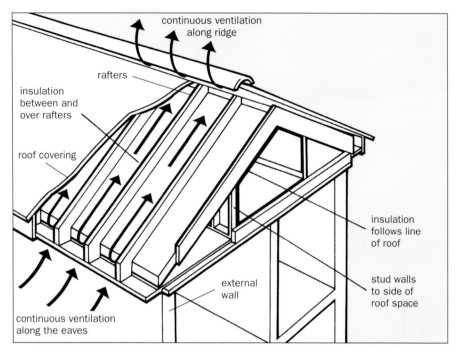

continuous ventilation along ridge

rafters

insulation between and over rafters

roof covering

insulation follows line of roof

external wall

stud walls to side of roof space

continuous ventilation along the eaves

LEFT: **This picture of a hip before the tiling and gutters are added shows the eaves ventilation strip, which hangs off the edge of the roof.**

Julian Owen Associates Architects

BELOW: **Mechanically fixed ventilated ridge.**

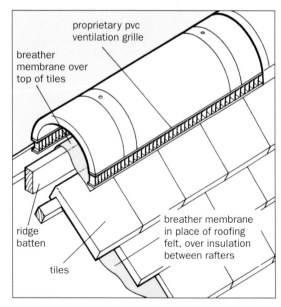

proprietary pvc ventilation grille

breather membrane over top of tiles

ridge batten

tiles

breather membrane in place of roofing felt, over insulation between rafters

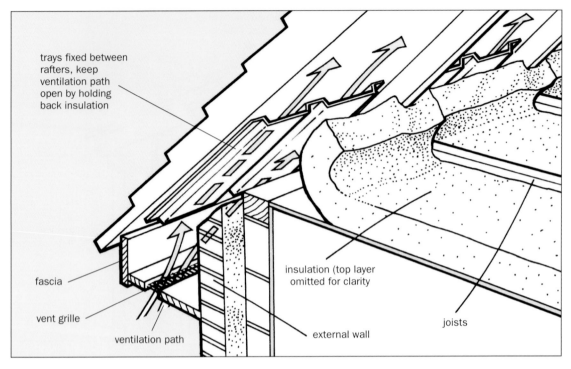

trays fixed between
rafters, keep
ventilation path
open by holding
back insulation

fascia

vent grille

ventilation path

insulation (top layer
omitted for clarity

external wall

joists

Roof ventilation at the eaves where insulation is between the rafters.

on the outer surface of the insulation. If these damp conditions are prolonged, there is a risk of rot, mildew and other undesirable consequences, such as the efficiency of the insulation reducing as it gets saturated. So there has to be a way of removing this moist air before too much condensation occurs and there are two strategies for doing this.

The traditional way of removing this unwanted moist air is to ventilate the gap between the top of the insulation and the underside of the roofing felt. The disadvantage of this method is that as well as installing ventilation at the ridge and eaves levels, you need to allow an air gap of 50mm above the insulation. This pushes the inside face of the insulation further into the room, reducing the headroom. Roofing felt is designed to catch the rainwater that might find a way between the roof tiles, and then drain it down into the gutter. Moist air will not pass through it as it does through the plasterboard and insulation. Although an underlay such as felt is required by modern Building

Insulation fitted between the rafters of a roof.
Julian Owen Associates Architects

Regulations, older houses may well not have any roofing felt. It is not necessary under the Building Regulations to provide a felt underlay to an existing roof where the covering is not being renewed. Some older roofs without felt were originally constructed with 'torching', which is cement filler spread under the joints of tiles. Because tiles tend to move slightly in the wind over time the torching drops out. There is little benefit in replacing the torching and the extra ventilation that results helps to dispel the moisture-laden air.

An alternative to ventilating the space above the insulation is to replace the roofing felt with a breathable membrane. Because this would be an expensive operation, it is only worth doing if the roof covering is going to be replaced anyway. This membrane is designed to perform the same task as the felt in preventing the rain passing into the roof structure, but also allows the damp air to pass through it, significantly reducing the risk of condensation. It is well worth considering the use of a breathable membrane for any new sections of roof where the ceiling is to follow the line of the rafters.

Whatever the insulation that is chosen for the roof, it is advisable to clad the underside of the ceiling in foil-backed plasterboard. The foil acts as a vapour check, that is it resists the passage of moist air through it. If the joints between the boards are properly formed the risk of condensation is greatly reduced. Foil-backed plasterboard is essential if the room is to be used as a bathroom or utility room, where there will be steam produced.

An important function of insulation between and over the rafters that is often overlooked is that it also keeps heat out in summer. This is expected to become a far more serious problem in the UK than it is at the moment, with some experts predicting that most houses of traditional construction will need some form of air conditioning by 2020. A south-facing roof tends to heat up far more quickly and to higher temperatures than with other orientations and this can lead to overheating problems in the summer. A thicker layer of insulation will prevent the heat from working its way into the room from the hot tiles.

Staircase Construction

The design options for staircase layouts have already been covered Chapter 4. When it comes to the construction stage, the most important issue is ensuring there is sufficient space and headroom to fit the staircase in the chosen location. Ideally, a clearance of 2m is desirable, although the regulations will allow it to be reduced to 1.8m on the sides in certain circumstances. Staircases are usually pre-fabricated as a kit by a specialist manufacturer and assembled on site by the builder or self-builder. At some point in the building programme it will be necessary to confirm the exact dimensions of the opening that the staircase will have to fit into and the overall rise from the lower to the upper floor. It is vital that these measurements are highly accurate and to confirm them finally only after the opening has been formed in the loft floor. If this is not possible, the staircase designer must build in some tolerance to allow for inaccuracies. This is particularly important with very old buildings, where floors are not necessarily dead level and the walls may not be at 90 degrees to each other in plan.

The simpler the plan of a staircase, the easier (and cheaper) it is to build.
Julian Owen Associates Architects

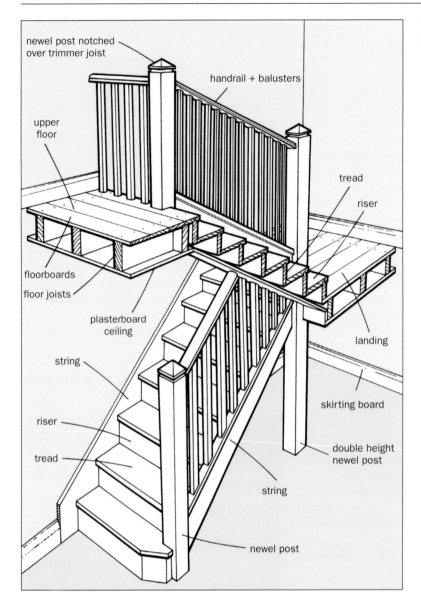

Typical staircase construction.

newel post notched over trimmer joist

handrail + balusters

upper floor

tread

riser

floorboards

floor joists

plasterboard ceiling

string

landing

riser

skirting board

tread

double height newel post

string

newel post

The simplest way to form the string, or main supporting elements of the staircase, is as straight boards running up the flight and concealing the ends of the treads and risers. A more expensive but better looking alternative is to cut the line of the top of the string to follow the steps up. This is more complex to construct and unlike with the straight string the balusters are of varying length. The blocking, brackets and wedges shown in the drawing are important to get right. This is to ensure that the structure of the staircase is robust – they also reduce the tendency of the treads to creak when stepped upon.

Internal Walls

The ideal internal wall, which will provide good sound insulation and a good base for securing fixings such as shelves, is masonry, for example concrete blockwork, with a two-coat plaster finish.

Stud walls under construction.

Julian Owen Associates Architects

If there are any existing masonry walls in sound condition that suit the layout of the newly created rooms they can be retained, provided that they can be made good and finished to meet current fire regulations. It is not good practice to build a new block wall off a timber floor, so in the roofspace there are only two ways of building new masonry internal partitions. Either there has to be an existing masonry wall immediately below the line of the new wall, or if this is not the case, a new steel beam has to be put in place to support it. To avoid these complications, most of the internal walls are likely to be made from either timber or metal studwork. Metal studs are lighter than timber but also slightly more expensive. Both can be cut with an appropriate hand saw. A timber stud wall is slightly less hollow than one made of steel, but neither, in their simplest form, is a good insulator against sound. This is fine for cupboards, but any walls to bedrooms or bathrooms can be made better at reducing sound transmission by filling the voids between the studs with sound-absorbing mineral wool.

If any heavy fittings are to be fixed to the wall, the ideal strategy is to plan where these are going to go in advance and provide extra studs in the wall. This will enable the fixings to be secured straight into them once the wall covering is in

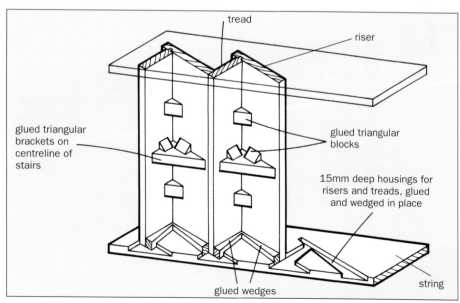

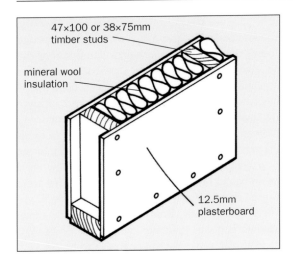

47×100 or 38×75mm timber studs

mineral wool insulation

12.5mm plasterboard

ABOVE: **Internal partition with mineral wool for sound insulation.**

RIGHT: **Filling joints in plasterboard cladding to a stud wall.**

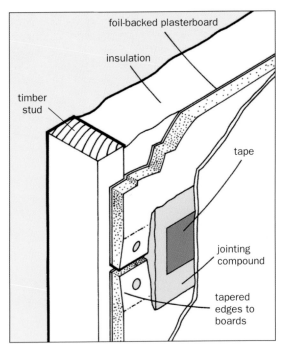

foil-backed plasterboard

insulation

timber stud

tape

jointing compound

tapered edges to boards

place. Otherwise the fixtures will have to be positioned to suit wherever the studs have been located. Provided that the loads are not too excessive, special fixings that are designed for use in plasterboard may be used. The joints in the plasterboard sheathing to the studs can be taped if it will be finished with wallpaper, but if the wall is to be painted a thin coat of plaster or skim is preferable.

Walls that form the sides of the stairwell or landing of a fire-escape staircase need special construction to ensure that they provide at least 30 minutes' fire resistance. A staircase will be a fire escape route if the house has an existing first floor. It is relatively easy to achieve this level of resistance if the wall is made of either brick or blockwork, which are inherently resistant to fire. With stud partitions, the wood, which has a tendency to burn, needs to be protected properly by non-flammable plasterboard sheathing. This can be achieved by ensuring that the thickness of the plasterboard is 12.5mm rather than 9.5mm and that it has noggins at all edges, fixed to studs of at least 38mm × 75mm.

Another crucial internal wall for a house that is semi-detached or in a terrace is the party wall, which separates the attic space above a property from the space next door. Modern regulations require that a new house must have very robust party walls, with good resistance to the passage of fire and sound. For older properties these walls are invariably poorly built of common bricks and often have large gaps between the top of the party wall and the underside of the roof.

It is essential that walls in this condition are properly upgraded. Simply fixing a sheet of plasterboard on one face of the wall is wholly inadequate. Apart from the issues already mentioned, assuming that the space next door has not been converted, the insulation will be at ceiling level and so the dividing wall will also have to be insulated. If the wall is one whole brick wide, that is 215mm, the surface should be treated with a sand/cement render and all gaps between the top of the wall and the roof packed with mineral wool before dry lining. One way of dry lining is to use a frame of studwork with voids filled with insulation and a plasterboard cladding. The alternative is a proprietary system of plasterboard sheets that have insulation and a vapour barrier bonded to their backs, held in place with a strong plaster-based adhesive (known as 'dot and dab' in the construction industry). If the wall is only half a brick thick, that is 105mm, an independent stud wall with two layers of plasterboard with staggered joints and mineral wool insulation in the voids should be constructed.

If the house is made entirely of a timber frame, or there is no party wall between the lofts of neighbouring houses, a more heavyweight construction is required, as well as advice from an experienced builder or architect to ensure that the finished wall will comply with current regulations.

SERVICES

Lighting

Fortunately lofts have a built-in advantage when it comes to daylight levels. The amount of light that comes into a room clearly depends on its size, but also how much direct light from the sky is allowed in. Most ground-floor and even first-floor windows receive most of their light by reflection off the surrounding buildings and landscape. Higher windows, such as those on a second-floor loft conversion, often look out mainly on to the sky, so admit a great deal more daylight. The same applies to sunlight, so too many windows looking southeast, south and southwest should be avoided to reduce solar gain and the overheating that results. Where the headroom in a roofspace is very restricted, the feeling of being in a cramped space can be partially offset by ensuring that there is plenty of daylight and views out.

Basic solutions that are adequate for artificial light in a normal, straight-sided room may have to be rethought for a space that has some sloping walls. A pendant, or hanging, light bulb with a shade around it may be impractical because it will be too low for people to walk underneath. Standard wall-

In a roofspace, you are more aware of the sky. The Velux Company Ltd

Whole-house ventilation ducts may be too large to fit between the rafters.

Julian Owen Associates Architects

mounted uplighters may be inappropriate on sloping ceilings because they cannot be mounted high enough to avoid shining directly into the occupant's eyes and so need to be mounted on the walls that are vertical up to at least 1.8m. Bulkhead fittings, or units that are fixed directly to the high point of the ceilin, which is usually flat, are often used. Freestanding standard lamps can be quite effective, as can fittings designed to sit on a desk or table and direct light upwards to reflect off the surrounding ceilings and walls.

It is especially important to light the staircase well and ideally direct some natural daylight into this area to give it a warmer, less enclosed character.

Ventilation

The simplest way to ventilate the rooms is to ensure that there are enough openable windows to allow fresh air directly into it. This is particularly important where the roof is south facing because it will heat up more than a normal room in summer.

The ventilation of fresh air into the new rooms can be achieved artificially with a whole-house mechanical ventilation system. These systems are increasingly popular, particularly with people who suffer from allergies and asthma, because they removed particles from the air before circulating it. They also come with a heat exchange system as standard, which uses the heat of the stale air being exhausted to heat the fresh air on its way into the building – a helpful energy efficiency measure.

The ducts for these have to be quite large and finding unobtrusive routes through the structure of a loft conversion can be complicated. The ideal route for the ducts, some of which must be at high level, is between the rafters. Unfortunately they have to compete with the roof insulation and in some situations there may not be space to snugly fit them out of the way, especially if essential structural bracing is in the way, as in the photograph on the left So if a mechanical ventilation system is to be used, the actual sizes of the ducts, including any integral insulation surround, should be ascertained and the routes through the construction plotted carefully in advance.

For bathroom or utility areas a more basic mechanical ventilation system can be provided. This is a requirement of the Building Regulations. It is relatively easily achieved by an off-the-shelf extractor fan unit with a pull cord. This can be mounted in a vertical window (not a rooflight) or a vertical section of external wall. Sometimes this is not possible and it has to be mounted in the ceiling, with the exhaust air exiting through the roof covering. This is achieved by connecting a flexible plastic duct to the unit and a special tile that incorporates a ventilation outlet. The latter come in many shapes and sizes, some of which make an unsightly lump that is undesirable on a prominent roof. The better types are 'in line' and use discreet grilles in the gaps between ordinary tiles or between the ridge tile and the rest of the roof and are almost invisible from the ground.

Heating and Water Supply

A common practical problem that arises with a loft conversion occurs when there is a large existing water storage tank in the roofspace. Some heating systems also have a small expansion tank to relieve pressure. Sometimes it is possible to incorporate at least the expansion tank into the layout of the rooms, but generally there is not room for a large water tank. Where there is no space for the tanks the boiler will need to be replaced. Cold-water taps that were fed from the water tank will need to be connected to the mains supply.

Another disadvantage of this older-style 'gravity-fed' heating system is that it relies on the water tank to provide a head of water. In other words, the flow through the taps is dependent on the height of the tank in the loft. The higher the tank in relation to the tap, the greater the pressure. If you want to fit any kind of appliance, such as a sink or WC, the top of the tank must be higher than the taps themselves. If any bathroom fittings are to be fitted in a loft conversion they would need to be connected to the mains water supply. For example, in a loft space, if the tank is just above head height the pressure will not be very high and water will not flow readily through the taps, let alone a shower. It is possible to obtain electrically operated shower units and water heaters that are connected to the mains, but some appliances, such as thermostatic shower valves, will not work if the pressure is less than around 2 bar.

Most modern houses are built with a 'mains-pressured' or an 'unvented' central heating system. This is where all the cold taps and the water that flows through the boiler to the hot taps come directly from the mains supply. Sometimes there is no water storage at all and the cold water from the mains is heated instantaneously as it flows through the boiler straight to the taps. This is known as a 'combi' or combination boiler. Other more complex systems incorporate hot-water storage in a cylinder. These systems do not need a water tank to store water, or a smaller expansion tank to take overflow from the hot water storage. Apart from not needing any tanks the other benefit of changing an existing boiler to a pressured system is that instead of being dependent on a tank

position above the taps to get pressure, it comes straight from the water main. The pressure is set by the mains water supply system in the area, so provided the mains pressure is adequate for the system installed, a shower fitted in the roofspace should work without any problem.

Some of the mains pressure systems require a minimum pressure to be provide by the water company, typically 2.5 bar. Unfortunately in the UK there is no obligation on the water companies to ensure that this pressure is available. In some areas, particularly on higher ground, there is not enough pressure to keep unvented systems working efficiently. Before any type of unvented system is fitted, the plumber must check that the local pressure is appropriate. If it is vital to the success of the loft conversion that a shower is fitted, or that the water tanks are removed, the mains pressure should be checked with the water supplier before any design work is finalized.

Generally it is desirable to conceal pipework but care should be taken and allowance should be made for access to taps, valves and other fittings. The triangular spaces between the vertical walls and the eaves are ideal for this purpose. Any heating pipes should be well lagged. If the pipes are to be concealed within the depth of the floor the floor joists will probably have to be notched to allow then to pass through. Ordinary floor joists are usually safe to notch as shown in the diagram. If

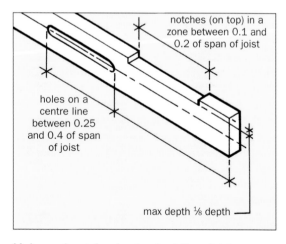

notches (on top) in a zone between 0.1 and 0.2 of span of joist

holes on a centre line between 0.25 and 0.4 of span of joist

max depth ⅛ depth

Holes and notches in standard floor joists.

the floor joist is part of a trussed rafter or attic truss, however, it should not be notched without expert advice from the truss designer or a structural engineer.

If you want a relatively low initial cost and to avoid having to run pipework around the rooms to supply heating and hot water, the alternative to extending the existing central heating system is to fit electric night storage heaters. In appearance the heaters are similar to water-filled radiators. The electric element heats to quite a high temperature, around 600°C to 700°C, and this is absorbed by and stored in the bricks. The heaters radiate heat throughout the day and are comparatively expensive to run. Care in siting the heaters is required: the units have bricks inside, making them heavy, and most have to be wall mounted.

The easiest forms of heating of all to install are radiator panels that work directly from a plug socket, which can be left to radiate heat in a similar way to a normal radiator, or fans that blow air across a heated element. Unfortunately, these are also the most expensive to run and will send most electricity bills 'through the roof' if used as the main source of heating, even if they are fitted with a timer to ensure that they do not continue to run when the heat is not needed.

In a similar way, hot water can be created by running cold water from the mains through an instantaneous water heater, with similar cost implications. Electric heating should be considered if the rooms are only going to be used occasionally and the budget for the conversion is very tight.

Energy Efficiency

Energy conservation is the first and most effective strategy in creating an energy-efficient house – in other words, reducing the amount of heat lost through the roof and walls. The easiest way to do this is to limit the area of the windows and make sure that the insulation level in the new construction is significantly higher than the minimum requirements of the Building Regulations. However, once you have used the most effective insulation and it has reached a thickness of around 200mm, the benefits of increasing the depth reduces significantly, and the loss of headroom caused by the

Photovoltaic panels are expensive to fit but will save energy. Julian Owen Associates Architects

increase in the overall thickness of the roof construction may be undesirable if space is very limited. So if there is still money to spare after increasing the insulation to this level, it is worth looking at the technological solutions available. Another cost-effective way of reducing energy use is to ensure that there is good control of the radiators by fitting thermostatic valves to them. These valves will shut the radiator off when the room temperature reaches a set level. If the room is not being used, the valve can be turned down to keep the room temperature above freezing.

Aside from the conventional arrangement of a gas- or oil-fired boiler and radiators in each room there are some alternatives that are worth considering before assuming this is the only option. Underfloor heating can be fitted above the insulation between the floor joists quite easily during construction and solves the problem of trying to locate space for radiators.

You could also consider harnessing the power of the sun with solar panels. It is likely that there will be scaffolding up and work being carried out on the roof as well as alterations or replacement of the heating system, so it will cost less to fit a panel at this time than at any other. There are two options. One is a wet system that uses thin pipes, painted black, running under a glass sheet. Water or liquid is run through the pipes, which readily warm up, even on overcast days, thanks to the glass trapping the heat. This type of panel is relatively cheap and is used to supplement the main source of heat, usually a conventional boiler. It will only work if some kind of storage of the hot water is available, such as a cylinder or heat store. The more sophisticated alternative is the photovoltaic panel, which converts the sun's energy into electricity that can be used to supplement the electricity provided to the house through a mains connection or stored in a battery. Solar voltaic panels are relatively expensive and in the UK will typically not provide sufficient electricity to supply a normal house. If a registered installer is used, the UK government provides grants that can help to make the installation of solar panels more cost-effective.

There was a fashion in the UK for installing wind turbines to the gables of houses at the turn of the century. This has largely come to an end in suburban areas, where the wind speed is completely inadequate to make it worthwhile and some buildings sustained structural damage because the fixings were not properly designed. In exposed rural areas they are a more viable option but even then will take a long time to pay back their cost by saving electricity.

Electrical Installation

All significant work altering or adding to the existing electricity supply around the house must be certified by a qualified, registered electrician. This is a requirement of the Building Regulations. The electric sockets, switches and appliances in the new rooms created in the loft will be connected to the existing supply either by extending the existing ring circuit or, more likely, by the creation of a new one. To add a new circuit there has to be a spare miniature circuit breaker (MCB) or space for one to be added to the consumer unit. The consumer unit is located close to the point that the mains

A free-standing wind turbine is a better option than trying to attach one to a house-sized roof.
Julian Owen Associates Architects

electrical supply enters the house and usually has a row of MCBs, which should ideally be labelled to indicate to which part of the house they relate – upstairs lights, downstairs sockets and so on. If there is no MCB available, a new consumer unit may be needed.

Service Penetrations through the Roof Covering

It is sometimes necessary to pass flues, chimneys and soil vent pipes through the roof covering to the outside air. This work must be carried out carefully because poor workmanship will result in leaks that can wreak havoc with the interior construction and finishes. The traditional method of flashing the junction between pipe or wall and roof covering is the most reliable way to reduce the risk of such damage. Failure of the flashing around an existing chimney is a very common problem in older properties and if the water getting through is just a trickle, it may not be immediately obvious whilst the loft is unheated, with unplastered walls

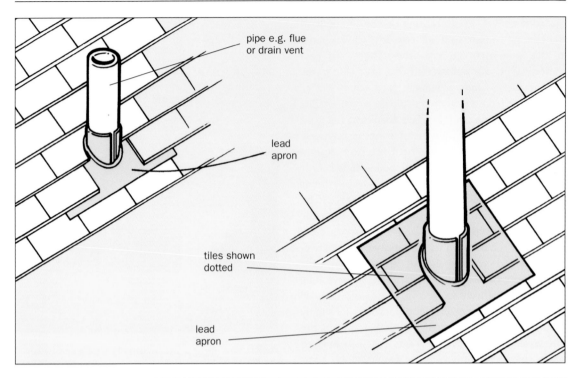

pipe e.g. flue
or drain vent

lead
apron

tiles shown
dotted

lead
apron

ABOVE: **Flashing
around a pipe
penetrating a
roof.**

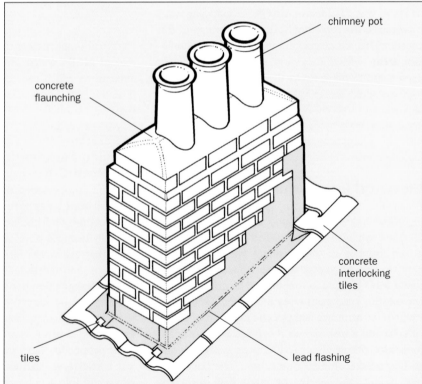

chimney pot

concrete
flaunching

concrete
interlocking
tiles

tiles

lead flashing

RIGHT: **Flashing
detail around a
brick chimney.**

and only used for storage. Even a small amount of water can cause long-term damage once the new rooms have been created, so it is sensible to get the condition of the flashing checked.

Chimneys are also prone to losing their pointing externally and very occasionally the walls are not sound below the line of the roof as well. The consequences of the latter are serious if carbon monoxide is leaking through the walls of the chimney and so should also be checked thoroughly. If the chimney is not being used the best solution is probably to remove it altogether, at least down to the floor level, but this can significantly alter the appearance of the house from the outside. If you are in a conservation area, you will need approval from the planning department to demolish a chimney.

Drainage

There are two main types of drainage to be considered – run-off from the roof, known as surface water, and the product of sinks, wash basins and toilets, known as foul water. In newer properties in the UK, the foul water and surface water are directed to separate underground drainage systems, known as a separate system. In older properties the two types of water run into the same drain and this is known as a combined system. Even if the system is combined below ground, the Building Regulations require that foul and surface water must be kept separate above ground. However tempting it may be to run the outlet from a sink into a nearby rainwater downpipe rather than create a new foul drainpipe, it is not permissible and may generate unpleasant smells around the house.

Surface water drainage will hopefully not be affected at all by the conversion, unless there are major changes to the shape of the existing roof. New dormers need gutters, but these can usually be drained straight on to the existing roof. If the area of the roof does not increase, there will not be any extra surface water running through to the drains.

If new bathrooms or toilets are being created in the roofspace, getting the drainage to the existing system can be a major challenge and may even require a new drain to be laid below ground, with a new connection and manhole. It is possible to run drains almost horizontally through the house and quite often a bit of careful planning can allow you to connect to an existing soil pipe. If you hit the worst case and it is not possible to reach the existing drains, for example because the staircase location blocks the way, an alternative is to use a pump. This works by pumping the waste water and other products from bathrooms to a high level and then through a relatively narrow plastic pipe at a slight gradient.

SPECIFICATIONS

The construction of a building is planned and described in two ways. Apart from drawings showing how the different elements of the building goes together, there is written information that describes or specifies the type, quality and description of all the materials and components that are shown in the drawings. The importance of specifications should not be underestimated. The drawings are required by building control and larger-scale drawings may also be produced if you employ an architect to design the project for you. But drawings alone do not determine the quality of the finished job. Many people converting their homes have been disappointed on completion because they either did not look closely enough at the specifications, or they were never provided when the builder was taken on.

It is particularly important to ensure that the specifications are sufficiently detailed when comparing builders' prices. A very brief specification that does not fully describe the fixtures, fittings and finishes leaves plenty of scope for the builder to cut costs once the price has been agreed and the job is underway. Items not listed in the specification may be charged as extras and any increases in quality above the most basic may also lead to a demand for more money.

If there are any items that are particularly important to you, such as the style or model of the wash basin or the type of ironmongery, they should all be agreed before a fixed price quotation is accepted.

Typical Items to be Included in a Detailed Specification

If the items listed are not described in your builder's quotation, it is reasonable to ask for them to be specified before signing on the dotted line, particularly if they involve aspects of the work that are important to you. *See* Chapter 7 on contracts for the meaning of some these items.

Excavations (if needed for new drains and so on)
- Can any waste spoil be disposed of on site?
- Topsoil to be retained and reused on site?

Floors
- Will they be boarded in chipboard or tongue and groove softwood?
- Is underfloor heating required?

Walls
- Will they be timber or metal studwork?
- High level of insulation or minimum required by Building Regulations?
- Will dormer wall be clad in tiles, lead, render or formed from brick?
- Any specialist brickwork, for example type of sills and heads, dentil courses.

Pitched Roof
- How will the roof structure be adapted?
- Will any new roof tiles closely match the existing roof covering?
- What is the tile material, for example clay or concrete?
- Tile colour and type, for example plain or interlocking?

- High level of insulation or minimum required by Building Regulations?
- Valleys formed from lead or plastic?
- Will any service penetrations through the roof be concealed with special tiles or just pass through and be visible?
- How will the roof be accessed? Will proper scaffold be erected or will the roofers try to access the roof just from ladders? The latter may be against health and safety rules.

Flat Roof
- Standard construction or specialist, such as single ply, zinc or lead.
- How will the roof be protected from the sun, for example white chippings or reflective paint?

Internal Doors
- Construction, for example flush, pressed fibreboard, natural timber, mortice, tenon and wedged.
- Finish, for example self-finished, painted, stained or varnished.
- Ironmongery type, for example brushed aluminium, brass finish, plastic.
- Openers, for example handles or knobs.
- Locks, for example mortice locks, bolts.

External Doors and Windows
- Construction, for example UPVC, softwood, hardwood.
- Glazing, for example safety glass, triple glazing, argon-filled units.
- Style, for example plain casements, cottage style, Georgian, real or fake leaded lights.
- Ironmongery finish and type.

Joinery
- Staircase construction, for example natural timber or MDF and plywood.
- Staircase joinery style – handrails, banisters and newel posts, open or cut strings.
- Fitted cupboards and airing cupboard construction and appearance.
- Skirtings, trims and architraves – style, profile and material, for example MDF or softwood.

Sanitary Goods
- Manufacturer and model number where possible.
- Taps, for example chrome, brass finish, monoblock, thermostatic mixer.
- WC suite lid type.
- Vanity units.

Heating System
- Will the existing system be thoroughly checked?
- Can the existing boiler cope with the extra demand of new rooms to heat?
- If new boiler required, what type, for example combination, mains pressured, condensing?
- Will the boiler system have rust inhibitor added when refilled after the work is completed?
- Heating method, for example underfloor, radiators, air blown, perimeter heating.
- Will all work to the heating system or gas supply pipes be carried out by a qualified plumber? Note: this is actually required by law. The approved body that regulates a plumber's work used to be called CORGI. This name is quite well known but it no longer applies – the regulating body since 1 April 2009 has been Capita Gas Registration and Ancillary Services Limited, which runs a scheme that is now called 'Gas Safe'.

Electrical Services
- Number of all sockets, lights, and switches for each room, located on a plan if possible.
- Types of fitting, for example security lights, wall mounted, pendants, bulkhead fittings.
- Special circuits, for example for electric cooker.
- Other wiring, for example computer networking cable, TV sockets, security system.
- Work must be carried out by a qualified electrician. Test certificate to be issued on completion. As with gas installations the Electrical Contractors Association, which used to be the body that governed the certification process, has been replaced since April 2009 by a subsidiary company of that organization called EC Certification Limited. This is the name that any certification should be issued under.

Surface Finishes
- Is decoration of all surfaces inside and out included?
- Will all making good of existing surfaces damaged by the work be included?
- Walls – papered or painted?
- Ceiling – any textured finishes?
- Flooring, for example quarry tiles, laminated, carpeted.
- Wall tiling, where and to what extent?

External Works
- Will any areas of the garden and land surrounding the house be made good if they are affected by the works?
- What is the location of areas available to the contractor for storage?

CHAPTER 7

Getting the Loft Conversion Built

Once you have obtained the necessary local authority approvals and found the right builder for your project you will be almost ready for building work to start. But there are still one or two issues that need to be addressed first. The price that you have been quoted may be higher than you were hoping for or can afford and some negotiation may be necessary; you should have a proper written contract that clarifies the services that the builder is going to provide for you; and you can start preparing for the demands and disruption that will be inflicted on you as a result of major construction work being carried out on the house where you and your family are living.

Most conversions are a job for the professionals. Room Maker Loft Conversions

BUDGET

However carefully and cautiously you plan your project, there is still a risk that you will be over budget when you finally get quotes from builders. This is one of the reasons that it is essential to ensure that those prices have all been prepared on exactly the same basis, using the same highly detailed information. This way, you can compare the quotes directly and decide which company you will pick to negotiate a price reduction. Always bear in mind that items that are not adequately described and leave a builder to make an assumption will make a price comparison more difficult. The builder who submitted the lowest quotation may simply have assumed a much lower quality than the others and the price will therefore be deceptively low. It is worth asking the chosen builder for a price reduction but reputable builders

are unlikely to do this without some negotiation. You may get them to reduce their price if you omit some of the work, or reduce the quality of the specification. If the two lowest contractors are very close in price, or some other factor, such as a shorter build programme, makes them equally attractive to you it is reasonable to discuss cost reductions with both – provided that they are both aware of what is going on.

If a builder who is not the lowest asks what the others have tendered and then offers to undercut them, it is advisable to avoid further dealings with this firm. Such tactics are dishonest and disreputable and it is a sure sign of the way in which that builder is likely to run the rest of their business, including the work to your house.

If you do go over budget, be reassured that you are in good company, including not only many others with home improvement projects but also teams of experienced professional advisors working on large construction projects. Do not panic. It is possible to reduce cost significantly, unless you have been grossly over-optimistic.

Over-Specification

One common reason that a project goes over budget is that the specification is too high. In other words you have chosen too many nice things. This is an understandable misjudgement before you know exactly how much they will actually cost. If this is your problem, it is painful but relatively easy to solve. You will have to omit some things and reduce the cost of others. The last items to cut are the construction and materials that make up the main fabric of the building, unless they are particularly extravagant. The cost of finishes and fixtures can be reduced and they can be upgraded at a later date. The main structure is very difficult to alter once built.

Wrong Prices Tendered or Wrong Contractors Selected

Sometimes not enough tenders are returned, or the ones that are come from contractors who are not that keen to get the work and are priced unrealistically high (a practice known as 'cover pricing'). Re-tendering to a fresh set of contractors can help in these situations. It is a step worth taking if the prices are so high you will otherwise have to give up on a project. All you have to lose is the cost of a few weeks' wait, but you may get better prices the second time around.

Inflation

Even the chancellor of the exchequer (whatever he may say) does not really know exactly what will happen to the economy between the start of your project, when you prepare your initial budget calculation, and later, when you find out what builders are proposing to charge you. If you lose out due to a rising market you may be able to get your mortgage provider to make up the difference.

How to Save Money

Decorations and Finishes
- Reduce the number of different colours and finishes.
- Take out any special finishes, use plain white finishes and do the internal decoration yourself.
- Omit more expensive floor coverings, such as natural wood, and use basic vinyl and carpet until you can afford to upgrade.

Internal Doors and Ironmongery
- Cheap internal doors can be replaced very easily in the future, one at a time. Keep the better doors for where they are most on show, for example off the landing and hallway, and use cheap flush doors elsewhere.

Joinery, Skirtings and Trims
- If there is any decorative joinery make it less elaborate.
- Replace hardwood with softwood, or, if it is painted and indoors, with MDF.
- Built-in cupboards and wardrobes can be taken out of the contract and temporarily replaced with free-standing flat-pack or second-hand furniture.

Electrical Installations
- The difference between a desirable electrical layout and a serviceable one is often significant. Reduce the number of sockets and mini spots.
- Use cheaper light fittings that can be replaced as long as the concealed wiring is in the right position.

Sanitary Ware
- This is often an item where fantasy can overtake rational thought and the reduction of the specification to cheaper models is relatively easy to achieve.

Special Features
- If you selected underfloor heating, solar panels or surround-sound TV, reassess how badly you want them.

LEGAL MATTERS

Before signing a building contract, it is worth appreciating the essential legal principles that will be in operation. The government passes new laws and case law changes over time, but in the UK the interpretation of legal rights and who has transgressed them is often a matter of judgement and opinion rather than a black-and-white issue. Consequently the advice contained in this book is very general and should not be used as a basis for sorting out a specific legal issue. If there is any doubt, consult a solicitor.

Some Definitions

There are definitions that are useful to know when dealing with a building contract of any kind.

Quotation A fixed price for the work that is to be carried out. To be effective, it has to be tied into a detailed description of the work, usually in the form of drawings and specification. If this is not done, the builders are free to reduce the specification should they wish to increase their profit. The ideal is to get a quotation for all the construction work, based on an accurate, thorough set of specifications and drawings. This is not always possible where an existing building is involved, because some aspects are unknown until the existing construction is exposed. However, the quoted price should not increase unless the builder can show that either you have changed your mind, or the extra work could not reasonably have been predicted when it was calculated.

Estimate This is an approximation by the builder of the cost of the work. The price is not legally binding if you employ a builder based on an estimate. A contract based on an estimate carries a lot of risk for you, because once on site the cost for the job can be increased significantly and, unless you can prove they are particularly unreasonable, you will be obliged to pay up.

Employer Although you may be referred to as a 'client' or 'customer', in a strict legal sense you are the employer under the contract. If you have a spouse, partner or someone else who wishes to take equal responsibility they will only be a joint employer if you both sign the contract, or if they are identified in it with your signature being 'on behalf of' yourself and the other person.

Contractor (sometimes called the 'main contractor') This is whoever you employ directly to do building work for you – the builder. This includes people or companies that have specialist trades, such as plumbers, plasterers and electricians, who would otherwise be subcontractors if they fitted the description below.

Subcontractor This is anyone who works on your house who is employed by the main contractor rather than directly by you. This does not include employees of the main contractor. For example, a plumbing subcontractor may be employed on a fixed price by a contractor who does not have these skills in house, but a joiner may work for the builder as an employee with a weekly wage.

Agent This is someone who is named in the contract as being able to issue instructions on your behalf. If you employ an architect to manage a project they are usually named as the agent. There should only be one person or company named and all your instructions should be issued by them, rather than you.

Contract This is a legal agreement usually between two parties. In the UK it does not have to be in writing unless it involves the exchange of land. So if you ask a builder to do a job for you after he has told you how much it will cost, you may have agreed a binding contract even if there is no letter or contract confirming it. Because verbal contracts, by definition, have no permanent record, they can easily lead to disputes. Many disputes are caused unnecessarily because there is not enough detail in the written contract. A simple letter from the builder stating a price is inadequate for this type of project.

Party to a contract The employer or the contractor – that is you or the builder.

Guarantee If the building work is the subject of a guarantee and is substandard, you will be compensated in some way, usually with a payment or the work being put right at no cost. Guarantees are only as good as the company backing them, so an independent guarantee from a large insurer is valuable, but a thirty-year guarantee from a small limited company that could go into liquidation or be wound up well within that period is worth little in the long term.

Variation This is an aspect of the building work that is changed or added from what was agreed when the contract was signed. It may lead to an extra cost or a saving or neither.

Agreeing the Building Contract

Never, ever agree to engage a main contractor without a proper written contract from an independent source. It is not necessary to employ a solicitor to draft one especially for you – there are standard contracts available, some of which have been developed by committees with representatives from all the main bodies involved in the construction industry. This organization is called the Joint Contracts Tribunal, or JCT. Their contracts are fair to all sides and are specifically designed to anticipate the most likely problems and stipulate how they should be dealt with. Do not use a contract prepared on behalf of one of the contractor organizations however keen the builder is for you to do so. Unsurprisingly, these tend to favour the contractor heavily in comparison to the JCT and other independently prepared varieties. Unfortunately, a simple letter stating that the work will be done for a stated price is wholly inadequate in these litigation-obsessed times and the lack of detail that results stacks the odds very heavily in favour of the contractor.

There are three main JCT contracts, available online or by ordering from most bookshops:

JCT Minor Work Building Contract This contract is only appropriate if there is an architect or similar professional running the contract on your behalf. You cannot use this contract without naming someone to act on your behalf in this way and it should never be used in any other circumstances, for example, nominating yourself as the contract administrator. It is really for larger projects, but can be used for smaller jobs if necessary.

JCT Building Contract for a Home Owner/Occupier This excellent document is designed for a wide variety of domestic alteration projects and has an award from the Plain English Campaign. It comes in two varieties, one for use with an architect or similar consultant and one for use without this assistance. It includes all the essential requirements of a building contract but does not deal with some of the problems that may arise with larger projects – for example there is no provision for deducting money if the contractor overruns the agreed date for completing.

JCT Contract for Home Repairs and Maintenance This is for very small-scale repairs or building works. It allows for an hourly rate to be paid or a lump sum, and for only one payment at the end of the project. It is not recommended for work that is likely to take more than a month to complete.

On signing the contract, the employer (you) takes on certain duties, mainly concerned with payment, but also takes the ultimate responsibility and risk for the contract. Much of the management work can be delegated to an architect if you choose to employ one to help on site. In this respect having work done to your home is very different from buying a house from a developer and being simply 'a customer'. After you have signed a contract, and everyone is clear about their responsibilities, it can be put away, and hopefully there will be no need to refer to it again. But if there is a dispute it will give you much more security and a good chance of resolving the problem without having to resort to lengthy and expensive legal action.

Tip

Make sure that you explain to builders invited to tender which contract you will want them to use, and the main points of it, such as liquidated damages and so on. Otherwise the selected contractor may use the introduction of your contract terms as the basis to renegotiate the price upwards.

Unfair Terms

Assuming that the building work is being carried out on your home, and that you are not a construction professional, the UK law should give you extra protection in the form of the Unfair Terms in Consumer Contracts Regulations 1999. Because you are not a professional developer, the law recognizes that you do not have specialist knowledge of the design and construction process and also places more onus on the people that you employ to do the work to explain the implications of the contract and to ensure that you agree to them.

All the contract terms should be clear to you and most importantly, if a nasty catch has been concealed in the small print, the courts will not enforce it. Clauses printed on the back of a con-

---

Key Terms of a Building Contract

The following are some of the issues that should always be included in a building contract for a project of any size or complexity.

The parties Who you are, and the name of the builder. You may think this is obvious, but some builders have more than one company. And sometimes parties to contracts have used the fact that they have been wrongly described in a contract to avoid their liabilities.

Identification of the works A summary of the scope of the works is particularly important if the contractor takes on other work outside this contract, for example landscaping.

Contract documents It is essential to record the specific drawings, by number and revision letter, as well as the version of the specification. These may be different from the tender documents if there have been revisions to price since tenders were received.

Agent If you are using an architect or similar professional to manage the contract on your behalf, you must make clear what powers they have in the contract with the builders. You should also have a matching, separate written agreement with this agent.

Contract sum This has to tie in directly with the contract documents, and must reflect any post-tender changes. If it is a fixed price, this should be clearly and unambiguously stated.

Project duration and liquidated damages Many of the problems that arise between employer and builder are due to late completion of the work. The contract should state the time that work is to start, and when it is to be finished. A useful clause to have is one that states that any unwarranted delays will give you the right to make deductions from money due to the builder, usually a set amount for each week of overrun. These deductions are called 'liquidated damages'. This description means that they are set at a pre-agreed level and cannot be altered without the agreement of you and your builder, so you cannot ask for more that the stated figure. The amount of liquidated damages must be a reasonable calculation of the expected costs – if you pick a very high figure as an incentive to the builder to finish on time, the courts will not enforce it. Liquidated damages are sometimes wrongly referred to as 'penalties'.

Payment terms Contractors are usually paid every four weeks, or at specific stages in the job, for example when the external shell is completed to make the roof watertight again. A small amount should be held back until the end of the job, usually 5 per cent, and of this a smaller amount should be kept until six months after work is finished (usually 2.5 per cent of the total bill). These are all standard requirements in typical building contracts used in the UK construction industry.

Variations These are items of the work that are omitted, changed or added after the contract has been signed.

Insurance The contractor must have and maintain adequate insurance, but this may not be extended to cover items that belong exclusively to you and are stored on site, unless you ask for it. It is essential to talk to your own insurers and tell them the details of the contract before the work starts, and ensure that there are no gaps between the cover that the builder holds and your own.

Solving disputes There should be a description of what the parties can do if there is a dispute and what to do if it cannot be settled.

---

tractor's quotations in small, faded grey letters that say something along the lines of 'we reserve the right to increase our prices during the course of the works and the client will be bound to pay any such increase when it becomes due' or 'we accept no liability for any of the materials or goods supplied as part of this contract' (both real-life examples) are unlikely to be enforced should you choose to disregard them. These clauses are unfair and not a part of usual business practice in the construction industry. Also, if a term of the contract is written in obscure legal jargon and is not understandable to the average person, it will be difficult for the contractor to hold you to it by taking you to court.

Sale of Goods Act and Supply of Goods and Services Act

There is a certain kind of legislation that is designed to add extra terms to a contract between a consumer and a supplier of products. These are called 'implied terms' and automatically apply to a contract even if they were not discussed or written into it. The above two pieces of legislation apply to the supply of goods and services and therefore to a building contract for work to your home. It gives you basic rights that are not unreasonable to expect. For example, the goods supplied should match the description you agreed when the contract was signed, should be in good condition without defects, are safe, and should be able to do the job that is expected of them. Services must be provided with reasonable skill and care and the provider is entitled to reasonable payment. Some unscrupulous suppliers or service providers may try to exclude these conditions. If they do at the time the contract was agreed this would not be enforceable, thanks to the legislation that is designed to prevent unfair terms.

PREPARING FOR WORK TO START

After many months of preparation you will reach the final and most crucial stage of the project, when building work begins. The success or failure of the construction stage will probably have been

If the whole house is to be surrounded by scaffold and there are also major internal alterations to other floors, would you really want to stay in the house during the building work? Julian Owen Associates Architects

decided well before you reach this point. Things will go wrong, because that is what happens on a building site – even the most thorough planning cannot cover every eventuality. But if you accept that there will be problems, and have an idea of how you will approach them, you have every chance of dealing with them successfully. All of this section applies if you are using a single main contractor, but much of it also applies if you are self-managing separate trades or doing a large proportion of the work yourself.

Once the contract is signed, you are almost ready for building work to start. But there are a few matters to be dealt with first.

Will You Move out of the House?

You will hopefully have made this decision much earlier, but may have modified your plans in the light of the tenders that you received. If the work involves more than just the loft and particularly if it affects all the key rooms – the kitchen, bathroom and toilets – it will be much less stressful and more comfortable if you can afford to move out for most of the building programme. If there is not enough in your budget, or you are concerned about security, or it would prove inconvenient in some other way, you will need to plan the programme of work carefully and will want a sympathetic builder. In most cases, it is possible to rig up basic facilities, or phase the work to keep a minimum number of rooms available to live in.

Tip

Regardless of what the builder says, always allow for at least a 20 per cent overrun on the completion date and have a contingency plan if it is longer. If you are building or managing the project yourself instead of using a contractor, allow for a 50 per cent overrun and have a contingency plan if you run completely out of time or enthusiasm or find you have less skill at building than you believe.

Start a Site File

During construction, efficient management of information will be helpful. If you have not already done so, create a project file, with the following sections for correspondence and notes:

- Contact details of everyone involved (on a sheet at the front)
- Copy of contract documents
- Site meetings
- Client
- Architect
- Engineer
- Contractor
- Subcontractors
- Planning department
- Building control and Regulations
- Utilities – gas, water, drainage, electricity, telephones, IT
- Suppliers and manufacturers

Pre-Contract Meeting

Before a contractor occupies the site, it is a good idea to have a meeting to discuss the way that the project is to be run, which can be combined with the signing of the contract at the end. It is impor-

tant that you are reassured that this project, which is to be run in your name, will be well managed and will cause as little inconvenience to your neighbours as possible. Most important of all, the site must be as safe as possible. The builder, agent (if there is one) and client should all be represented.

The best-run projects are based on good communication between all parties, and this is the time to arrange some regular project meetings, where you should make notes and record important decisions in writing. You do not necessarily have to be present at all of them if you are using an architect to manage on your behalf, but in that case make sure that you are kept informed of all the important discussions.

Health and Safety on Site

A building site is one of the most dangerous environments to work in and one of the most dangerous places on a building site is at high level. There have been many deaths and countless

A roof is one of the most dangerous places to be at work. Julian Owen Associates Architects

---

Standard Agenda for Pre-Contract Meeting

Introductions Full names and contact details of everyone present.

Contract
- Commencement and completion dates
- Programme. Detailed breakdown of each trade and subcontractor.
- Insurance. Ask for photocopies of the relevant documents.

Local Authority
- Planning approval. If is needed check it is in place and that any conditions have been satisfied. If it is not needed, check that confirmation of this has been received in writing from the local authority planning department.
- Building Regulations. Check that full plans approval has been received and the building control officer will be notified that work is about to start.

Site
- Sign boards. Where will they be erected, if at all?
- Storage. This can be a significant issue.
- Extent of the working area.

Communications
- Contractor contact on site. Name and mobile phone number.
- Client contact. Which member of your family is to be the main contact?
- If there is an agent, note that instructions will be issued through them to the builder.

Information
- Information required. The contractor may need further drawings or specifications or decisions from you to progress the work.
- Details of subcontractors – names and addresses.

Payment
Every four weeks or at agreed stages in the work.

Health and Safety
- What measures will the contractor have in place to manage health and safety?
- Is the site easily accessible to children and other members of the general public, and will steps be taken to keep it safe and secure?

---

injuries suffered by people falling from a height or having things being dropped on to them from above. It is essential that any builder who works on your property complies with current health and safety requirements. The basic requirements are:

- Anyone on the site where there is work going on higher than waist level should be wearing a proper hard hat.
- Scaffolding should be properly constructed and certified as such by the specialist firm who erect it.
- Anyone on site should be wearing safety boots.
- Anyone working at height should be protected from risk of falling, for example by secure handrails and toe boards attached to the scaffolding or safety harness.

- No one, including the family, should be allowed into the area of the work without complying with these rules.
- Young children should never be allowed on to a building site and it should be secure enough to prevent them from easily gaining access when the site is unattended.

It is important to let the contractor know well in advance that you expect the health and safety rules to be followed and that they should allow for this in their quotes.

The sad truth is that you may well find that some or all of the above rules are blatantly ignored by your contractor. This is often the case and it is the main reason that the casualty departments are regularly kept busy by the construction industry. Not following the health and safety rules saves money and it may be that part of the benefit of that saving is passed on to you, the customer. But before you take the money and shut your eyes to the increased risk of accidents, think about the possible consequences for your family. If that is not enough to worry you, think about the risk that you will run if the health and safety inspector decides that you are complicit in any breaches of the criminal law that applies if someone else is injured or killed.

Party Wall Act

If the work that you are about to undertake affects a shared wall with your neighbour the party wall legislation will apply to your project. Typically the wall between the two roofspaces may be affected, particularly if there are gaps around the junctions between the tops of the walls and the underside of the roof. These gaps will have to be filled for fire protection and also to provide sound insulation. The best source of information on the Party Wall Act is to be found on the government website www.communities.gov.uk/publications/planningandbuilding/partywall. A copy of an explanatory booklet can be downloaded or it can be obtained by post for free by ringing the publications telephone number (0300 123 1124).

If the Party Wall Act does apply to your project, your best option is to obtain written consent from

Work starts on a project with the first delivery of materials. You should agree in advance where they are to be stored.
Room Maker Loft Conversions

A shared wall between you and your neighbour may cause the Party Wall Act procedure to be applied. Julian Owen Associates Architects

your neighbour. If this is not forthcoming, you may need professional help to settle any disagreements. If the procedure applies and you do not follow it, the worst case is that an uncooperative or awkward neighbour could get an injunction to stop work from proceeding until the due process has been followed.

Starting to Build

Do not be surprised if at 8am on the day work is due to start, no one arrives on site. The contractor should be committed to a completion date and has a right to start on the contractually agreed date, but not an obligation. A diligent builder will make sure that the last job is properly finished before moving onto the next – an attitude that you may be grateful for when it is your turn. A telephone call at 8.30am demanding to know why there are no workmen on site will not help diplomatic relations.

Architects' Certificates

There are various certificates that are either required or can be requested in the course of the building work. If you have an architect or other consultant managing your project on site there are several types of certificate that may be produced.

Issued by: Julian Owen Associates Architects

JULIAN OWEN ASSOCIATES
ARCHITECTS
27a Queens Road,
Beeston, Nottingham
NG9 2BO
t 0115 922 9831
f 0115 922 4636
e enquiries@julianowen.co.uk
www.julianowen.co.uk

Employer: Peter Griffin
Address: 12 Spooner Street, Nottingham NG9 2AB

Contractor: A Smith Builders
Address: 99 Cone Street
Denton, Borcetshire

**Interim
Certificate**

Job Ref: 1213

Works: Loft Conversion
Situated at: 12 Spooner Street, Nottingham NG9 2AB

Certificate No: 04

Issue Date: 08/12/08

Valuation Date: 12/11/08

Start on Site: 1st April 2008

Contract Sum: £37,732.00

We certify that, under the terms of the above mentioned contract, payment is due from the Employer to the Contractor as detailed below:

	£
Total Value of the Works:..........	£52,200.00
Less Retention of 5%.................	£2,610.00
Balance......................................	£49,590.00
Less Total Previously Certified..	£35,845.40
Net Amount for Payment...........	£13,744.60

In Words: Thirteen Thousand Seven Hundred and Fourty Four Pounds and Sixty Pence.

All Amounts Exclusive of VAT

Signed: _____   Date: 08/12/08

(On Behalf of Julian Owen Associates Architects)

Distribution	Original to:		Copies to:				
	[*] Employer		[*] Contractor		☐ Engineer		[*] File
			☐ Sub Contractor		☐ Quantity S		☐

This is not a Tax Invoice

JOAA2003

A typical payment certificate as issued by architects. Julian Owen Associates Architects

Five Golden Rules for a Building Project

- Never pay for any work, materials or fittings in advance except for expensive specialist items.
- Agree amounts and dates for payment before work starts.
- Make regular checks on the work for quality control.
- Always record key events in writing and ensure that the builder receives a copy.
- Make the builders quote a completion date and hold them to it.

Interim Certificates

The architect issues these at regular intervals throughout the building programme, either every four weeks or when key stages in the building are reached. Interim certificates have only one purpose. Once issued by the architect, you have to pay the stated amount to the contractor for the work that he has completed to date. Five per cent is deducted from the value of the work certified as completed, and you retain this until the end of the job.

Interim certificates help you to plan your cash flow, but most of all they ensure that the contractor knows that his progress and workmanship are being closely monitored.

Practical Completion Certificates

The date when the affected areas of the house can be reoccupied is crucial. This is usually referred to as 'practical completion' and should be recorded in the contract you signed with the builder. Some contracts state that it is for the architect to decide whether or not this completion date has been achieved. If it has been achieved, the practical completion certificate can be issued. If there is a liquidated damages clause, and the contractor has not provided a good reason why the completion is later than agreed, you have the option of deducting money in compensation, although this is only recommended as a last resort.

Whether or not you use an architect, you can build in a safeguard against any outstanding items

not being completed, or hidden defects not immediately apparent appearing at a later date. Release half of the 5 per cent you have been holding back and keep the remaining 2.5 per cent for six months. During this time, any defects that become apparent have to be made good before the final amount is paid over.

Final Certificate

The final certificate is normally issued after six months of occupation. Before the architect signs it, the contractor must make good any defects or errors that may have become apparent after you moved in. He is then entitled to the final 2.5 per cent of the contract value.

Other Certificates

The certificates listed above are all issued by architects. In addition to these, there are several other kinds of certificate that you should be aware of, as follows.

Completion Certificate

Building control officers will issue a completion certificate at the end of a project, but sometimes only if they are asked to when the full plans application was made. This is an essential document when you come to sell the house, so always ask for it and keep it safe. However, should it be shown

A final certificate is issued six months after the work has been handed over, so that you can live in and use the space before being sure that it is defect-free. The Velux Company Ltd

that the building control officer has somehow failed to spot work that is not in accordance with the regulations, you are unlikely to be able to get any form of compensation.

Warranties/Guarantees

Some manufacturers provide warranties or guarantees for their products, which are worth having, especially if the company is large and well established. Should the material or product be defective, it may be easier to claim on this guarantee than it is to track down a builder. They are invariably qualified in some way, usually to the effect that the installation by the builder and the use to which it has been put has to be strictly in accordance with the manufacturer's recommendations. In reality, this allows a lot of scope for insurers to avoid paying out. If one of these warranties is available, make sure that it is made out in your name, not that of the builder's.

Subcontractors may also issue guarantees. These are fairly meaningless unless they are underwritten by a third-party insurer of sufficient size and reliability for you to be sure that they will still be around for thirty years, when the guarantee finally runs out. The terms under which the guarantee will pay out should also be scrutinized – often catastrophic failure is needed before this will happen, as opposed to simple poor performance. If a guarantee is from the installer, it is only effective whilst that company remains in business. If the owners wind it up after a couple of years and start another similar but separate business, the guarantee will be worthless.

WHAT IF SOMETHING GOES WRONG ON SITE?

One thing that is certain with any building project is that not all things will go according to plan. Part of your management strategy for the project should assume that this is the case. With careful planning, the right advice and a bit of luck, nothing serious will go wrong. If it does, and you are at risk of being out of pocket, you will need to take action. The best solution is to keep on speaking terms with everyone involved, get the problem resolved before you apportion blame and try to negotiate a solution that involves the offending party compensating you in some way. If you have used one of the standard contracts, there will be provisions that set out what you can do if you reach an impasse. For example, you can start an adjudication, which is a quick, if often temporary, fix. The alternative might be to embark on legal action, which is far more lengthy and expensive, and should be a very last resort, ideally not to be embarked on before the work has been completed.

The Top Five Risks and How to Deal With Them

Going over Budget

Most projects end up costing more than was hoped for at the beginning. There are many pressures on the budget (not least your desire to achieve the best possible result) and it is an impossible job to predict it accurately in the early stages of a project. Careful planning and thorough preparation can significantly reduce the risks, as well as ensuring that you have a watertight contract and a reputable builder. If you hit unexpected extras in the course of the work, you will have to use funds from your contingencies. If these are not enough, you may have to do some negotiating to reduce the specification or scale of the work, or carry out some of it yourself.

Delayed Start or Excessive Delay on Site

Sometimes there are genuine reasons for the contractor not coping, especially if it is a small business and it relies on one or two people to keep the operation running. If you think that this is the case, confront the problem and try to agree revised dates, rather than letting things drift. It is not unheard of for a contractor to shift resources to another project in the last few weeks because there is often more profit at the beginning of a new job than the end of an old one, particularly if they have underestimated the time and cost. If you think that this is happening, do not wait for things to slip to a serious stage before complaining and do not accept vague reassurances. Insist on a revised programme and confirm your concerns in writing to the most senior person in the firm.

Poor-Quality Workmanship

Any building work can only be as good as the person on site doing it. But even the most conscientious worker will not produce their best if they are not properly supervised. All building sites need a robust foreman present every day to check progress and stop bad work from being left or concealed. This is a growing problem now that most builders do not have many full-time employees but instead rely on subcontractors, who may have less motivation or skill than the contractor's own staff. You can employ an architect to make spot inspections as work progresses, but this is not always cost-effective on a small project. You are entitled to good-quality workmanship and should insist on it. If a contractor is not supervising adequately, or trying to pass off bad work in the hope that you will not see it, you are entitled to delay paying for those aspects of the work until they have been put right.

Poor-Quality Materials

This may not be the contractor's fault if you have either not specified the type or quality beforehand, or you have chosen a contractor whose price is unusually low. You should make it clear at the start if there is something that must be from a particular manufacturer or at least suggest a name, followed by 'or equivalent' so that you are not tying them down to one possibly overpriced supplier, but setting a level of quality expected. If something is not of sufficient quality in your opinion, proving it is not always an easy matter. One way is to find an objective standard of quality from a respected trade association or an independent organization such as the British Standards Institution (BSI) or the National House-Building Council (NHBC).

Unreasonable Expectations

Of course, this would not apply to readers of this book, but some building contracts get into serious problems because the homeowner is unreasonable, demanding a far higher standard than the particular builder who has been employed would normally provide. If you expect near perfection this is not in itself unreasonable, provided that you make this very clear when you ask for prices and are prepared to pay for it. Not many builders who carry out small projects to alter private houses can achieve excellence in everything that they do – the old adage mentioned earlier that 'you can have any two out of price, quality and speed' is very true. If you want the very best quality you will have to seek out a builder with high standards and quite rightly pay a premium for it. If you try to apply these standards to the average reliable, responsible small works building contractor for an average price, without warning them beforehand, the result will be misery all around.

The Contractor

If you are unhappy with the contractor, bear in mind that unless you are very near the end of the project, it will be a major disaster for you if they walk off the job however much they are in the wrong. Get professional advice if you are not already using it. Ask the senior management to change the site operatives if you have a problem with an individual. If you or your architect decide to hold back payment, make sure that you follow the rules set out in the contract to the letter. If you want to prevent the contractor from continuing on site, do not do so without consulting a solicitor. However distressing it gets, as long as you are not paying anyone in advance, you should have the upper hand financially. Remember that the contractor has a lot to lose as well, and will be just as keen as you to set things right.

Your Professional Advisors

If you employ an architect, they must have professional indemnity insurance and a detailed, written appointment letter. Most non-architects are not so tightly regulated. Be clear what responsibilities you are delegating and the limitation of the service that is being provided. If a proper contract has been signed, it will give the options for resolving disputes and how to terminate your agreement. As with the contractor, it is essential to follow the procedures set out in the contract.

Legal Action

By far and away the best solution to a dispute is to reach a compromise with the other parties and move on. The alternative will involve financial risk and stress. Many disputes escalate because a personal battle develops between individuals who become locked in a struggle to prove they are right and the other side is wrong. In these circumstances it is very difficult to be objective, so if you feel that this situation is developing it is vital to get an independent, detached opinion. This may be from a friend or colleague experienced in these matters, or more formally from an architect or solicitor who is not directly involved.

Unfortunately, the legal processes do not decide disputes on the basis of who is right and who is wrong, but on which of the parties probably has the law on their side – quite a different thing all together. Someone can be entirely unreasonable, but if they can show that they have apparently acted within the contract you will not win a case against them. For this reason, if you are in a dispute it is vital to behave in a reasonable way, to follow the requirements of the contract and to make sure that you record what you do in writing to all parties. For example, if you refuse to allow a builder onto the site without following the procedure set out in your contract, you will place yourself on the wrong side of the law, regardless of how unreasonable the contractor's behaviour has been.

If things have deteriorated to the point that you are forced to abandon any hope of settling things amicably there are a number of legal avenues that you can take; the options are partly dependent on the wording of the contract.

There is a 'quick fix' solution, which has been designed especially for building contracts, called adjudication. This only applies to private householders if it is expressly mentioned in the contract. An adjudicator is nominated and both sides are given three or four weeks to convince this person, usually an experienced construction professional, of the merits of their case. The adjudicator will reach a decision, for example that one side is to pay the other some money, or that some of the work is defective. This decision has to be acted on immediately, but it is ignored and overridden if the

If you use the services of an architect or designer to certify the work on site, ensure that they are suitably qualified and carry indemnity insurance. Julian Owen Associates Architects

case goes to a court or arbitration (see below). Despite the short deadline and potential unfairness of this process, the vast majority of cases that are put before an adjudicator go no further once a decision has been reached. This probably happens because both sides have had a taste of the unpleasantness and expense of any kind of legal action and resign themselves to the loss that they are going to suffer. The dispute can go to adjudication even if it is not provided for in the contract so long as both sides agree to this.

If your contract has provision for it, you can put your case before an arbitrator. This person is trained and qualified to make decisions on legal disputes and it is usually an alternative to going to court. The arbitrator acts as a judge in many ways,

Once completion is reached, you still need to check for snags. The Velux Company Ltd

but has specialist knowledge about the construction industry and some flexibility regarding the running of the arbitration process. It was conceived as a cheaper and quicker way to resolve disputes than a full-blown court case, but in recent times has often turned out to take longer, and some legal experts advise avoiding it.

If your claim is valued at less than £5,000 (in 2009) you could consider the small claims court. This is a user-friendly procedure (as much as court can be) and you do not have to have a solicitor to represent you. If your claim is over this amount you will have to go to the county court or high court and accept the considerable cost that results.

If you would like some outside intervention but do not want to get tied up in legal knots, you could try alternative dispute resolution or mediation. This process needs the co-operation of the other party, and involves a trained professional who talks to both sides, establishes the common ground and tries to develop a compromise that both sides can live with. Some of the professional bodies, such as the Royal Institute of British Architects, offer this service as do independent bodies such as the Centre for Effective Dispute Resolution.

Needless to say, you should not try to halt a contract or start any kind of legal proceedings without getting advice from a solicitor with experience in construction disputes.

REACHING COMPLETION

The building work may have been continuously monitored by the builder's management team, yourself, the building control officer and possibly

---

Snagging Checklist

Pitched Roof
- Roof slates or tiles complete, undamaged, unmarked and properly bedded.
- Vent tiles/eaves in place, fly screens fitted.
- Main edges, such as the ridge and line of the eaves straight.
- Flashings in place and properly fixed, with adequate lap and wedged into brickwork.
- Weep holes above cavity trays, DPC and openings.
- Ventilation openings adequate.

Rainwater Drainage
- Valley gutters are clean and free from debris.
- Gutters and stop ends located correctly, sufficient brackets and falls in right directions.
- Gutters clear of rubbish.
- Roof underlay laps into gutter.

Brickwork
- Pointing complete, gaps created by scaffolding made good.
- Clean, no mortar splashes.
- Mortar and brickwork consistent in colour.
- Perpends (vertical joints between the individual bricks) are in line, one above the other.

Downpipes
- Fixed securely.
- Locations match the drawings.

Overflow Pipes
- Visible.
- Correct length.
- Sealed at exit point.

Windows and Doors Externally
- No chips or splits or other damage.
- Frames sealed at edges.
- Glass clean and not scratched.
- Beading securely fixed.

Ceilings
- Corners are straight.

an architect as well, but once the contractor tells you that the work is finished, arrange a formal inspection tour. You should have a defects period agreed, and hold a retention on any amount due, but once the builder leaves the site it is harder to get any faults put right quickly. In theory, you should not have to 'snag' a building, because it is supposed to be complete, but even if the work has been immaculate, your idea of a defect may not be seen as a fault by others. Unsurprisingly, the

Paintwork and Staining
- Finished with all coats applied, especially where hidden, for example on tops of doors, under window sills
- Free from patches.
- Cleaned down.
- Smooth surface, free of plasterboard joints, popped nail heads and cracks.

Plasterwork
- Smooth, even surfaces.
- Gaps made good around service penetrations.
- Junctions and corners straight.

Windows Internally
- Painted properly.
- Timberwork undamaged.
- No scratches or marks on the glass.
- Open and close smoothly.
- No distortion in the frame.
- Trickle ventilators working.
- Compliance with escape requirements on first floor and above.
- Window locks and keys available (if specified).

Doors Internally
- Painted properly.
- Timberwork undamaged.
- Open and shut when handle turned.
- Should not pull open without operating the handle.
- No distortion or twisting in the frame.
- Door has an equal gap around the frame.
- Ironmongery and locks clean and as specified and locks are working properly,

Skirtings and Architraves
- Level, with clean line along the top.
- Undamaged, with no dents or marks and painted properly.

Floor Finishes
- Tiling complete, even, regularly spaced and sealed at joints.

- Vinyl smooth and even with no bubbles or lumps.
- Clean.
- Timberboard surface floor smooth, clean and ready for carpet or other covering.
- No creaks (these will always gradually get worse if not picked up early).

Services
- Pipes supported with plenty of clips.
- Radiators securely fixed, clean, with bleed points accessible.
- Switches and sockets clean, level and secure.

Staircases
- Balustrading, newels, handrails securely fixed.
- Surface varnish or paint complete, clean and undamaged.
- Equal risers and goings.

Bathrooms
- All fittings clean, working and without chips or blemishes.
- Taps working.
- Toilets flush.
- Plugs and other attachments present.
- No leaks to plumbing.
- Worktop unblemished.
- Cupboard doors fitted square and secure.

Plumbing
- No leaks.
- Pipework securely fixed.
- No airlocks in pipe bends.

Electrical
- All fitted appliances working (such as cooker, heaters).
- Mechanical ventilation working.

Gas and Fires
- Appliances operate properly.
- Ventilation available as required by Building Regulations.

process of snagging can lead to disagreements, but it is not in your interests to fall out with the contractor at this stage. If the work has been of a good standard so far, a little tact will go a long way, but do not be afraid to insist if there is something that you are unhappy with. You will probably be looking at it every day for the next few years, and however trivial it may appear to anyone else, you will always see it. It is not necessarily a defence for the contractor that it has been there for several weeks or even months – any interim payments are not legally conclusive evidence that you or your architect have approved the work.

Less reputable foremen prefer to let a lot of snags go, get the client to do all the snagging and see what they can get away with. If there are a lot of snags, it is advisable to refuse to accept completion, ask the contractor to let you know when the building is really finished, then leave the meeting.

Before you let the contractor leave the site, ask for all the documents that will help you and future owners maintain the building, covering aspects such as:

- Heating
- Alarm system
- Appliances
- Electrical layout and fittings
- As-built drawings

Also make sure that you have the names and addresses of all the key suppliers and subcontractors, some of whom may agree to come back for routine maintenance.

You also need to be sure that all the necessary approvals and certificates are in place, along with any suppliers/manufacturer's guarantees, such as:

- Building Regulations Certificate (may be sent to you directly from the council)
- Gas appliances certified under the Capita Gas Registration and Ancillary Services Limited 'Gas Safe Register Scheme' (formerly CORGI)
- Electrical work certified under the EC Certification Limited certification process (formerly Electrical Contractors Association)

- Guarantees from suppliers of appliances
- Guarantees from suppliers of laminate and other specialist floors
- Warranties from any specialist features or components, such as built-in home cinema.

After Completion

Once the building work is agreed as 'practically complete' you can occupy it. But as you start to live in it, some defects or small faults will probably come to light that need to be rectified. A 2.5 per cent retention should be kept for six months after completion for what is called the 'latent defects period'. During this time any defects that arise as a result of the construction must be put right by the contractor.

Since signing the contract, there will have been changes and modifications to the design, unexpected extras and other matters that will have caused the original contract value to be amended.

Once the work is completed, it is time to relax and enjoy the new spaces that have been created. The Velux Company Ltd

The end result will be worth the effort. The Velux Company Ltd

It is not unusual for the contractor to still be calculating and agreeing these with you well into the defects liability period. Hopefully, by the time this period has ended, you will have agreed the amount due and a final account can be prepared to tie up all the loose ends. If the contractor has done a good job, worked hard, and delivered the project to you more or less on time, it is better not to haggle too much over minor items. At the end of the project, you should look at the whole picture. If you are satisfied with the completed project and it is at a reasonable price, the builder probably deserves to be paid without having to justify every extra cost in great detail.

RIGHT: **Your house will be changed for ever by loft conversion.** The Velux Company Ltd

CHAPTER 8

Two Examples of Successful Loft Conversion

ARCHITECT-DESIGNED CONVERSION OF A NOTTINGHAMSHIRE BUNGALOW

The existing bungalow from the front.
Julian Owen Associates Architects

The existing bungalow from the rear.
Julian Owen Associates Architects

The loft before conversion.
Julian Owen Associates Architects

This project is an illustration of a classic bungalow conversion. Originally built without any consideration of the need for a first floor, the simple roof spanning over the full depth of the plan was ideal for converting. All that was needed to be added to the original roof shape were two dormer windows, front and rear. The front dormer provides an extra bit of space for the larger bedroom and the rear dormer allows room for a small bathroom – an essential requirement to avoid midnight trips that will disturb the other occupants. The staircase was originally intended to run into the hallway by stealing space from the front bedroom. After some consideration, it was decided that the bedroom was not essential and so the stairwell was combined with that space by removing the wall

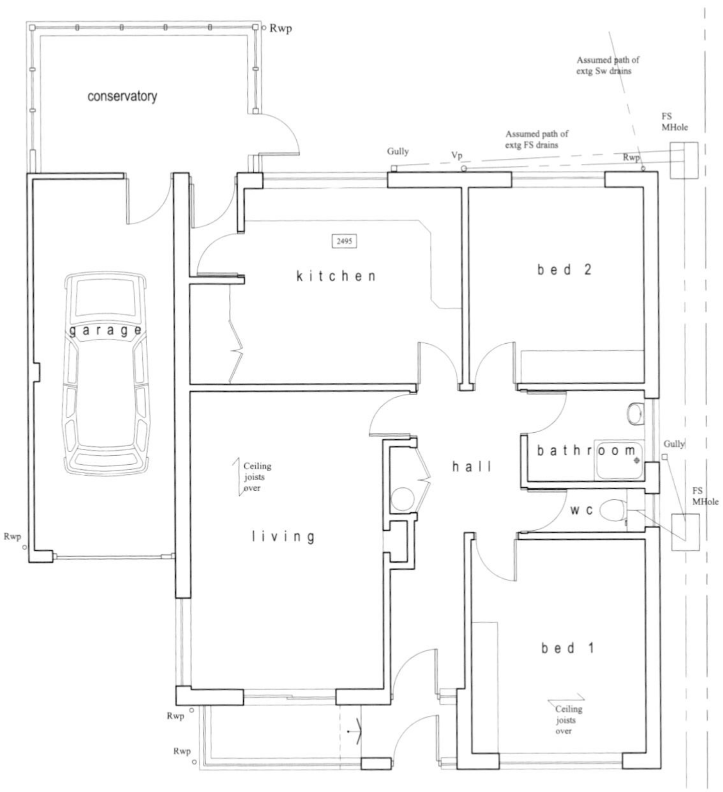

Ground floor plan of the house before conversion. Julian Owen Associates Architects

conservatory

Rwp

Assumed path of extg Sw drains

FS MHole

Gully

Vp

Assumed path of extg FS drains

Rwp

2495

kitchen

bed 2

garage

Ceiling joists over

living

hall

bathroom

Gully

wc

FS MHole

Rwp

bed 1

Rwp

Rwp

Ceiling joists over

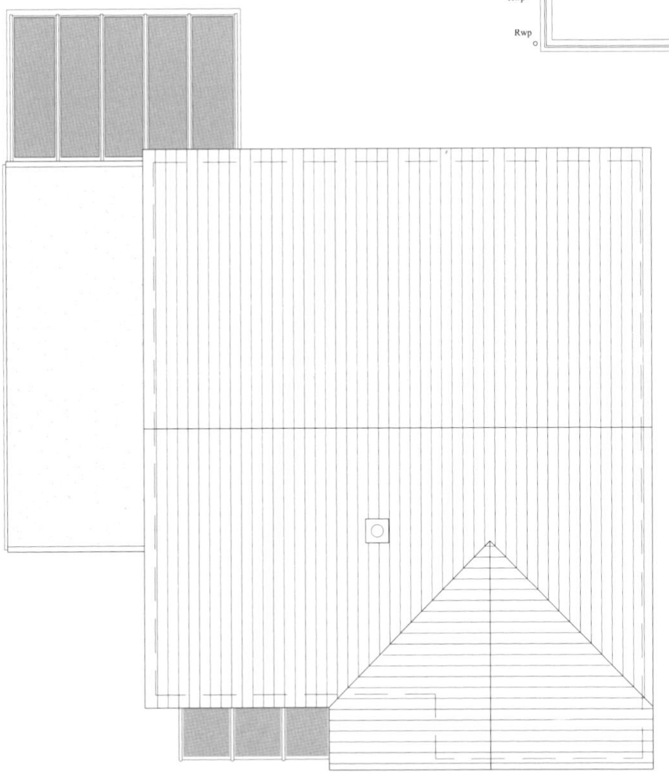

Roof plan of the existing bungalow. Julian Owen Associates Architects

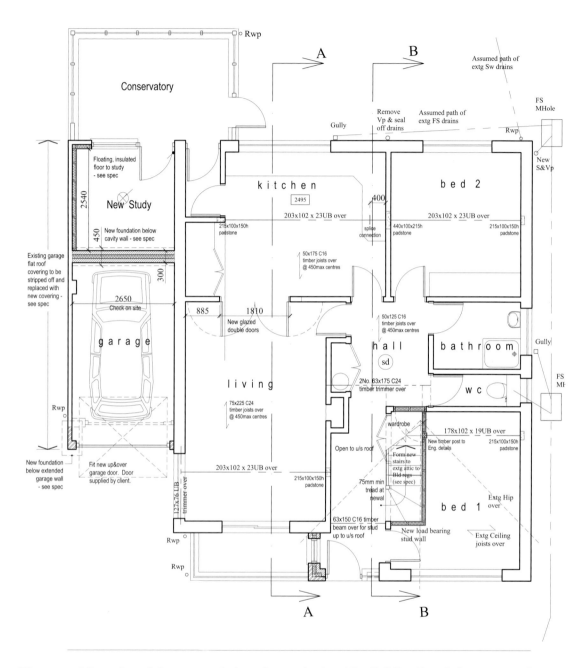

The ground floor plan of the proposed alterations, submitted for Building Regulations approval.

Julian Owen Associates Architects

The loft is boarded out and the rafters are cut ready for the construction of the dormer windows. Julian Owen Associates Architects

The internal structure is altered and new timbers are added. Julian Owen Associates Architects

The new dormers are built up off the existing structure. Julian Owen Associates Architects

New purlins are added to compensate for the existing ones that have been removed.
Julian Owen Associates Architects

The new dormers and the rest of the existing roof are insulated. The existing water tank is kept in use during the work until the boiler is replaced. Julian Owen Associates Architects

The space between the low level internal side walls and the eaves is useful for storage and to run services. Julian Owen Associates Architects

Towards the end of the project, the ceiling is removed ready for the formation of the new staircase. Julian Owen Associates Architects

The finished staircase. Because this is a bungalow, the Building Regulations requirements for a fire escape are not so onerous and the stairs can finish inside a living area. Julian Owen Associates Architects

The conversion seen from the rear of the house. Julian Owen Associates Architects

The converted loft seen from the front garden. Julian Owen Associates Architects

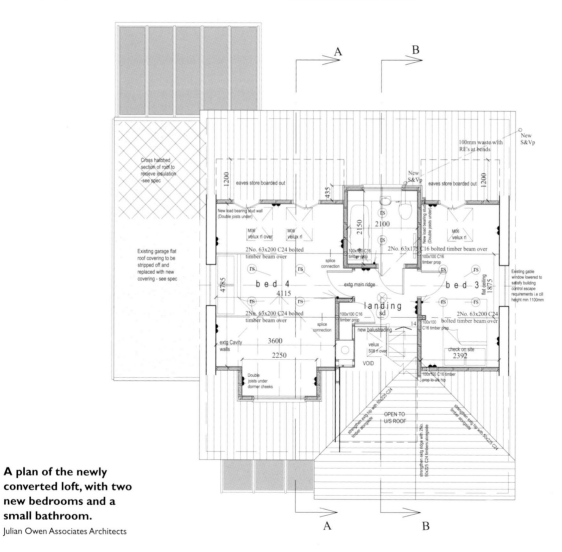

A plan of the newly converted loft, with two new bedrooms and a small bathroom.

Julian Owen Associates Architects

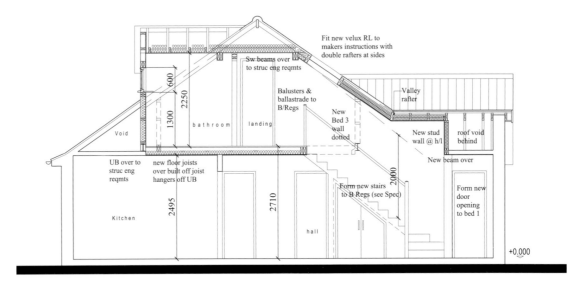

A section through the bungalow, used to work out the structural design and ensure that there is headroom where it is needed. Julian Owen Associates Architects

between the bedroom and the hallway, creating a spacious new living area.

Because the loft conversion is at first-floor level the Building Regulations do not require the staircase to be fire protected or lead directly to the outside. If the conversion was at second-floor level, as happens when the loft of a two-storey house is converted, this arrangement of the plan on the ground floor would not be permissible.

The scheme was designed and managed on site by Nick Jones of Julian Owen Associates Architects and the building work was carried out by Trent Valley Plumbing and Building Ltd of West Bridgford, Nottingham.

Sample Specification for the Conversion of a Bungalow Loft

Floor
- Floor joists to structural engineer's specification mounted on joist hangers hung off new steelwork or timber binders to structural engineer's requirements.

- 22mm t & g (tongue and groove) or 22mm chipboard flooring (glued and screwed).
- 100mm rockwool insulation or equivalent to fill floor void for sound insulation.

Pitched Roof
- Dormer: at existing roof cut back roof rafters and suitably trim below and between for new dormer window. Form new pitched roof over of 50 × 125mm sw (softwood) g/s grade joists at 450mm intervals, to be insulated with board infill, minimum 135mm deep in total with 50mm air gap over rafters.
- Tile colour to closely match existing, lap and gauge to manufacturer's instructions on tanalized 25 × 38mm sw battens, roofing felt or similar.
- Vent ridged tiles for cross-vent purposes to roof. Roof pitch to match existing dwelling.
- Dormer cheeks to be constructed from sw grade timbers with two rows staggered noggins, externally clad with ply.
- Ply to receive breathable underlay, battens and vertical tile hanging. Provide tilting fillet and

code 5 lead flashing at junction between dormer and existing roof.

- Studwork infilled with 100mm insulation board. Cut rafter ends between new dormer and eaves to be fixed to studwork uprights.
- Valley construction to be 50 × 125mm boards on diminishing rafters at maximum 450mm centres on valley board with code 5 lead flashing.
- New roof (U value 0.2W/m² K) to be insulated with insulation board, minimum 135mm deep total, 90mm between rafters and 45mm fixed across face of joists all with minimum 50mm air gap over. Roof ventilation to be afforded by 25mm continuous gap along full run of eaves, and vented ridge to allow equivalent of 5mm continuous gap.
- Preservative treatments to all roof timbers.
- All new structural and external timbers to be treated with Vac Vac organic solvent preservative treatment.
- Exposed existing timbers and joinery to be preservative-treated on site.
- Re-treat all timber that is sawn, drilled, planed or otherwise exposed after initial treatment.

Structural Steelwork
- Any structural steel required to be in accordance with engineer's design and specifications. Engineer's information must be read in conjunction with this specification and Julian Owen Associates drawings.
- All steelwork to have minimum end bearing of 150mm and laid on pads indicated by structural engineer.
- 30 minutes' fire protection to all steel beams with fire protection board.

Plasterboard, Plaster, Internal Walls
- Ceilings to be lined with 12.5mm plasterboard with joints covered with jute scrim and skim coat.
- Noggins to all edges.
- Any internal studwork partitions to be constructed with softwood studs, double-staggered soleplate and head.

- Studs to be at maximum 450mm centres with at least two lines of noggins in their height.
- One layer of plasterboard internally on one or both sides as required.
- Stagger all joints, cover joints with scrim and apply skim coat to plasterboard surface.
- All voids to be filled with mineral wool sound-absorbing quilt.
- 13mm two-coat plaster to internal walls.
- Use renovating plaster where an existing external wall is becoming an internal wall.

Stairs
- Construct new timber staircase, as indicated on drawings.
- Fourteen equal risers and goings with maximum pitch no greater than 42 degrees.
- Minimum clear width 700mm and minimum headroom to be 2,000mm.
- New timber handrail 900mm above stair pitch.
- No gaps greater than 100mm between any balusters.

Windows
- At existing roof supply and fix new roof windows, to manufacturer's instructions. Provide double rafters to sides of windows.
- Any new and/or replacement windows to be double-glazed in UPVC window frames, where indicated; style and openings to satisfy building control and owner's approval and to meet minimum U value 1.8W/m²K.
- Any habitable room on upper floors to be provided with an opening window suitable for escape, that is minimum 0.33sq m openable area, minimum 450mm high and 450mm wide, with a sill height of no more than 1,100mm.
- Habitable rooms to have min 1/20th of floor area as openable window and as indicated by drawing requirements.

Doors
- Fit new interior paint-grade doors, where indicated on plans, with one pair of hinges and lever handle and rose.
- New bathroom to have internal bolt, sited above the reach of small children.

Glazing
- Double glazing 24mm overall thickness with inner pane of 4mm minimum thickness, low 'E' coated glass.
- Any new glazing in critical locations such as windows, doors, door side panels within 800mm of finished floor level to be kite-marked toughened safety glass (see Diagram 1 of Document N of the Building Regulations).

Ventilation
- New bathroom to have mechanical ventilation to provide 15 l/s extract, operated by a pull-cord switch.
- All new windows to have adjustable trickle vents.

Sanitary Fittings
- New waste connections if required at upper floors to connect to existing 100mm diameter soil and vent pipe.
- Client to supply new bath, shower, sink, WC suite and all bathroom fixtures and fittings.
- Client to confirm appliances and fittings before installation.
- Fit new WC suite with all necessary fixtures and fittings with 75mm trap minimum and 50mm seal.
- Fit new wash hand basins with 32mm diameter trap with minimum 75mm seal, and all necessary brackets, fixtures and fittings.
- Bath/shower to have 40mm diameter trap with minimum 75mm seal.
- Fit shower unit at height suitable for client (to be agreed on site).
- Fit shower rail/curtain or screen to client's choice.
- Carry out all plumbing work necessary to install fittings, allowing for stopcock to cistern, anti-return valves, isolation valves etc., all to the approval of water authority.

Foul Water Drainage
- As required lay new drain, 100mm clay drains, bedded in accordance with Document H of the Building Regulations, encased in 150mm con-crete below new slab and suitably bridged using concrete lintels where any walls cross drains.
- Minimum fall 1:40 to break into existing drain via new manhole.

Surface Water Drainage
- As existing.

Heating System and Hot and Cold Water
- Supply mains cold water to WC and to other appliances as required.
- Plumb in hot-water supply to new bath, shower and wash hand basin from existing hot-water system.
- Adapt existing system as necessary to achieve properly balanced system.
- Plumb in any new radiators below window sills where possible from existing central heating system if possible. Fit adjustable thermostatic valve to any new radiators.
- The gas service to be installed in accordance with the Gas Safety (Installation and Use) Regulations by an approved installer.
- Heating system to provide a temperature of 21°C internally for living areas, 22°C in bathrooms and shower room and 18°C in circulation areas, assuming external temperature of −1°C.
- System to be designed with 10 per cent margin on radiator sizes over the heat loss for intermittent operation and 20 per cent margin on boiler capacity.
- Include all usable space in attic rooms for heating to 21°C.
- Any new flue to any new proposed boiler to be sited in accordance with regulations.
- Anti-corrosion fluid to be put in the system.
- All pipe runs to be concealed in floor or ceiling voids where possible, or otherwise boxed in with moisture resistant MDF casing ready for decoration.

Electrics
- Provide and fit lights and switches as indicated on the plans.
- Provide light fittings that will only take 40 lumens per circuit-watt.

- Provide double power points as indicated on the plans, client to confirm locations before installation.
- All work in accordance with Table 4 of Document L1 of the Building Regulations and with current regulations.
- Fit electric shower if client requests, all in accordance with current regulations.
- Mechanical extractor, wired into lighting circuit, including external grille and anti-backdraught flaps.

Fire Prevention Requirements
- Mains-operated self-contained smoke alarms to be installed in accordance with the paragraph 1.8 of Document B of the Building Regulations.
- The smoke alarms to be wholly mains operated, on an independent circuit permanently wired to a separately fused circuit at the distribution board.
- To be minimum of one alarm on each floor, as indicated on the plans. Ground-floor smoke alarm to be positioned within 7m of the doors to the kitchen and living room, and within 3m of bedroom doors, measured horizontally.
- Alarms to be interconnected so that detection of smoke by any one unit operates the alarm signal in all of them.

A LOFT CONVERSION IN THE WEST COUNTRY – A DIARY IN PICTURES

Joinery
- New skirting, architraves to match existing dwelling as required.

Floor and Wall Finishes
- Make good all damaged existing finishes, wall coverings, plaster, joinery etc., and repaint and or repaper to match existing as required.
- Extent of new tiling to bathroom to be agreed with client.
- All other areas to be finished with two-coat emulsion, colour to client's choice.
- Paint all new woodwork with primer and two coats gloss paint.

Scaffold is erected to allow access to the roof space. Attic Designs Ltd

- Floor finishes as requested by client.

Important Note
The information above is a reduced version of a typical architect's specification, provided for illustrative purposes only and is not intended to be used for actual projects. Neither Julian Owen nor Crowood Press offer or imply any warranty as to the accuracy of these specifications. Professional advice must be sought before the incorporation of any of the above information into a real project.

Steel beams installed along with new floor joists. Attic Designs Ltd

The chimney is in an inconvenient place and is removed. Attic Designs Ltd

The props supporting the purlins are also removed. Attic Designs Ltd

The roof window framing is constructed, prior to the removal of the roof covering. Attic Designs Ltd

The structure of the dormer window is formed. Attic Designs Ltd

The insulation is fitted over the rafters. Thin foil insulation has to be used in conjunction with insulation board to comply with the regulations. Attic Designs Ltd

The roof windows are installed and the insulation fitted around them. Attic Designs Ltd

Plasterboard is fixed to the underside of the roof and to the walls. Attic Designs Ltd

Decoration cannot start until the skim coat over the plasterboard has thoroughly dried out. Attic Designs Ltd

The new dormer window looks over the rear garden and provides extra headroom inside.
Attic Designs Ltd

The design and conversion of a bungalow was carried out by Attic Designs Ltd of Wellington, Somerset. Where a dormer extension to the roof is at the rear of the property planning permission is not normally required unless the site is in a conservation area or an area of outstanding natural beauty.

ABOVE: **The two roof windows to the side let plenty of light into the rooms.**
Attic Designs Ltd

LEFT: **A bedroom fitted into a converted loft by the same company.**
Attic Designs Ltd

Glossary

Adjudication A quick and inexpensive method of dispute resolution resulting in an immediately enforceable, non-binding dispute settlement by an adjudicator.

Architect, chartered A registered architect who is also a member of the Royal Institute of British Architects.

Architect, registered Professional who has obtained sufficient qualifications to be registered with the government to use the title 'architect'.

Architectural technologist Draughtsman who deals with the practical side of building design. Membership of the Chartered Institute of Architectural Technologists (CIAT) indicates training and qualifications.

Architrave Strip of wood, usually decorative, which surrounds a door opening and conceals the joint between the plaster and timber lining.

Barge board This board follows the line of tiles at the gable end of the roof to conceal the joint between roof and wall.

Batten Timber strip to which roof tiles are fitted.

BBA Certificate British Board of Agrément Certificates are awarded by a government-backed organization to products as a sign that they are safe and appropriate for stated uses in a building.

Binder Spans between cross walls to provide intermediate support to ceiling joists.

Breather membrane Sheet material often used in timber frames, which keeps water out of a building but allows water vapour, which may be trapped inside the structure, through to evaporate into the air.

BSI The British Standards Institute is a government-backed body that issues guidance and recommendations for all kinds of organizations and businesses on their products and services. If companies comply to their standards they may use the BSI kitemark logo.

Building control officer (BCO) Local authority official who checks buildings comply with the Building Regulations.

Building Regulations Minimum standards for construction and design set by the government and illustrated by a series of booklets called Approved Documents.

Computer-aided design (CAD) Two- and three-dimensional models can be created on a computer to give an idea of how a design may look and work out a schedule of components needed.

Coping Protective capping to the top of a wall.

Corbelling Successive projecting courses of brickwork.

Cresting Decorative detail that runs along the top of a ridge.

Damp-proof course (DPC) Prevents moisture from rising up through the walls into a room.

Delegated powers The process by which planning applications are decided without going to the local council's planning committee.

Door, flush A door with a smooth face, usually with a veneer of good-quality wood concealing a carcass of cheaper construction.

Eaves The edge of a sloping roof, where the gutter is usually fixed.

Embodied energy The energy that has been used to incorporate a material into a building, including the energy used manufacturing it, transporting it to the site and dealing with it after the building is demolished.

Estimate An informed guess, a rough price.

FENSA Fenestration Self-Assessment Scheme, which allows contractors to install windows without requiring inspection by a building control officer.

Finial Decorative pointed feature at the end of a ridge of a roof.

First fix The point at which electric cables and pipework are put into position, usually once the building is watertight and before plastering.

Flashing Metal sheet used to deflect water at junction between roof and wall.

Gable Vertical triangular section of a wall between two roof pitches.

Glass, laminated A sandwich of glass and reinforcement that looks like normal glass but is designed to bend rather than shatter if hit with force.

Glass, obscured Glass that allows light through but has a pattern on to reduce visibility.

Glass, toughened Glass that is treated to be tougher that normal glass and harder to break. When it is broken it shatters into small, regular pieces that do not have sharp edges.

Glazing bar Horizontal support for a panel of glass in a window.

Hip Sloping section of roof between two other roof pitches, an alternative to a gable.

HIP Home Information Pack, a legally required summary of information on a house when it is sold, including legal issues, local authority records and energy performance.

Humidity The amount of water vapour in the air. If very damp or humid air comes into contact with a cold surface condensation results.

Jamb The side of an opening in a wall for a door or window.

JCT contract Contract that has been produced by a collaboration of all the professionals involved in building work, including clients, builders and architects.

Joist Support for floor and ceiling.

Lean-to Single-pitch roof, usually butting up to a solid wall of a house; sometimes called a mono-pitch roof.

Line drawing A drawing that is created using single lines to describe mass and shape of objects, usually black and white with no shading, texture or colour.

Lintel Concrete, timber or steel beam over an opening to support the wall above.

Low 'E' glass Glass that is treated to help to trap more heat from the sun in a room.

Making good The finishing touches that bring work up to scratch, remedial work to existing surfaces and finishes affected by the work.

Microporous paint Coating for timber that looks like paint but 'breathes' like a stain finish.

Mitre Angled joint (similar to a joint in a picture frame).

Noggin Short wooden stiffeners inserted between joists.

OS Ordnance Survey, the only reliable source of larger-scale maps such as 1:1250.

Payback period Length of time that a cost-saving measure needs to cover the initial cost. For example, if extra insulation costs £500 to fit and saves £100 a year in fuel, the payback is five years.

Permitted development Changes and additions that you can make to your house without needing formal planning approval from the local planning authority.

Pitch Slope of roof.

Procurement route The way that a building project is managed, for example DIY or design and build.

Purlin Horizontal beam fixed part way up a rafter to prevent sagging.

Quote A fixed price that is binding.

Rafters Series of structural timbers rising from eaves to ridge to support pitched roof covering.

Reveal Vertical side of door or window opening.

RIBA Royal Institute of British Architects.

RICS Royal Institute of Chartered Surveyors.

Ridge Apex of a roof, where two pitches meet.

Roof truss Prefabricated structural timber framework to support roof.

SAP rating A number that indicates to building control officers how much energy a building loses. The closer this number is to 100 the less energy is wasted.

Screed Layer of fine concrete used to provide smooth surface prior to floor finish.

Second fix The point at which radiators, sockets, switches and so on are fixed prior to decoration.

Sill Bottom horizontal member of a door or window frame.

Soffit The underside of a projection, for example the underside of a roof between the eaves and the wall of the house.

Solar gain The build-up of heat that occurs in a room when sun shines into it through glass.

Specification List of materials and procedures need to complete a building, sometimes with a description of the standard of work that is expected.

Sustainable construction Building in a way that reduces the damage to the environment. Similar to 'green' or 'environmentally friendly' building.

Thermostatic valve (TRV) A valve that switches a radiator on when it gets below a chosen temperature and off when it goes above that temperature.

Tie bar Horizontal metal bar that ties the eaves of a roof together, running at ceiling level inside a conservatory.

Trickle ventilation Air that is allowed to flow into a room via adjustable grilles, usually fitted in window frames.

U-Value This number describes the insulative properties of a construction. The lower it is the better it is at insulating.

Valley Line which follows the lowest point where two roof pitches meet.

Vapour barrier Used in timber frames and on the back of plasterboard, usually to prevent moisture-laden air getting from inside the building into the structural walls.

Vernacular Design that uses local traditional building style and materials.

Wallplate Typically 100 × 50mm in size, this softwood section supports the rafters and ceiling joists. It is bedded on mortar on top of the external wall. Modern wallplates are fixed to the wall with steel straps with the rafters and ceiling joists nailed to them.

Window board Flat shelf that butts up to a window frame internally (sometimes also called the window sill).

Window, casement Window with hinges on the side.

Window, sash Window that slides vertically up and down.

Window, top hung Window with hinges at the top.

Recommended Reading

Magazines

Build It + Home Improvement (Inside Communications Media Ltd)
Lots of case studies and practical advice on building new and altering existing houses.
www.buildit-online.co.uk

Grand Designs (Media 10 Ltd)
A tie-in with the Channel Four TV series.

Homebuilding & Renovating (Ascent Publishing Ltd)
A good-quality publication that deals with all kinds of domestic building projects, including loft conversions.
www.homebuilding.co.uk

Self Build and Design (Waterways World Ltd)
A good source of ideas for design as well as more practical matters.
www.selfbuildanddesign.com

Books

The Loft Conversion Project Guide (Construction Products Association)
This technical book for the construction industry has been prepared by a consortium of manufacturers, suppliers and government and trade organizations. It is intended to be a definitive technical guide and is pretty close to being this.

The Property Makeover Price Guide (BCIS)
An excellent guide to approximate prices for getting items of building work completed on a home by a builder, with detailed price breakdowns as well as general costs per square metre for early estimating.

Coulthard, Sally, *The 10 Best Ways to Add Value to Your Home* (Pearson Education Ltd, 2008)
This book covers more than just loft conversions, but sets out how to assess whether your project is likely to make money in a direct and readable manner.

Coutts, John, *Loft Conversions* (Blackwell Publishing Limited, 2006)
Designed more for professional builders and architects, this is a comprehensive guide to the practical side of loft conversions. A key source of the information in this book.

Grimaldi, Paul J, *Getting the Builders In* (Right Way Books, 2003)
Useful tips on how to select, appoint and manage building contractors for alterations to your house.

Hymers, Paul, *Home Conversions: The Complete Handbook* (New Holland Publishers (UK) Ltd, 2003)
A reasonably priced paperback that covers all types of conversion, including lofts.

Mindham, C N, *Roof Construction and Loft Conversion* (Blackwell Publishing Ltd, 2006)
Well-established text book on the structural and constructional considerations of carrying out a loft conversion.

Owen, Julian, *Home Extension Design* (RIBA Publishing Ltd, 2008)
A general guide to the design of house alterations, including advice on project management.

Owen, Julian, Chilvers, Peter and Hill, David, *Before You Build* (RIBA Publishing Ltd, 2007)
A short guide to the planning and building regulations, along with advice on how to approach the design and project management of a house alteration project.

Pearson, David, *The Gaia Natural House Book* (Gaia Books Ltd, 2004)
An excellent book for anyone interested in sustainable or 'green' building and designing for healthy living.

Rock, Ian Alistair, *Loft Conversion Manual* (Haynes Publishing, 2008)
Very useful book for anyone contemplating a DIY project.

Weiss, Barbara and Hellman, Louis, *Do It With an Architect* (Mitchell Beazley, 1999)
An excellent and humorous guide to getting the best out of your architect.

Index